Twayne's English Authors Series

EDITOR OF THIS VOLUME

Kinley E. Roby

Northeastern University

Dorothy L. Sayers

TEAS 281

Dorothy L. Sayers

DOROTHY L. SAYERS

By Mary Brian Durkin, O.P.

Rosary College, River Forest, Illinois

TWAYNE PUBLISHERS

A DIVISION OF G. K. HALL & CO., BOSTON

Copyright © 1980 by G. K. Hall & Co.

Published in 1980 by Twayne Publishers,
A Division of G. K. Hall & Co.
All Rights Reserved

Printed on permanent/durable acid-free paper and bound
in the United States of America

First Printing

Library of Congress Cataloging in Publication Data

Durkin, Mary Brian.
Dorothy L. Sayers.

(Twayne's English author series; TEAS 281)
Bibliography: p. 189 - 200
Includes index.
1. Sayers, Dorothy Leigh, 1893-1957—
Criticism and interpretation.   I.   Title.
PR6037.A95Z65   823'.9'12   79-21271
ISBN 0-8057-6778-9

For my sister Margaret and my brother Bob
and in loving memory of John, Joe, Bernard and Philip Durkin

Contents

About the Author

Sister Mary Brian Durkin of the Dominican Congregation of Sinsina-wa, Wisconsin is an associate professor of English literature at Rosary College, River Forest, Illinois. She received her Master of Arts degree from the University of Wisconsin, then continued her studies at the University of London, and at Oxford University under an IIE grant. After directing graduate theses at Villa Schifanoia, Rosary College of Fine Arts in Florence, Italy, she instituted and directed the first years of the Rosary-in-London program, a semester of studies abroad.

Her previous publications include articles in *American Literature*, *Milton Studies*, *Literature in Transition*, and the *Christian Century*. She is presently engaged in research on Muriel Spark.

Preface

"I am a writer," stated Dorothy L. Sayers forthrightly, "and I know my craft." This introductory study is designed for readers eager to learn about the writings, craftsmanship, and ideals of this versatile author.

The first chapter deals with pertinent biographical material; the second, with her early novels. Although *The Documents in the Case* is a collaborative effort with Doctor Eustace Robert Barton, who supplied the medical details, I have considered it in this chapter for several reasons. The manuscripts at the Marion E. Wade Collection at Wheaton College, Wheaton, Illinois, indicate that the characterization, dialogue, and plot are undoubtedly the work of Miss Sayers; secondly, written in the epistolary style of Wilkie Collins's *The Moonstone*, which she considered a work of genius, *Documents* is her experimentation in combining the novel of detection with the novel of manners. Also, her other collaborative efforts, three novels written with various members of the Detection Club, are out of print at this time, so it seemed wise to treat *The Documents in the Case* as a significant early study of her development as a novelist. Chapters on her later novels, the short stories, dramas, essays, translations of the *Divina Commedia*, and essays on Dante follow in chronological order.

Limitations of space prevented a consideration of her first two volumes of poetry and later occasional verse, as well as her noteworthy translations, *Tristan in Brittany* and *The Song of Roland*. However, in the study of her dramas the strengths and weaknesses of some of the early poetry can be seen; the vigor and freshness of her translations of Dante's epic mirror the power found in the other translations not considered here. In the study of the detective novels, I have not stressed to what extent these follow the rules set forth by Ronald Knox and other early practitioners of the art of the mystery story but have attempted, instead, to indicate the stylistic techniques which brought her closer to the goal which she so frequently discussed: raising the detective story to the literary status of the novel of manners. Throughout this study of the various genres which she engaged in during her writing career, I have called attention to some of the significant themes which, discernible in early works, become dominant motifs in her most mature works, notably her attitude toward various aspects of integrity: the integrity of work, of the mind, of right relationships with others, one's self, and with God. Convinced that the remarkable resurgence of interest in the writings of Dorothy L. Sayers comes, not from any desire to dabble in the trivia of her life but from a genuine esteem for her talents used to entertain, to instruct, and to inspire, I present her as a lay theologian, scholar, author, and Christian humanist whose writings have in many ways a greater relevance for her audience today than in the past.

I wish to express my deep appreciation to Miss Olivia Gollancz, who kindly allowed me to spend many hours reading letters and notes written by Miss Sayers to her friend and publisher, Mr. Gollancz. To Muriel St. Clare Byrne, O.B.E., I am indebted for the many glimpses she gave me of Miss Sayers's personality and character. I am particularly grateful to Doctor Barbara Reynolds for her inspiring lectures on many facets of Miss Sayers's artistry and ideals of scholarship; to Doctor Clyde Kilby, curator of the Marion E. Wade Collection, Wheaton College, Wheaton, Illinois, and the former secretary, Miss Barbara Griffin, for their gracious assistance in helping me to utilize the wealth of Sayers material in the library; and to Lieutenant Ralph Clarke of the Dorothy L. Sayers Literary and Historical Society, Witham, England, for his generosity in sharing his knowledge and primary materials with me on my visit.

I am deeply indebted to the staff of the Rosary College library for untiring assistance, particularly Sister Mary Field, Eulalia Brown, Kathleen Heim, and Debby Walsh. Words can not express my appreciation for the solicitude shown by Agatha Vincent during my research days in London, and to Anne Kenny and Sister Marie Thomas Keating for their sustaining encouragement and interest. To Keetz Keneagy and Marcia Pappalardo for assistance that brought more weariness than compensation, my gratitude. I gratefully acknowledge the supportive interest of my colleagues, particularly the assistance of Sister Jocelyn Garey, and the generosity of Sister Candida Lund, president of Rosary College, River Forest, Illinois for granting me a sabbatical year to continue my research in England.

SISTER MARY BRIAN DURKIN

Rosary College, Illinois

Acknowledgments

To Anthony Fleming and the estate of Dorothy L. Sayers for permission to quote from the novels, dramas, essays, and short stories. This privilege was kindly arranged by Mr. A. Watkins, of A. Watkins, Inc.

To Rutgers University Press for permission to quote from *The Christian Tradition in Modern British Verse and Drama* by William V. Spanos.

To Biblo and Tannen for permission to quote from *Murder for Pleasure* by Howard Haycraft.

To *New Blackfriar's* Press for permission to quote from book reviews by Kenelm Foster, O.P.

To Harper & Row, Publishers, Inc., for permission to quote from *The Man Born to Be King, The Emperor Constantine, Introductory Papers on Dante, Further Papers on Dante,* and *Mortal Consequences* by Julian Symons.

To William B. Eerdmans Publishing Company for permission to quote from *Christian Letters to a Post-Christian World*, essays selected and introduced by Roderick Jellema.

To the estate of Vera Brittain for permission to quote from *Testament of Youth*. This privilege was extended by Shirley Williams, M.P.

To the editor of *Comparative Literature* for permission to quote from Theodore Holmes's review of Sayers's translation of the *Divina Commedia*.

To Doctor Barbara Reynolds for permission to quote from the Foreword, *The Divine Comedy: Paradise*.

To David Higham Associates LTD for permission to quote from Dorothy L. Sayers's translations of the *Divina Commedia*, Penguin edition.

To the University of Pennsylvania Press for permission to quote from *Religion in Modern English Drama* by Gerald Weales.

Chronology

1893   Dorothy Leigh Sayers, the only child of the Reverend Henry Sayers and Helen Leigh Sayers, born June 13, Oxford, England.

1897   The family moves to Bluntisham Rectory, Huntingdonshire.

1909   Dorothy enters Godolphin School, Salisbury, as a boarder.

1912   Attends Somerville College, Oxford University.

1915   Wins First Class Honours, Master of Arts in Modern Languages.

1916   *OP I*, a small volume of poems published by Blackwell's, Oxford.

1917   Serves as coeditor of *Oxford Poetry*, also in 1918, 1919. Learns the publishing trade at Blackwell's, Oxford.

1918   *Catholic Tales and Christian Songs*, a second book of verse.

1919   Assists Eric Whelpton at Les Roches, a boys' school in southern France.

1920   Receives the Master of Arts degree in Modern Languages with the first group of women to be granted degrees by the University of Oxford.

1922   Joins Benson's Advertising Agency, London, as a copywriter.

1923   *Whose Body?*, her first novel.

1924   Gives birth to a son.

1926   *Clouds of Witness*. Marries Captain Oswald Arthur (Mac) Fleming.

1927   *Unnatural Death*; U.S. title: *The Dawson Pedigree*.

1928   *The Unpleasantness at the Bellona Club*; *Lord Peter Views the Body*, a collection of twelve short stories; edits *Great Short Stories of Detection, Mystery and Horror*, an anthology; U.S. title: *The Omnibus of Crime*, 1929.

1929   Moves to Witham, Essex. Cofounder of the Detection Club, London. *Tristan in Brittany*, verse and prose translation of *The Romance of Tristan* by Thomas the Anglo-Norman in the twelfth century.

1930   *The Documents in the Case*; coauthor, Robert Eustace, pseudonym. *Strong Poison*, the novel that begins Wimsey's romance with Miss Vane.

1931   *The Five Red Herrings*; U.S. title: *Suspicious Characters*. *Great Short Stories of Detection, Mystery and Horror*, Second series; U.S. title: *The Second Omnibus of Crime*, 1932. *The Floating Admiral*, a detective novel written by certain members of the Detection Club, including G. K. Chesterton, `Agatha Christie, Ronald Knox.

1932   *Have His Carcase*.

1933   *Murder Must Advertise*; *Hangman's Holiday*, short stories, *Ask a Policeman*.

1934   *The Nine Tailors. Great Stories of Detection, Mystery and Horror*, third series; U.S. title: *The Third Omnibus of Crime*.

1935   *Gaudy Night*.

1936   *Tales of Detection*, editor. *He That Should Come*, a Nativity play broadcast on Christmas. *Busman's Honeymoon*, a three-act drama coauthored with Muriel St. Clare Byrne, O.B.E., produced in London.

1937   *Busman's Honeymoon*, revised as a novel, the last in the Wimsey series. *The Zeal of Thy House*, written and produced for the Canterbury Festival.

1939   *In the Teeth of the Evidence*, short stories. *The Devil to Pay*, produced at the Canterbury Festival. "The Wimsey Papers," wartime essays appear in the *Spectator, Double Death*.

1940   *Begin Here*, a wartime essay, book length. *Love All*, a farce, on London stage.

1941   *The Man Born to Be King*, a radio play-cycle of twelve plays, broadcast monthly. *The Mind of the Maker. The Golden Cockerel*, radio dramatization of Pushkin's tale.

1944   *Even the Parrot*, exemplary "talks" for children.

1946   *The Just Vengeance*. Lichfield Festival play. *Unpopular Opinions*, twenty-one essays.

1949   *Creed or Chaos?*, a collection of seven essays. *The Divine Comedy*, Cantica I, *Hell*, a translation, Penguin Classics series.

1950   Awarded an Honorary Doctorate of Letters by the University of Durham. Her husband, "Mac" Fleming, dies.

1951   *The Emperor Constantine*, Festival of Britain drama.

1952   Appointed churchwarden, St. Thomas, Regent Street, London.

1954   *Introductory Papers on Dante*.

1955   *The Divine Comedy*, Cantica II, *Purgatory*, translation.
1957   *The Song of Roland*, translated from the French. *Further Papers on Dante*. "Christian Belief about Heaven and Hell," in the *Sunday Times*, January 6. Dies suddenly at her home in Witham, December 17.

CHAPTER 1

Biography—"I Am a Writer . . ."

DOROTHY L. Sayers was born in 1893 at Oxford, where her father, the Reverend Henry Sayers, was Headmaster of Christchurch Cathedral Choir School. Her mother, Helen Mary Leigh, was the grand-niece of Percy Leigh, cofounder of *Punch*. When Dorothy was four and a half years old, her father accepted a living at Bluntisham-cum-Earith in Huntingdonshire, an isolated parish in the bleak Fen country.[1]

One morning when she was about six and a half years old, her father appeared in the nursery, announced that he thought it was time that she began to study Latin, initiated her into the mysteries of case and gender, and ended the lesson with the admonition to learn the declension of "mensa" for the session the next day. Years later, lecturing before the Association for the Reform of Latin Teaching, she confessed that the adventure appealed to her immensely: "It seemed to me that it would be a very fine thing to learn Latin, and it would place me in a position of superiority to my mother, my aunt, and my nurse. . . ." [2] Tutored by a French governess, Dorothy was proficient in that language at the age of thirteen, when she began to study German. As a boarder at Godolphin School for Girls in Salisbury, she enjoyed her lessons in French, German, piano, and violin, but she was miserable during the two years spent there. Tall, awkward, almost bald as a result of a severe illness, she suffered from shyness and had little rapport with the other students. Some hint of her unhappiness is revealed in a letter written years later to her friend and publisher, Victor Gollancz. Upbraiding him for allowing the letter "L" in her name to be omitted in an advertising blurb, she wrote: "My feeling about this is no doubt unreasonable, but the fact remains that 'Dorothy Sayers' has unpleasant associations for me and I do not like it. It is, if you like, a Freudian complex associated with my school days. . . . It produces in me a reaction of humiliation and depression and *I don't like it*." [3]

She studied assiduously for the Oxford entrance examinations, won a Gilchrist scholarship, and in 1912 entered Somerville, a woman's college at Oxford. Vera Brittain in her memoirs gives this intimate picture: "I took an immediate liking to Dorothy Sayers, who was affable to freshers and belonged to the 'examine-every-atom of you' type. A bouncing, exuberant young female who always seemed to be preparing for tea-parties, she could be seen at almost any hour of the day or night scuttling about the top floor of the Maitland building with a kettle in her hand. . . ." [4] Her second and third years at Oxford were better spent; in 1915 she took First Class Honours in Modern Languages, but the degree of Master of Arts was not formally conferred until 1920, when the University of Oxford finally capitulated and granted degrees to women.

Her first book, *OP I*, a slight volume of verse, was published in a series for young, unknown poets by Blackwell's in 1916. Her second, *Catholic Tales and Christian Songs*, 1918, in the same series, showed greater originality in subject matter and techniques. From 1916 until 1922 she held a variety of positions, teaching modern languages in Hull, working at Blackwell's as a reader, spending some time in southern France assisting a friend, Eric Whelpton, at a boys' school, and then small jobs in London. Undoubtedly the most rewarding experience was her work at Blackwell's, where she learned facets of the publishing business while coeditor of *Oxford Poetry* for the years 1917, 1918, 1919. During those years she plunged once again into the activities of university life. Doreen Wallace recalls:

I, a Somerville student, became one of her closer friends in those days. I have never known anyone so brimful of the energy of a well-stocked mind; even at 24, when I knew her first, she knew an enormous amount about all sorts of subjects unconnected with old French literature, which was her alleged "special," and nothing would content her but fact. There was, however, a lighter side to this impressive character. Long and slim in those days, she loped round Oxford looking for fun. Some of the fun was our Rhyming Club—one minute to produce the rhyming line, no matter whether sense or nonsense, and I drawing the pictures. . . .

Once, in Dorothy's rooms in Long Wall Street, Osbert and Sacheverell Sitwell turned up in uniform at a Rhyme Club session; but they were silent and aloof, having then no heart for nonsense. . . . I mention these occasions to show that Dorothy Sayers in her early twenties was a focal point for the young people of literary importance there.[5]

These years of study and employment at Oxford had a formative influence on her life and career, for it was there that she experienced the joys of scholarship and became aware of her own creative gifts. *Gaudy Night*, 1935, with its setting at Shrewsbury, an imaginary college for women at Oxford University, closely modeled on life at Somerville, reveals her knowledge of the university milieu as well as her deep regard for the ideals upheld there.

When her father exchanged his parish for an even poorer living at Christchurch, Wisbech, deeper in the Fen country, she found the rectory uninviting and crowded, but as the only child she was favored with a study-bedroom, where she spent pleasant hours during vacations and periods between jobs, avidly reading the works of Conan Doyle, Edgar Wallace, and other masters of mystery stories. When chided for reading such material, she stoutly defended her choice, declaring, "Oh, that is where the real money is!" She did not confide that she was mulling over ideas and writing rough drafts of a novel about an amusing, titled Denver family living in that district of the Fens.

Her training at Blackwell's enabled her to secure a position as a copywriter at Benson's, an advertising firm in London. Gregarious by nature, she enjoyed the camaraderie and creativity at Benson's, where she wrote jingles, coined slogans, and launched sales campaigns with gusto. In 1923 her first novel, *Whose Body?*, introduced Lord Peter Wimsey, second son of the Duke of Denver, a debonair sleuth whose quick wit and deductive powers delighted her readers so much that she immediately began to write a sequel. In September of that year she took six months' leave from the agency, ostensibly to finish the second novel but in reality to retire to the privacy of Christchurch rectory, where she managed to hide from most members of the household the fact that she was pregnant. The child, a son, was born in a nursing home in Bournemouth early in January 1924. Although she registered the birth under her own name at Somerset House, London, where the record was available for anyone to see, she never divulged even to her most intimate friends that the child was her own.[6] She placed him in the care of a distant relative, provided generously for his material needs and for excellent schooling. She made him sole heir to her literary estate, but never gave him love or companionship, a mystery more puzzling than any found in her novels.

Returning to Benson's, she published *Clouds of Witness* in 1926, and that same year married Captain Oswald Atherton Fleming, a journalist. She continued to write about Lord Peter Wimsey: *Unnatural Death* appeared in 1927; *The Unpleasantness at the Bellona*

Club in 1928. That same year, short stories, previously published in magazines, were gathered together under the intriguing title, *Lord Peter Views the Body*. She also edited the first of three monumental anthologies of mystery stories, adding scholarly introductions that trace the rise and development of the genre. *Great Short Stories of Detection, Mystery and Horror*, volumes one, two, and three, are better known in the United States as the *First*, *Second*, and *Third Omnibus of Crime*. *The Romance of Tristan*, by Thomas the Anglo-Norman, she translated in verse and prose as *Tristan in Brittany* in 1929.

While editing the anthologies, Miss Sayers spent considerable time studying the stylistic techniques of the masters Edgar Allan Poe, Sheridan Le Fanu, and Wilkie Collins, whose novel *The Moonstone* she termed a masterpiece of mystery, detection, and characterization. Collaborating with Robert Eustace, she wrote *The Documents in the Case* in 1930, an epistolary novel modelled on *The Moonstone*. After that experiment, she was no longer content to write just a mystery story, and decided to combine the detective story and the novel of manners in the style of Collins. Fearing that Lord Peter would not fit into this type of novel, she planned to provide him with a love affair, marriage, and then oblivion. For that reason, she began Lord Peter's romance with Harriet Vane, whom he defends in the murder trial described in *Strong Poison*, 1930; then she discovered that she simply could not treat her sophisticated sleuth like a mere puppet to be jerked off stage summarily. To do such a thing would be to violate the code of artistic integrity which she propounded in her essay "Gaudy Night," and to commit the same fault that she accused Dickens of perpetrating: manipulating characters, such as Micawber, making them perform acts that are utterly out of character in order to bring the story to a pleasing end. To bring Lord Peter and Harriet together, she had to change him, and so she set about the transformation, "chipping away," as she described it; while doing so, she succeeded in her ambition to make her novels more than mere whodunits.

The essay "Gaudy Night" reveals that she gave so much thought to effecting this transformation that Peter quite took over her life; formerly, as she says, he was just a periodic visitor, but gradually he became a "permanent resident in the house of my mind." [7] Planning episodes for the next book, she was obliged to consider the possible effect of these on his future; then, too, there was the Wimsey family, in-laws, friends, and even Wimsey's children. Her friends entered into the sport, tracing the Wimsey genealogy back to the Crusades; spoof pamphlets, supposedly written in the eighteenth century, mysteriously appeared; when Mr. Scott-Giles, Fitzalan Herald, wrote to her about a minor error in a title given to the Duke of Denver, he was drawn into the fun. He designed the family crest for the Wimsey family: "three silver mice on a field sable and the 'domestick Catt' couched menacingly on the helmet wreath. Two armed Saracens supported the shield, beneath which ran the mocking and arrogant motto: 'As my Whimsy takes me.' " [8]

The Detection Club, founded in 1929, was another source of amusement and stimulus. At the initiation ceremonies, the president, G. K. Chesterton, with mock-solemnity accepted from the candidates their promise that in their writings the detective would solve crimes by his wits without reliance on Divine Providence, Mumbo-Jumbo, or Feminine Intuition; that they would use with moderation such devices as "Death-Rays, Hypnotism, Trap-doors and Chinamen," and that they would always "honour the King's English." [9] When Miss Sayers became president she introduced bizarre elements that added to the fun. She contributed chapters to the three "round-robin" novels written by club members: *The Floating Admiral*, 1929; *Ask a Policeman*, 1933; and *Double Death*, 1939.

With indefatigable energy and zest she wrote and lectured for the BBC, reviewed mystery stories for the *Times Literary Supplement*, continued to write fiction, and lectured to various groups on topics ranging from "The King's English" to "Aristotle on Detective Fiction." Mary Ellen Chase gives this intimate picture:

There can be few plainer women on earth than Dorothy L. Sayers, and the adjective is an extremely kind one. She seemingly had no neck at all . . . a florid complexion, very blue, near-sighted eyes, and wore eyeglasses that quivered. Her thinning hair rarely showed evidence of care . . . she had small taste in dress, favouring what used to be known as "georgette," often purple by some unfortunate choice of color, with too much lace in all the wrong places. She was large, raw-boned, and awkward. Just as I have never seen a less attractive woman to look upon, I have never come across one so magnetic to listen to. [10]

Stimulated by an appreciative public, she continued to write but endeavored to give her detective fiction the literary merits characteristic of the novel of manners. With the exception of *The Five Red Herrings*, 1931, she wove into her later novels significant themes closely integrated with plot and character, while continuing to transform Lord Peter into a more humane person. In *Have His Carcase*, 1932, she made penetrating comments on the necessity of integrity in human relationships, for in that novel Harriet, resentful that she is under obligation to Lord Peter for saving her from a murder charge, wrestles with her feelings of inadequacy and indebtedness. In the next two novels she does not appear, but Miss Sayers still "chips away" at Lord Peter's transformation. In *Murder Must Advertise*, 1933, she places him in a milieu which she knew so well: the competitive world of advertising where, as a copywriter, he solves mysteries of murder and dope-peddling. The theme is as pertinent today as it was then—the ethical problems involved in advertising: the promotion of shoddy goods and the creation of false needs in order to stimulate production and consumption. *The Nine Tailors*, 1934, set in the flat, wind-swept Fen country, shows the strange workings of Providence in the parish of Fenchurch St. Paul, where massive bells ring out messages of death, flood warnings, and joyful tidings, circumstances which reveal new aspects of Lord Peter, who assists Providence in solving not one but several puzzles.

In a collection of short stories,*Hangman's Holiday*, 1933, Miss Sayers introduces a new detective, the dapper wine salesman Montague Egg. He also appears in a later collection, *In the Teeth of the Evidence*, 1934. After leaving Benson's advertising agency in 1931, she continued to write and to lecture. *Gaudy Night*, 1935, and *Busman's Honeymoon*, 1937, which first appeared as a drama coauthored with Muriel St. Clare Byrne, brought to a climax the romance of Lord Peter and Harriet Vane. Although Miss Sayers announced firmly that there would be no more Lord Peter Wimsey tales, nevertheless in several short stories she portrays the couple as happy parents of three children, and she began a sequel to *Busman's Honeymoon*, five chapters of which are in the Marion Wade Collection at Wheaton College, Wheaton, Illinois.[11] In 1939, she wrote a series of articles for the *Spectator*, utilizing the Wimsey family as a device to comment on the war.

When the monetary success of these novels and short stories freed her from undue financial worries, she quickly turned to the scholarly pursuits which had always interested her, notably apologetics and drama. In 1937 the Friends of Canterbury Cathedral produced *The Zeal of Thy House*, her poetic drama retelling the story of the architect who rebuilt the cathedral choir after the great fire in 1174. Her version of the Faust legend,*The Devil to Pay*, was given at the 1939 Canterbury Festival. In the next decades she wrote two festival plays, *The Just Vengeance*, 1946, and *The Emperor Constantine*, 1951. Her most memorable dramatic work is *The Man Born to Be King*, 1941–42, the life of Christ retold in twelve fifty-minute radio plays, commissioned and produced by the British Broadcasting Company.

In lectures, letters to the press, radio talks, poems, and essays, she continued to expound Christian dogma and its relevance to war-torn England. "The Dogma Is the Drama," "Creed or Chaos?", "Why Work?", "How Free Is the Press?", and "The Other Six Deadly Sins" are among the many lectures that were later published in inexpensive pamphlets, then gathered into collections: *Unpopular Opinions*, 1946, *Creed or Chaos?*, 1949, and in posthumous publications. She approached the task of making religion meaningful with a zeal that sometimes shocked the conventionally orthodox. Addressing the Archbishop of York's Conference at Malvern in 1941, she insisted that the churches spent more time "nosing out fornication" than in condemning intellectual corruption, denounced legalized adultery but paid scant attention to cheating, and acquiesced "in a definition of morality so one-sided that it has deformed the very meaning of the word by restricting it to sexual offenses." [12]

Lecturing on the capital sins, she boldly stated:

The Church says Covetousness is a deadly sin—but does she really think so? Is she ready to found Welfare Societies to deal with *financial* immorality as she does with sexual immorality. . . . Is Dives, like Magdalen, ever refused the sacraments on the grounds that he, like her, is an "open and notorious evil-liver"? Does the Church arrange services with bright, congregational singing for Total Abstainers from *Usury?*[1]

Never one to criticize without making an effort to alleviate the conditions which she deplored, Miss Sayers devoted her time, energy, and talents to eradicate the liberalism, lethargy, and laxity which vitiated postwar society and seemingly undermined the strength of the Anglican Church. When St. Thomas parish of Regent Street was reorganized after the war, becoming the parish of St. Anne, Soho, she was a vital force in the Society of St. Anne, an unusual organization which served as an inquiry center, a discussion club, and a drama society. As Chairwoman, she organized the first production of Christopher Fry's *A Sleep for Prisoners*, and directed several of her own plays. In 1952 she was appointed churchwarden. Minutes of the parish meetings reveal her interest and zeal in promoting intellectual activities. Informally associated with C. S. Lewis, Charles Williams,

and J. R. R. Tolkien, she was able to draw them and other intellectuals into the seminars, discussions, and drama festivals. Val Gielgud
recalls her zest for such activities: "No combination of air-raids and
general discomfort availed to keep her away from every rehearsal of
her broadcast play cycle, *The Man Born to Be King*. I doubt if she was
ever happier than when presiding over the charade-like ceremonial
of the Detection Club. She saw the whole business of actors and
acting through the rosiest-coloured spectacles . . . and behind a
facade occasionally forbidding there was an immense friendliness." [14]
(The fact that she wore the flowing robes designed for G. K. Chesterton when he was president of the club indicates her size; she was no
longer the slender girl who loped down High Street, Oxford, whis-
tling Bach, but her enthusiastic, fun-loving spirits were not dimin-
ished.) Appearing in the *Spectator* in 1939 and 1940, the "Wimsey
Papers" show that she could chuckle over human blunders. Miss
Climpson, a friend of Lord Peter, deplores that the children, hastily
evacuated from the cities to safer spots, were bereft of books, pens,
and paper, implying that the government had wretchedly bungled
the whole business of organizing and distributing supplies. Lord
Peter, after seeing a placard, "Berlin Suppressed Churchill,"
announced that if Berlin could do that, it could accomplish anything,
and England might as well lay down her arms at once." [15]

    Although involved in lecturing, writing, broadcasting, as well as
various club and parish activities in London, she found time to spend
quiet weekends in Witham, Essex, where she had purchased a cot-
tage for her mother after her father's death. It was evident by this
time that she was destined to be the breadwinner, for her husband,
"Mac," was content to live in Witham, earning small sums as a
photographer and painter of miniatures. During World War II and
later years, she spent more and more time in Witham, reserved and
even irascible to her husband and neighbors when engaged in writing
and research, friendly and interested in the town and its doings when
pressures lifted. Friends recall how she plodded along High Street, a
fur coat carelessly slung over her shoulders, as she set off to buy meat
for her many cats. The coat was a present to herself, a memento of an
occasion that delighted her: the conferring upon her in 1950 of an
Honorary Doctorate of Letters by the University of Durham. She
was, she admitted, particularly pleased by the citation which acknowledged "admiration of her art, gay and grave, and a deep regard for
her sincerity." [16]

    It was this same enthusiasm and exuberance that started her on her last, and many would say, her greatest intellectual achievement. Familiar with Dante's works through *The Figure of Beatrice* by her friend Charles Williams, she had put off reading *The Divine Comedy* because, she admitted: ". . . after all, fourteen thousand lines are fourteen thousand lines, especially if they are full of Guelfs and Ghibellines and Thomas Aquinas. . . . Besides, the world had always hinted that Dante, besides being great, grim, religious and intellectual, was also 'obscure.' " [17] It took an air-raid warning to get her started. Snatching up a book to read in the shelter, she discovered after settling down, that she had picked up a volume of the Temple edition of the *Inferno*, with Italian on one side, English on the other. "I can remember nothing like it since I first read *The Three Musketeers* at the age of thirteen," she declared. "However foolish it may sound, the plain fact is that I bolted my meals, neglected my sleep, work, and correspondence, drove my friends crazy . . . until I had panted my way through the Three Realms of the Dead from top to bottom and from bottom to top; and that, having finished, I found the rest of the world's great literature so lacking in pep and incident that I pushed it all peevishly aside and started out from the Dark Wood all over again." [18]

In order to read the poem in the original, she armed herself with an Italian grammar, a dictionary, and an English crib and mastered the study in six weeks. From then on her ambition was to make *The Divine Comedy* available to readers who, like herself, had avoided it because they lacked an understanding of the language and of Catholic theology, scholastic philosophy, Italian medieval history, the system of courtly love, and all the other studies so necessary to appreciate fully this masterpiece. At the end of the war she asked Dr. E. V. Rieu, editor of the Penguin Classics, about the possibility of a new translation for the common reader. Given the green light, she proceeded to set about this formidable task, determined to achieve not only a competent translation utilizing Dante's own verse form, the *terza rima*, but one with commentaries, footnotes, maps, diagrams, and glossaries that would clarify unfamiliar concepts and make the poem relevant to modern readers. Dante's *Inferno* appeared in 1949; *Purgatorio*, in 1955. Characteristically, she preferred the English titles. "Hell," as she said, "is a good, strong word!" The scope of her intensive study can best be indicated by reference to her scholarly volumes: *Introductory Papers on Dante*, 1954, and *Further Papers on Dante*, 1957. Many of these papers were originally delivered as lectures at Summer Schools of Italian at Jesus College, Cambridge.

She had completed twenty cantos of the *Paradiso* at the time of her sudden death, December 17, 1957. The work was finished by her friend and Dante scholar, Dr. Barbara Reynolds, of Girton College, Cambridge, who wrote in the Foreword of *Paradiso*: "It is probably true to say that between 1949 (the date of the publication of her translation of the *Inferno*) and the present day, 1962, the *Divine Comedy* has had more English-speaking readers than it ever had over a comparable length of time in all its history. That would not have displeased Dante. . . ." [19]

Such comments would not have displeased Miss Sayers, either. Just a few weeks before her death in 1957, in a rarely granted interview, she spoke with humorous resignation of Lord Peter Wimsey as her "breadwinner," but insisted that his exploits were not her real métier. "By instinct, preference, and training," she declared, "I am a scholar—a medieval scholar." She added wryly, "When I finished *Purgatory*, and wanted some relaxation before I started the next volume, I translated *The Song of Roland* (1957); I didn't write a detective story." [20]

Although she spoke disparagingly about her fiction at times, it was evident that she was proud of the fact that her detective novels were regarded as some of the very best to come out of what is often called the Golden Age of Detective Fiction, the years between the two World Wars. Yet she never wanted her novels to overshadow her more scholarly writings. When the BBC televised many of her novels, her fiction became better known in the United States, but during these same years her other writings also grew in popularity. Students read her translation of the *Divine Comedy* and her helpful essays; many study groups utilized her writings available in posthumous publications, such as *The Poetry of Search and Statement*, 1969; *Are Women Human?*, 1971; *A Matter of Éternity*, 1973; *Christian Letters to a Post-Christian World*, 1969, reprinted under the title *The Whimsical Christian: 18 Essays*, 1978. Interest in her themes and craftsmanship incresed to such an extent in the 1970s that her reputation truly encompasses her achievements in the way that she wished that they might be. Not only as a writer of detective fiction of significant merit, but as a dramatist, minor poet, Anglo-Catholic apologist, and Dante scholar-translator, she is now recognized as a Christian humanist who, revering the integrity of the word, left writings that have a particular relevance for these times.

CHAPTER 2

The Early Novels—Murder and Mirth

IN *Whose Body?*, published in 1923, Miss Sayers introduces Lord
Peter Wimsey, amateur investigator of crime, whose personality,
eccentricities, and powers of ratiocination are developed in novels
and short stories over a span of years.[1] Popular in the 1920s and
1930s, he became as famous as Conan Doyle's Sherlock Holmes, W.
H. Wright's Philo Vance, and Agatha Christie's Hercule Poirot.

Lord Peter is the second son of the fifteenth Duke of Denver,
deceased. The eldest son, Gerald, present Duke of Denver, manages
the family estate on the borders of the Fen country in Norfolk, leaving
his younger brother free to pursue his own interests. Miss Sayers
wisely endowed her hero with a quick mind and wit, freedom from
binding ties, and a large fortune. He has a tastefully furnished flat at
110A Piccadilly, and a valet, Bunter, competent and indefatigable.
Wimsey's special hobbies are book-collecting and criminal investigation. The latter, which brings the family name into law courts and
sensational newspapers, is frowned on by his brother and snobbish
sister-in-law Helen, but his mother, the Dowager Duchess, views his
sleuthing as a wholesome outlet, a release from the bouts of nerves
and depression which have afflicted him since the war.

Lord Peter looks the part he plays—the debonair, wealthy bache-
lor-detective. He has gray eyes, hard and keen, a narrow chin, a long,
receding forehead, sleek blond hair; he assumes a slightly foolish
expression, at times accentuated by a monocle. Although not very
tall, he gives the impression of strength. A graduate of Balliol, he took
first honors in history, won fame at Oxford as a cricketer, is renowned
as a connoisseur of food and wine, an amateur musician of surprising
skill, a collector of incunabula, and an avid sleuth. In *Whose Body?* he
does not possess all these characteristics; one of the delights of
following the Wimsey novels is the discovery of facets of his personality and character that deepen or change.

In the essay "Gaudy Night" Miss Sayers tells that in creating Lord
Peter she envisaged for him "a prolonged and triumphal career, going

on through book after book amid the plaudits of adoring multitudes," but after *Whose Body?* she realized that he was a mere puppet. She decided to operate on him, making him into a more "complete human being, with a past and a future, with a consistent family and social history, with a complicated psychology and even the rudiments of a religious outlook. . . . I laid him out firmly on the operating-table and chipped away at his internal mechanism through three longish books." [2]

Change him she did, indeed, providing him with an entry in *Who's Who* and a biography, supposedly written by his uncle, Paul Austin Delagardie. This traces Peter's life from childhood to his forty-fifth year, when he falls in love with Harriet Vane, on trial at Old Bailey. That story is told in *Strong Poison*.

In *Whose Body?* Miss Sayers reveals her ability to create an original plot, build tension, sustain suspense, and establish characterization. The first two chapters introduce the mystery of two bodies, one lost; one found. Just before rushing off to an important book sale, Lord Peter has a phone call from his mother, explaining why Mr. Thipps, the architect, cannot come to work: " 'He was so upset, poor little man. He'd found a dead body in his bath . . . with nothing on but a pair of pince-nez' " (8, 9). Sending Bunter to the sale, Wimsey dashes off to view the corpse in the bath. That evening his friend Parker, from Scotland Yard, comes to discuss another strange case: Sir Reuben Levy, a Jewish financier, has disappeared from his home; his personal effects, including all his clothes, even his eyeglasses, are there undisturbed. Murder is suspected.

When Inspector Sugg from Scotland Yard is confronted with an unidentified corpse and also a missing one, he jumps to the conclusion that they are one and the same person, despite Lord Peter's remonstrances. Parker assists Lord Peter with the case of the corpse with the pince-nez and receives help in return. Examining Sir Reuben's clothing and measuring the depression in the bedclothes, Wimsey deduces that someone returned in the late evening, used brushes, slippers, and bed, but that it was not Sir Reuben. Furthermore, Bunter discovers two sets of fingerprints on several articles. The body in the bath smells of carbolic acid, is discolored with flea bites, and has bad teeth; it could not be Sir Reuben from Park Lane.

These points are established in the first four chapters; in the remaining nine, Lord Peter traces the owner of the unusual pince-nez, finds that his suspicions concerning Sir Reuben's business rival,

Mr. Milligan, are false, and learns from his mother that, years ago, Sir Julian Freke, an eminent surgeon and scientist, had courted and expected to marry a girl who suddenly rejected him and eloped with Sir Reuben Levy. Lord Peter ponders: jealousy could be a motive for murder, but was it likely that so esteemed a person as Sir Julian Freke, after so many years, would commit such a deed? Rejecting the suspicion, Lord Peter tries to forget the case by reading Sir Julian's newest publication, *Physiological Bases of the Conscience*, a treatise contending that mind and matter are one, and that all ethical values should be, and soon will be, obsolete. Arguing that man's conscience is of little or no value and that it will disappear in the next decades, Freke insists that ideas of good and evil will vanish or become relative.

Pondering the terrible state of society if such a condition ever comes to pass, Lord Peter realizes that such beliefs would be an ideal doctrine for a criminal to hold, for a man who believed that conscience could be totally eliminated would stoop to any crime. Suddenly Lord Peter realizes that Sir Julian Freke has the moral outlook, the motivation, and the ability to perpetrate murder.

Miss Sayers presents his enlightenment in terms of intuition and associational psychology:

> . . . the scattered elements of two grotesque conundrums, flung higgledy piggledy into Lord Peter's mind, resolved themselves, unquestioned henceforward. . . . a single ruddy hair—lint bandages—Inspector Sugg calling the great surgeon from the dissecting-room of the hospital . . . the smell of carbolic soap. . . . all these things and many others rang together and made one sound, they swung together like bells in a steeple. . . . (168)

In the long denouement, evidence is secured, the mystery of the body in the bathtub is solved, and Sir Julian Freke is arrested.

Despite Howard Haycraft's view that Lord Peter in *Whose Body?* is "only a shadowy outline, a vague, affected caricature of the Wimsey known to thousands today," [3] and Miss Sayers's admission that he "played the silly ass," nevertheless this first novel establishes several personality and character traits which do not change over the years. It also reveals his lifestyle, his family relationships, as well as his associations with Bunter, Parker, and minor characters, such as Freddy Arbuthnot and Inspector Sugg, who appear in many novels. In later years, Lord Peter's hair turns gray and his deportment is less flamboyant, but his ebullient spirits, his delight in quoting literary gems and making impromptu parodies, remain unchanged.

Lighthearted loquacity is one of his notable characteristics. Miss Sayers often masks his feelings by using banter and persiflage. His disgust over Inspector Sugg's obtuseness is revealed in his comment: "Parker, acushla, you're an honour to Scotland Yard. I look at you, and Sugg appears a myth, a fable, an idiot-boy, spawned in a moonlight hour by some fantastic poet's brain" (34). Suspicious of Mr. Milligan's association with Sir Levy, Lord Peter thinks of a ruse to watch him closely; he invites him to speak at a church benefit: " 'How I did it' kind of touch, y'know—'A Drop of Oil with a Kerosene King'—'Cash, Conscience and Cocoa' and so on. It would interest people. . . . We'd really appreciate it very much if you'd come and stay a day or two and just give us a little breezy word on the almighty dollar" (62).

Two character traits evident in this first novel remain constant throughout Lord Peter's career. The first is his concern for the elderly and those less fortunate than himself, evinced here by his solicitude for Mrs. Thipps. Although his motives are not purely altruistic, he goes to a great deal of trouble to bring her to his mother's home, the Dower House, Denver Castle, at two o'clock in the morning, knowing that his mother will cosset her, while preventing her from interfering with the investigations of Scotland Yard. The second, more prominent trait is his intense dislike of bringing a criminal to justice. Once the mental challenge to outwit the criminal is met, the code of sportsmanship instilled during his public school training makes him unwilling to continue the pursuit. Parker, whose middle-class background, red-brick university education, and position at Scotland Yard create no such scruples, lashes out when Lord Peter confesses that he does not feel like "playing the game" any longer because somebody is going to be hurt. Reminding his friend that he ought to drop this "playing-fields-of-Eton complex," Parker continues: "You want to be consistent, you want to look pretty, you want to swagger debonairly through a comedy of puppets. . . . You want to hunt down a murderer for the sport of the thing and then shake hands. . . . Well, you can't do it like that. Life's not a football match. You want to be a sportsman. You can't be a sportsman. You're a responsible person" (158).

Lord Peter's scruples are genuine; sometimes he suffers so acutely after he has brought a criminal to justice that he collapses. For instance, after surmising the extent of Sir Julian Freke's perfidy, Lord Peter falls asleep, then awakens delirious, shivering and chattering wildly, under the delusion that he is in the trenches, waiting for Bunter to rescue his men.

Although Miss Sayers was dissatisfied with *Whose Body?* when she reread it years later, nevertheless it has features so well planned and executed that she utilized them in subsequent works. Lord Peter's apartment, for instance, remains unchanged until the last novel, when, as a married man, he moves to more spacious quarters. His library retains the same décor through many novels:

> Lord Peter's library was one of the most delightful bachelor rooms in London. Its scheme was black and primrose; its walls were lined with rare editions, and its chairs and Chesterfield sofa suggested the embraces of the houris. In one corner stood a black baby-grand, a wood fire leaped on a wide old-fashioned hearth, and the Sèvres vases on the chimney-piece were filled with ruddy and gold chrysanthemums. (26)

Permanent, too, is his invaluable sleuthing equipment: the monocle, worn jauntily at times, is a very powerful lens, which, he explains, is "jolly useful when you want to take a good squint at somethin' and look like a bally fool all the time." A silver matchbox is actually a small electric torch (flashlight); a walking stick has a sword tucked inside, a compass in the silver knob, and is marked off in inches, truly a "gentleman-scout's *vade-mecum*," as he terms it.

Mervyn Bunter, Lord Peter's valet, is one of Miss Sayers's best-drawn and beloved characters. His endearing traits are those of devoted service, loyal discretion, and competency. Although Lord Peter seems to accept Bunter's unremitting attendance with perfunctory appreciation, an occasional comment shows how much he values him. When Parker drops in to tell about the vanishing financier, Wimsey asks him to hold the news: "D'you mind if Bunter hears it, too? Invaluable man, Bunter—amazin' fellow with a camera. And the odd thing is, he's always on the spot when I want my bath or my boots" (29).

Responsible for Lord Peter's sartorial elegance, Bunter brooks no interference in this matter. Wimsey, late for a dinner party, and hoping to dash off without changing his attire, meets with stern resistance:

> "Not on any account, my lord. It would be as much as my place is worth."
> "The trousers are all right, Bunter."
> "Not for Lady Swaffham's, my lord. Besides, your lordship forgets the man that ran against you with a milk-can in Salisbury." (145)

A trustworthy and clever assistant, Bunter photographs footmarks, lifts fingerprints, prepares slides of incriminating objects, and ferrets out information discreetly. In the house of Sir Reuben Levy, he engratiates himself "below stairs," and while snapping photos of objects from the master's bedroom, gleans details about the personal habits of the missing man which confirm Wimsey's suspicions that it was not Sir Levy who occupied the room that auspicious night. Plying Sir Julian's man with Lord Peter's best port and cigars, Bunter extracts details of the surgeon's movements during the night of Sir Levy's visit and disappearance.

The Dowager Duchess is more fully characterized in later novels, but several traits, discernible in *Whose Body?*, do not change. Her maternal solicitude is evinced by her concern for Lord Peter's health and happiness and by her willingness to assist him in his sleuthing whether it involves sheltering the aged Mrs. Thipps, entering into the hoax concerning Milligan's talk at a charity bazaar, an affair which she supposedly is sponsoring, or comforting Lady Levy during the ordeal of the autopsy of her late husband.

The Duchess's tendency to chatter, jumbling incoherent ideas, irrelevant asides, and nonsequiturs in rapid succession, creates the impression that she is somewhat confused, but the truth is that her quicksilver mind slides from one thought to another, and she expects her listeners to keep pace with her. (Lord Peter's loquacity is an inherited trait.) When Sir Julian Freke appears in court, she confides: ". . . and I'm sure some Jews were very good people, and personally I'd much rather they believed in something, though of course it must be very inconvenient, what with not working on Saturdays and circumcising the poor little babies and everything depending on the new moon . . . and never being able to have bacon for breakfast . . ." (56, 57). (Because the Dowager at times sounds anti-Semitic, critics have accused the author of the same bias.)

I *Minor Characters*

Charles Parker from Scotland Yard is an excellent foil for Lord Peter. Like Sherlock's Watson, Parker listens respectfully to his friend's theories, marvels at his powers of observation and agility in discovering solutions to perplexing mysteries, then methodically works out his own conclusions. As a representative of Scotland Yard, he gives to Wimsey's unofficial activities a semblance of authoritative support. Despite the warning, "You'll never become a professional till you learn to do a little work, Wimsey" (73), Parker is obliged to undertake all the onerous tasks, gathering data, interrogating suspects, shadowing elusive figures, and examining possible clues. He serves not only as a Watson-figure on whom Wimsey tests his theories and suppositions, but also as a companion. His education and limited means do not prevent him from enjoying Lord Peter's varied interests, particularly his habit of tossing off literary quips, parodies, and allusions. Lecturing Lord Peter on his duty to complete a case, despite his compunction over bringing a criminal to trial, Parker obviously expresses the opinions of the author. Fond as she was of her hero, she could not approve of his irresponsible attitude; law and order must be maintained for the good of society. In *Creed or Chaos?* she asserts that, although the law shares human imperfections, yet it is necessary "as a protective fence against the forces of evil, behind which the divine activity of grace may do its redeeming work." [4]

Inspector Sugg from Scotland Yard appears frequently in the novels. In charge of the investigation concerning the body found in Thipps's bath, Sugg reveals his incompetency and overzealousness. Examining the corpse, he fails to notice such telltale signs as flea bites, callouses, and dirty toenails; he insists that the body must be that of Sir Reuben Levy and orders Lady Levy to return to England to confirm his opinion.

When Sugg discovers that both Mr. Thipps and the maid, Gladys Horrocks, have concealed pertinent information about their actions, he charges them with murder and places them under arrest. (Michael Underwood in *Crime in Good Company* notes that such an arrest would not be made until sufficient evidence was available to support such a charge, a mistake undoubtedly permitted by the author in order to accentuate Sugg's hasty bungling and ineptitude.) [5] In later novels, Sugg, a shade more competent, is treated with less scorn. His character and surly manner change very little, however. He continues to play the role familiar to readers of this genre, that of the obtuse, heavy-handed policeman who impedes, rather than assists, the investigations of the quick-witted, adroit detective.

II *Notable Writing Techniques*

The first novel shows Miss Sayers's talent for writing dialogue that reveals the personalities of the speakers and the relationship existing between them. Sitting in the smoking room at his brother's home, grinning over a letter from Bunter reporting his success in securing information, Lord Peter is rebuked by his brother Gerald:

"What on earth are you doing, Peter, sittin' there noddin' an' grinnin' like a what-you-may call it?" demanded the Duke, coming out of a snooze. "Someone writin' pretty things to you, what?"

"Charming things," said Lord Peter. The Duke eyed him doubtfully. "Hope to goodness you don't go and marry a chorus beauty," he muttered inwardly, and returned to the *Times*. (178, 179)

A technique that adds a touch of comedy is the use of a web of tangled sentences, clauses, dangling participles, and nonsequiturs, a jumble that may not express comprehensible ideas but implies a great deal about the character speaking. When Sir Julian Freke comes into the courtroom, for instance, the Dowager Duchess murmurs to Parker:

"So handsome, I always think . . . just exactly like William Morris, with that bush of hair and beard and those exciting eyes looking out of it—so splendid, these dear men always devoted to something or other—not but what I think socialism is a mistake—of course it works with all those nice people, so good and happy in art linen and the weather always perfect—Morris, I mean, you know—but so difficult in real life." (128)

This elliptical phrasing marks Lord Peter's lighthearted spoofing when he asks Mr. Milligan to talk at the church benefit: "My mother—most energetic, self-sacrificin' woman, don't you see, is thinkin' of getting up a sort of charity bazaar down at Denver this winter, in aid of the church roof, y'know . . . fine old antique . . . all tumblin' to pieces, rain pourin' in and so on—vicar catchin' rheumatism at early service . . ." (80). This technique is also employed to depict unusual settings and mounting tension. It dramatically evokes the eeriness of the graveyard during the exhumation of Sir Reuben Levy's body: "The sound of the spades for many minutes. An iron noise of tools thrown down. Demons stooping and straining. A black-bearded spectre at your elbow. Introduced. The Master of the Work-house. . . . The mortuary. Raw red brick and sizzling gas-jets. Two women in black, and Dr. Grimbold. The coffin laid on the table with a heavy thump" (224, 225).

Whose Body? was favorably received. The *Nation* commented: "Seldom has a murder been made so delightfully mysterious and rarely has the gentleman detective been cast in quite so attractive a guise as that of Lord Peter Wimsey to whom books in first folios and bodies in bathtubs are of equal interest." [6] Haycraft, in *Murder for Pleasure*, praised its original plot, articulate and amusing style, and the range of interesting subsidiary characters. [7] Such notices encouraged Miss Sayers to continue.

III   Clouds of Witness

Clouds of Witness, 1926, has a complex plot concerned with Lord Peter's efforts to clear his brother Gerald, Duke of Denver, of the charge of murdering Captain Denis Cathcart, fiancé of their sister, Lady Mary Wimsey.[8] The Captain's body was found near the hunting lodge where the Duke has been hosting a shooting party. He admits that after receiving a letter from a friend stating that Cathcart is a card cheat, he confronted him with the allegation and a violent quarrel ensued. Unfortunately, the Duke cannot find the incriminatory letter, and his gun is discovered close by the corpse which, he claims, he stumbled upon when returning from a stroll on the moors about three in the morning. He absolutely refuses to say why he was there at that odd hour. At the inquest, Lady Mary declares that she heard a shot at three o'clock, but the doctor who examined the body at 4:30 insists that the victim has been dead for three or four hours. The evidence establishes that the Duke of Denver had the motive and the opportunity for murder. Refusing to provide an alibi for those questionable morning hours, he is held in prison.

Lord Peter's enthusiasm for solving mysteries is slightly dashed, for his brother takes a dim view of his offers of assistance. Under his mask of insouciance, Peter's worry increases as the days draw closer to the trial in the House of Lords. With Parker from Scotland Yard, he discusses puzzling angles: had Gerald actually received a letter stating that Cathcart was a gambler and cheat? On whom had Cathcart squandered his wealth? Who hid the suitcase in the conservatory? Who dropped the bracelet charm, a diminutive diamond cat with emerald eyes? What about the bloodstains on Lady Mary's skirt? Was her malingering a trick to hide something or someone?

To Lord Peter, the questions seem endless and his visit to Grider's Hole, Mr. Grimethorpe's farm, creates further complications. Both Parker and Lord Peter agree that there must have been another person prowling about that eventful night; Peter suspects that the interloper was returning from an assignation with the beautiful Mrs. Grimethorpe while her brutish husband was away. Lady Mary's melodramatic confession that she killed Cathcart is brushed aside by her brother as something out of a "blood-and-thunder" novel, but it confirms his suspicions that she is trying to shield someone.

Despite the investigations of Parker and Wimsey, the date set for the Duke's trial before the House of Lords draws near without proof sufficient to establish his innocence. Convinced that Grider's Hole offers a clue hitherto undiscovered, Lord Peter and Bunter risk another trip there, but on the way, trapped in a murky fog, they stumble into a bog and Lord Peter sinks into quicksand. Rescued by Bunter, he is taken to Grimethorpe's farm, where he discovers a piece of evidence that will clear his brother's name but leaves another mystery to be solved: who did kill Cathcart? Handwriting on a blotter suggests a possible solution which necessitates Lord Peter's flight to New York to interview Cathcart's former mistress.

In the meantime, the Duke of Denver's trial opens in the House of Lords. Three hundred British peers, garbed in scarlet robes and ermine, assemble.[9] The Royal Gallery is filled; witnesses are marshaled; reporters fidget; the ceremony begins with a Proclamation of Silence. Then the Duke of Denver, looking "very small and pink and lonely in his blue serge suit, the only head uncovered among all his peers . . . listened to the Lord High Steward's rehearsal of the charge with a simple gravity which became him very well" (162). As the trial proceeds, tension mounts. Relief comes unexpectedly when Lord Peter Wimsey, grubby and grease-stained after a hazardous ocean flight, rushes in with a letter and deposition clearing the Duke of the murder charge.

Critics point out that *Clouds of Witness* is structurally weak, dependent on implausible coincidences and melodramatic scenes rather than on the ratiocinative powers of Lord Peter. Parker's discovery of the shop where the jeweled charm was purchased, the dangers of the trans-Atlantic flight, and the circumstances of Grimethorpe's death are indeed melodramatic, but they add suspense, tension, and elements of uncertainty that make the novel exciting and entertaining. Michael Underwood suggests that Parker plays an unusual role in the investigation: "The really curious thing is, though, that Parker spends the whole of his time working in conjunction with Lord Peter Wimsey in ferreting out evidence *for the defense*. In spite of all this when the matter finally comes to trial in the House of Lords, the Attorney-General is able to present a full and detailed case to the Peers. Where he got it from is the one unsolved mystery of the book."[10]

James Burleson states that this work is of little importance in tracing Miss Sayers's progress toward her goal of writing the novel of manners.[11] He fails to note the very significant changes in the portrait of Lord Peter. Miss Sayers's comments in "Gaudy Night" suggest why she considered these changes essential and how she went about making them. Dissatisfied with the portrait in *Whose Body?* of Lord

Peter as a slightly silly aristocrat, endowed with little else but a taste for savoring excellent foods and vintage wines and indulging in his hobbies, collecting rare books and sleuthing, she creates here a more believable individual, an erudite, humane sophisticate of thirty-three years: a scholar, a musician of skill and understanding, an expert in toxicology. She cites enough instances to make these accomplishments seem credible.

The author's knowledge of classical literature is cleverly utilized to suggest Lord Peter's erudition. Watching Sir Impey Biggs's profile, Peter thinks that it has "the severe beauty of the charioteer of Delphi, and was about as communicative" (61). On two occasions he thinks of Mrs. Grimethorpe as Medusa, beautiful and enchanting (74, 144). Despite his perilous position in the engulfing quicksand, he envisions Bunter grappling to rescue him, as a "very Gothic Theseus of a late and degenerate school" (156).

By showing Lord Peter's concern for his sister's happiness and for his brother's precarious embroilment with the law, the author makes her hero more mature and humane. Conscious that his sister is suffering emotionally and aware that they have grown apart during the war years, he makes every effort to reestablish a relationship based on affection and sincerity. Realizing that she is interested in Parker, who returns her admiration, Peter fosters the friendship, although cognizant that in doing so he will upset Gerald and his wife, Helen, who cherish class distinctions based on wealth and birth. Peter's approval of the burgeoning love affair provides the author with opportunities to comment indirectly on changing social standards and values in England.

Miss Sayers's experiences as a copywriter at an advertising agency made her familiar with sales jargon which she utilizes in describing Lord Peter's gambit to win over the surly farmhand guarding the gates at the Grimethorpe farm. Peter burbles: "Wherever I go throughout the length and breadth of the North Riding I hear of Mr. Grimethorpe. 'Grimethorpe's butter is the best'; 'Grimethorpe's fleeces never go to pieces'; 'Grimethorpe's pork Melts on the fork'; 'For Irish stews Take Grimethorpe's ewes'; 'A tummy lined with Grimethorpe's beef, Never never comes to grief' " (70). Under all this nonsense is Peter's indomitable courage and determination to continue to search for clues, despite all handicaps.

The portrait of the Duchess is changed considerably. Although she still chatters, jumbling ideas and asides in an almost incomprehensible manner, she is more shrewd, witty, and discerning. One of Miss

Sayers's most memorable characters, the Duchess reflects the common sense and integrity of her creator. Adroit at puncturing the hypocritical posturings of the younger generation, who prattle about social, economic, and religious freedom, she effectually silences her daughter's protests that Goyles was not contradicting Lord Mountweazle but was just refusing to kowtow to an older person. "To be sure," the Dowager replies, "when you flatly deny everything that a person says it does sound like contradiction to the uninitiated" (112).

Proud of his mother's discernment, Wimsey supports her view "that if all those new-fangled doctors went out of their way to invent subconsciousness and kleptomania, and complexes and other fancy descriptions to explain away when people had done naughty things, she thought one might just as well take advantage of the fact" (91). Examining the synthesis of Christian ideas in Miss Sayers's works, David Soper states that Lord Peter's comment is made in proud recognition of her moral wisdom which properly evaluates the pseudo-scientific cant and popular illiteracy so widely accepted as truth.[12] It also may be interpreted as the author's concern over society's permissive attitude toward sexual freedom. To many in the Duke of Denver's social set, his adultery seems less reprehensible than Cathcart's card-cheating; Lady Mary has had an affair and contemplates marriage to a man who fully intends to continue to keep a mistress, a situation less irksome to Lady Mary than the vapid social life from which she hopes to escape. These relationships are never condoned but become important elements in the theme of false loyalties and false standards. Sexual scenes are never detailed, but, like Lord Peter's risque jokes, they are left to the reader's imagination. John Raymond's confession in the *New Statesman* is more of a tribute to the chasteness of English publications than a condemnation of the Wimsey novels: "Re-reading Miss Sayers again this week, I remembered how we loved it all at thirteen, and how sophisticated we felt on the train that took us back to the grim Warwickshire prep school. . . ."[13]

Miss Sayers's skill in describing settings is evident in her graphic portrayal of the colorful pageantry in the House of Lords, the description of Mr. Murbles's rooms at Staple Inn, Mr. Grimethorpe's gloom-shrouded house, the hunting lodge, and the pubs and clubs which Lord Peter visits. In *Clouds of Witness*, Miss Sayers began the practice of introducing chapters with intriguing titles and significant quotations. Chapter one, "Of His Malice Aforethought," has an introductory quotation from *Othello*: "O, who hath done this deed?";

chapter four, "And His Daughter, Much-Afraid," has a quotation from *The Pilgrim's Progress*: "The women also looked pale and wan," an apt line to introduce Peter's encounters with Lady Mary and Mrs. Grimethorpe.

Less successful than *Whose Body?* because of an excessive use of coincidence and melodrama, nevertheless the novel reveals the author's techniques in establishing characterization, particularly the portraits of the Wimsey family. Symons in *Mortal Consequences* commented that some of the minor upper-class characters are "conceived in the terms of a sketch for *Punch*"; [14] one might add that the satiric thrusts at society and its postwar follies have the wit and verve that mark that publication.

IV   Unnatural Death

Unnatural Death, 1927, originally published in America under the title *The Dawson Pedigree*, concerns not one murder but three.[15] Lord Peter and Parker listen sympathetically when Doctor Carr tells them of his suspicions concerning the unexpected death of his former patient, a wealthy eccentric, Miss Dawson. Although she refused to make a will, she let it be known that her fortune was to be inherited by her grand-niece, Miss Whittaker, a nurse who had cared for her during her last illness. Although Miss Dawson had cancer, the doctor is disturbed at the suddenness of her death. Despite the fact that an autopsy showed nothing amiss, he suspects that Miss Whittaker hastened her aunt's death.

Investigating the case, Lord Peter discovers that, since Miss Dawson died intestate in 1925, the grand-niece is the legal heir, but if the death had occurred in 1926 when the New Property Act came into effect, the fortune would have passed to the Crown. He not only suspects foul play but events make him fear the perpetration of more evil. Parker remains skeptical, even when a serving girl, formerly employed in the Dawson household, is found murdered in Epping Forest. As murders and murderous attacks increase, Parker is drawn into the case, but in the meantime Lord Peter is assisted by Miss Climpson. The murder of Vera Findlater, friend and close companion of Miss Whittaker, convinces Lord Peter that the grand-niece is trying to eliminate every person who knows something about her aunt's death. The motive for the murders is established but how were these brought about?

By the middle of the novel, readers suspect that Miss Whittaker is the murderer, but their interest is held by numerous complications: multiple murders, problems involving the legacy, the continued machinations of the villain, and Lord Peter's efforts to outwit her. As coldblooded and ruthless as Sir Julian Freke in *Whose Body?*, she schemes to secure what she wants and succeeds in her last endeavor: she escapes legal punishment by hanging herself.

Praising its sustained interest, Edmund Pearson commented: "The excitement lies in the chase and detection. . . . As the story progresses, the victims increase in number and very much in virtue and attractiveness. Here the crimes are real crimes; the murderer is a wicked person." [16] Haycraft stated that, although the murders are ingenious, yet the reader is disappointed at the premature revelation of the culprit, for "in the perfectly constructed detective story the questions *Who?* and *How?* are answered simultaneously at the dénouement. That story . . . which confines its puzzle to the *How?* of the crime simply falls short of its avowed goal." [17]

True to her commitment to make Lord Peter a more genuine person and less the frivolous fool, Miss Sayers shows him, now thirty-seven years old, more conscious of the gravity of his avocation, sleuthing, and more worldly-wise, particularly in regard to his knowledge of women. He is aware, for instance, as Parker is not, that Mrs. Forrest is playing the role of a seductress; he is surprised not by her attempts to seduce him, but by her clumsiness and revulsion when embraced. When he realizes that she is almost physically ill after his light kiss, he determines to discover what is behind her story and her actions.

His sensitivity to problems of conscience is evident. He asks the Vicar, for instance, if it would be a terrible crime to hurry the death of a person who would die very soon at any rate, "just to give 'em a little push off so to speak—hurry matters on—why should that be a dreadful crime?" (228). The Vicar's response: "Sin is in the intention, not in the deed," and his explanation that it is bad for any human being to feel that he has the right to dispose of another person's life to his own advantage, are succinct statements of Christian thought, but the exchange flows easily, devoid of moralizing tones. Lord Peter's scruples are not overplayed. Counseled by the Vicar to do what is right in accordance with the law of the country and to leave the consequences to God, Lord Peter responds: "I know. Knock the man down but don't dance on the body. Quite. . . . I don't feel so rotten about it now. But I was getting worried" (230).

Accused by some critics of modeling Lord Peter Wimsey on P. G.

Wodehouse's Bertie Wooster, in this novel Miss Sayers deliberately calls attention to mannerisms and verbal flights of fancy that are similar to Bertie's. In the act of ringing for Bunter, Lord Peter pauses: "His jaw slackened, giving his long, narrow face a faintly foolish and hesitant look, reminiscent of the heroes of Mr. P. G. Wodehouse." Miss Sayers also parodies the style of Conan Doyle. Wimsey jokes with Parker: "I am baffled, Watson (said he, his hawk-like eyes gleaming angrily from under the half-closed lids). Even I am baffled. But not for long! (he cried with a magnificent burst of self-confidence)" (216).

As usual, Parker does the grubby, mundane work while Lord Peter engages in the less demanding but more exciting aspects of the case. Lunching in a dreary cafeteria, redolent with stale tea urns and fried fish, Parker reflects ruefully that Wimsey, "a vision in pale grey," is dining luxuriously at his club, confident and not at all abashed that the "lengthy, intricate, tedious and soul-destroying" tasks will be done by others.

V   Introducing Miss Climpson

One of the author's most entertaining and believable characters is Miss Alexandra Climpson, who assists Peter. He explains to Parker:

"She is my ears and tongue . . . and especially my nose. She asks questions which a young man could not put without a blush. . . . People want questions asked. Whom do they send? A man with large flat feet and a note-book. . . . I send a lady with a long, woolly jumper on knitting-needles and jingly things around her neck. Of course she asks questions—everyone expects it. Nobody is surprised. Nobody is alarmed." (42–43)

Miss Sayers employs a clever, stylistic device to suggest Miss Climpson's nervous energy, exuberance, and scrupulosity. Whenever the fussily precise spinster writes to Lord Peter, the important ideas in each sentence are heavily underscored in pencil; exclamation marks, interjections, and parenthetical comments are sprinkled profusely in every paragraph. Despite her idiosyncrasies, Miss Climpson is a discerning person who knows human nature and has the courage to express her moral views. Realizing that Vera Findlater is so captivated by Miss Whittaker that she is virtually her slave, Miss Climpson hints that it would be better if Vera lavished this love on a young man. When Vera protests that a great friendship not only keeps one from being self-centered but also makes one courageous enough to sacrifice one's life for a friend, Miss Climpson unequivocally denounces this attitude:

"I once heard a sermon about that from a most *splendid* priest—and he said that that kind of love might become *idolatry* if one wasn't careful. He said that Milton's remark about Eve—you know, 'he for God only, she for God in him'—was not congruous with Catholic doctrine. One must get the *proportions* right, and it was *out of proportion* to see everything through the eyes of another fellow-creature." (188)

The author's love and knowledge of literature are evident in her facile interweaving of literary quotations, allusions, songs, and parodies which become more numerous as her stories acquire the characteristics of the novel of manners. Her erudition colors Wimsey's jokes and responses. He quotes lines from Ingoldsby, taunts Parker by singing, "Back and sides go bare, go bare," refers to himself as Prince Florizel of Bohemia, recites Wordsworth to a bewildered telephone operator, quotes Dickens, and christens his Daimler "Mrs. Merdle," because "she doesn't make a row, but purrs along, creating no trouble" (71).

Each chapter is introduced with a provocative quotation suggesting the contents. Chapter VI, entitled "Found Dead," has a line from Chapman: "Blood, though it sleep a time, yet never dies" (63); Chapter XVI, "A Cast-Iron Alibi," is prefaced by a line from *Pickwick Papers*, "Oh, Sammy, Sammy, why vorn't there an alleybi?" (182); Chapter XXI, "By What Means?" is introduced by one succinct line from Beaumont and Fletcher: "Death hath so many doors to let out life" (240).

Miss Sayers continues to evoke personality and character by describing an individual's appearance. Parker's comments, for instance, reveal a great deal about Mrs. Forrest: "Tall, over-dressed, musquash and those abbreviated sort of shoes with jewelled heels and hardly any uppers—. . . . Heavily peroxided; strong aroma of orifan wafted out upon a passer-by; powder too white for the fashion and mouth heavily obscured with sealing-wax red; eyebrows painted black to startle, not deceive; finger-nails a monument to Kraska—the pink variety" (81).

Surnames are comically apt: Mr. Tredgold is pastor of the Anglican Church, S. Onesimus; Mr. Probyn is a retired solicitor; Miss Findlater finds out too late the treachery of her friend; the suspect, Hallelujah, has every right to be jubilant, for his innocence is established and he inherits unexpected wealth. However, the Gotobed sisters are far more prim and proper than their name implies.

Unnatural Death reveals the author's careful attention to structure and form. Part one, "The Medical Problem," probes the causes of two deaths; part two, "The Legal Problem," details the intricacies of inheritance under the New Property Act; part three, "The Medico-Legal Problem," brings the two aspects together in a crescendo of murder, assault, and the conviction of the criminal. Part two is slightly tedious. The lengthy reminiscences of the Coblings are uninteresting, and the involved points of jurisprudence explained by Mr. Towkington, an authority on the New Property Act, make one chapter, in the opinion of Erik Routley, "nearly unreadable." Insisting that it is a bad novel with a creaking plot, he claims that it would have been a good short story.[18] Few critics support this view, but some have questioned the credibility of the means of murder.

R. Philmore stated that, with the increased demand for detective stories, writers were forced to look for odder and odder methods of killing victims. Asked if the method of murder detailed in this novel was plausible, Doctor Yudkin answered that death by the means described seemed unlikely, but medical opinion varies. "Possible, but not probable," is the usual response.[19] "It would be pernickety," commented Julian Symons, "to condemn a book which is a compendium of clever touches (who else has thought of making not one set of false footprints, but three, as the villain does here?) on such a ground. The method was at least possible, and it would be ungenerous to demand certainty."[20]

Unnatural Death is a significant work, for here the author begins to write a detective story with the characteristics of the novel of manners. She emphasizes important themes: evil begets evil; inordinate love enslaves. Characterization is improved by a more humane portrayal of Lord Peter and the introduction of the sprightly Miss Climpson.

VI The Unpleasantness at the Bellona Club

The Unpleasantness at the Bellona Club, 1928, opens on Armistice Day with Lord Peter and Captain George Fentiman exchanging pleasantries about the sepulchral staidness of the Bellona Club, stronghold of their arch-conservative elders.[21] Complaining that the place reminds him of a morgue, Fentiman points to his grandfather, who habitually appears at ten in the morning, collects his *Morning Post*, and settles in his favorite chair until evening. Approaching General Fentiman, Wimsey draws the newspaper from the gnarled hands; they are stiff, lifeless, cold.

Examining the body, Doctor Penberthy announces that the death, which probably occurred some hours earlier, was caused by heart failure. Ten days later, Mr. Murbles, solicitor for the Fentiman family, visits Lord Peter to ask if he would be willing to undertake the task of investigating the precise time of the General's death. The disposal of a large fortune depends on that information. The General's sister, Lady Dormer, an aged eccentric, made a will dividing her wealth according to these terms: if her brother, General Fentiman, survives her, he is to inherit her fortune, and twelve thousand pounds is to go to a distant relative, Ann Dorland, who has attended Lady Dormer in her last illness. However, if the brother died before his sister, the fortune is to go to Miss Dorland, and a sum of fifteen thousand pounds is to be divided between the General's two grandsons, Major Robert, the elder, and Captain George Fentiman. After explaining all this, Mr. Murbles reminds Lord Peter that the General usually came to the club about ten o'clock; Lady Dormer died precisely at 10:37 A.M. on Armistice Day.

The conditions are clear: if the General died before 10:37, Miss Dorland inherits half a million pounds; if he died after 10:37, he has legally inherited the money which will go to his heir, Major Robert; Miss Dorland then will receive only twelve thousand pounds. As soon as Lord Peter undertakes the inquiry, he informs Doctor Penberthy that he knows that there were suspicious aspects of the *rigor mortis* when he found the body. He also noticed that there was an important item missing among the General's clothes. The question is, not *when* did the General die, but where, how, and by whose hand?

The questionable actions of the suspects add to the novel's suspense. Major Robert Fentiman disappears to search for the unknown Oliver, with whom the General allegedly spent the evening of November 10; George Fentiman's attack of war nerves seems suspicious; Ann Dorland's sudden decision to settle the inheritance question by dividing the money with the brothers looks like a ruse to prevent a postexhumation autopsy. Examining Miss Dorland's studio, Parker concludes that she has a peculiar interest in crime stories and has been experimenting with chemical poisons, but Lord Peter, studying her paintings, discovers a portrait that suggests an entirely different fixation. Learning that Doctor Penberthy planned to set up an experimental clinic for glandular treatments—to rejuvenate some of his elderly patients—and possibly his own fortunes—, and after winning Miss Dorland's affections, abusively jilted her when her inheritance was in question, Lord Peter does not have to take many steps to clear up the mysteries surrounding the time and manner of the General's death.

Disobeying the rule of "Fair-Play," in this novel Miss Sayers conceals two important pieces of information, but the astute reader has little trouble figuring out what these are. As one reviewer says: "All its developments came just a little too late to knock the reader off his chair . . . he needs no great nimbleness to keep anywhere from one to six chapters ahead of the story." [22]

Two minor characters are introduced as loyal friends of Lord Peter. The sculptress, Marjorie Phelps, helps him by introducing him to Ann Dorland's Bohemian friends. Salcombe Hardy, journalist, never quite sober but always inquisitive, is, according to Peter, worth his weight in pound notes to the *Yell*, a London newspaper. He frequently adds a comic note. After surreptitiously observing the exhumation and autopsy of the General, Hardy explains how he managed the feat: "I was on a family vault, pretending to be a recording angel."

Miss Sayers utilizes a barrage of elliptical phrases to highlight the effusiveness of Mrs. Rushworth, excited over London's newest craze, the scientific possibilities of rejuvenation by glandular therapy. She gushes enthusiastically: "So very wonderful about glands, isn't it . . . Are you devoted to young criminals, by any chance? And just to think that we have been quite wrong about them all these thousands of years. Flogging and bread and water, you know, and Holy Communion, when what they really needed was a little bit of rabbit-gland or something to make them just as good as gold. Quite horrible, isn't it" (181).

Literary quotations are not used to introduce chapter headings; the titles are terms from card games. "Hearts Count More than Diamonds" reveals that Lady Dormer, against her family's wishes, married for love rather than for money; "Lord Peter Plays Dummy" shows him listening, and observing the maneuvers of others. Although allusions range from Jove, Morpheus, Aristotle, Macbeth, and Oliver and Roland to the Cheshire Cat, the author curtails the use of literary quotations, modifying the erudite tone of the earlier novels.

Although mildly exciting, *The Unpleasantness at the Bellona Club* lacks Miss Sayers's usual verve and wit. Much of the dialogue is banal; even the comic scenes fall flat. Since her next novel is strikingly different, it is worthwhile to note here some similarities found in her first four. In each there is a suicide, or at least an attempt. Three members of the medical profession commit murders. Two are motivated by greed; three use physical violence to kill their victims. Such a summary suggests that these early novels lack variety and originality, but that is not the case. The plots are ingenious, creating suspense, tension, and excitement; characterizations of the Wimsey family, as well as Parker, Bunter, and Miss Climpson, are cleverly done. Nevertheless, Miss Sayers decided to forsake her usual style; her next work was an experiment in theme and structure.

VII   The Documents in the Case

The Documents in the Case, 1930, opens quietly: no crime, murder, or mysterious event has occurred.[23] The novel begins by simply unfolding the relationships which develop when a married couple, the Harrisons, become acquainted, then intimate with two young men who move into the maisonette above them. Matters develop to the point that the husband suffers a violent, painful death. Was it murder, an accident, or suicide?

Three aspects of the novel are unusual. No person from the Wimsey circle appears; Miss Sayers creates entirely new characters: Mr. Harrison and his second wife; their spinster servant, Agatha Milsom; John Munting, a writer; Lathom, an artist. The novel is one of collaboration; much of the scientific material is the work of Robert Eustace, pseudonym of Eustace Robert Barton, a physician who frequently assisted other writers by supplying medical information. The most remarkable feature of *The Documents in the Case* is its epistolary form, a compilation of letters, statements, and reports collected by Paul Harrison after his return from Africa, following his father's death. Refusing to accept the coroner's theory that his father died from accidentally eating poisonous fungi, and convinced that his stepmother had something to do with his father's death, Paul spends seven months collecting data to prove that he is right in his suspicions. By one means or another, all quite plausible, he secures incriminatory evidence: Agatha Milsom's letters to her sister reveal the tensions within the Harrison household; Munting's letters to his fiancée record Lathom's infatuation with Mrs. Harrison; her letters to Lathom, begging him "to do something—anything!" indicate that she instigated the crime. Placing the fifty-two documents in order, Paul Harrison sends them to the Director of Public Prosecutions, with a note requesting that the matter be given careful consideration.

The epistolary style allowed Miss Sayers to portray characters from various viewpoints. Every missive reveals the personality of the letter-writer, yet the recipient and readers of the novel may receive impressions quite contrary to those which the letter-writer intended to convey. Agatha Milsom, for instance, writes pages to her sister, recounting how the young, winsome Mrs Harrison suffers from the neglect and irascible temper of her husband. Mr. Munting, however, sees situations in an entirely different light. In a letter to her sister, Miss Milsom tells that, robed only in a kimono and pajamas, she stepped out on the porch to get a bottle of milk when she met Mr. Munting, "with nothing on but vest and shorts." When questioned, he explains that he was just going for a jog around the Square to keep his figure down, but suspicious Miss Milsom confides:

"I'm sure it doesn't want keeping down . . . and I think he only said it to attract my attention to his charming person, for his eyes were looking me up and down all the time in the most unpleasant way. I didn't say much to him, but got in as quickly as I could. I didn't want everybody to see him exposing himself there with me on the doorstep. I saw him afterwards from my bedroom window. . . ."(22)

The word "exposing," and the fact that the spinster moves to the window to continue gazing, insinuate aspects of her personality which Munting bluntly comments on in a letter to his fiancée. Describing his neighbor as a middle-aged female with a come-hither look in her eye, he states that she deliberately cornered him early one morning:

"She was prowling round the hall in rose-pink pajamas and a pale-blue negligée, pretending to take in the milk. I dawdled on the stairs . . . to give her a chance to run to cover but as she appeared to be determined, and the situation was becoming rather absurd, I marched out, and was, of course, involved in a conversation. I made myself as repellent as I could, but the good lady's curiosity would take no denial."(25)

In another letter, Munting describes Mrs. Harrison as a "suburban vamp," always acting a new role. When a news article extolls the satisfactions of being a woman in the business world, she works herself into a frenzy of longing to be employed once again, instead of leading a humdrum life of domesticity, but when she reads about the necessity of having a full physical and emotional life, "then she is the thwarted maternal woman, who would be all right if she only had a child" (42). When Munting mischievously says that he pictures her in a cloister, walking among the lilies in contemplation, she adopts the role: swathed in a long veil, she greets him the next day with a demurely chaste smile.

Mrs. Harrison revels in playing the part of the injured, neglected wife shackled to a Gorgon, as she calls her husband; at the same time she delights in a new role, the inspiration of her lover, Lathom, to whom she writes: "Besides, our love is the natural thing—it's the Gorgon who is unnatural and abnormal. . . . your hand was telling mine how true and right it was that the useless husband should be got out of the way of the living, the splendid wife and her lover and her child" (137). Miss Sayers wisely limits these sentimental outpourings.

Lathom and Munting are skillfully portrayed. By providing details about their early schooldays together, as well as showing their present attitudes and actions, Miss Sayers makes subsequent catastrophic events seem plausible, almost inevitable. She shows Munting, for instance, recalling his schooldays with Lathom, who even then was an extrovert and a notorious pilferer, unafraid to steal the headmaster's toasting forks to please some senior boy. This disregard for the property of others is a source of annoyance and embarrassment to Munting now, for Lathom barges into his room uninvited, at any hour, taking not only Munting's precious work-hours but also any item of clothing that he fancies. Seemingly a trivial incident, Lathom's borrowing of his friend's dressing gown and wearing it on a midnight visit to Mrs. Harrison's bedroom leads to difficulties.

Munting is a complex character who manifests Miss Sayers's concern for artistic integrity and self-knowledge that rightfully esteem one's own talents and those of others. He scrutinizes his own values, his relationships with others, and the true meaning of a good life. Honest in assessing his own failings, he admits to his fiancée that, before his novels became famous, he had envied the popularity and esteem which her writings merited. Like Wimsey, he is able to laugh at his own foibles and deficiencies, as well as those of others. Munting's most likable traits are his sincere esteem for individuals and his ability to overlook their faults, seeing instead their worthwhile attributes. Although he recognizes that much of the tension in the Harrison household stems from the husband's thoughtless, unimaginative treatment of his wife, nevertheless Munting values Harrison's better qualities and admires his scholarly writings on the selection and preparation of edible fungi, ordinarily unknown and neglected. Aware of Lathom's failings, Munting honors his intellect and his creativity. He even blames himself for not having been more helpful at the time of his friend's emotional distress: "Lathom is all light and dark—a Rembrandt. I am flat, cold, tentative . . . a labourer in detail. I caught no fire from Lathom, and I quenched his. . . . It was my fault that I did not help Lathom more . . ." (103–104). Sensitive to the rights of each person, Munting abhors love that is possessive, overdemanding, demeaning. He queries: "What dignity is there in life, if one is not free to take one's own risks. . . . people should set their own value on themselves and not 'live for others' or 'live only in their children,' or whatever it is. It's beastly" (49–50). The necessity for each individual to keep his or her own identity and independence, free from subservience to others, is a significant theme that appears frequently in Miss Sayers's writings. Here Munting echoes the thoughts of Miss Climpson in *Unnatural Death* when she speaks out against love that enslaves an individual; Lord Peter voices the same idea to Harriet during his courtship and after their marriage. Obviously it is a theme of importance to Miss Sayers.

Mrs. Harrison is a selfish, immature person whose sensuality colors all her judgments. She utters banalities about love, proclaiming that her passion for Lathom cannot be considered adultery, for it is so lovely and pure, yet she insists that she will be "dirtied and draggled" if she has to appear in a divorce court. She absolves herself and her lover from all guilt: "I can't believe it was a sin—no one could commit a sin and be so happy. Sin doesn't exist, the conventional kind of sin, I mean—only lovingness and unlovingness—people like you and me, and people like him" (136). When all is idyllic, she is positive that God approves of this liaison; when she fears that she is pregnant by Lathom, she laments: "How cruel God is! He must be on the conventional people's side after all" (139). Munting's suspicion that she is without moral standards is substantiated by her hints to Lathom to get rid of the Gorgon.

To convince her husband that she no longer cares for Lathom, Mrs. Harrison feigns listlessness. Outwardly torpid, she secretly enjoys a dreamlike existence filled with sexual fantasies. Her outpourings to Lathom reveal her self-willed abasement before her husband: "Oh, I do hate this cramping life—always telling lies and smothering up one's own feelings. But tyrants make liars . . . I feel myself turning into a cringing slave, lying and crawling to get one little scrap of precious freedom . . ." (132). She views this deception as a means of building an inner life for herself, "a lovely, secret freedom," a statement that emphasizes the specious reasoning which characterizes most of her relationships. Catching the nuances of self-love and self-pity in these outbursts, Miss Sayers parodies the sentimental romances of the pulps, and excoriates the type of woman who, uncertain of her own worth as an individual, willingly prostitutes herself in order to win love and esteem.

The Documents in the Case comes close to the author's ideal: a detective story not only rich in mystery and suspense but one that makes significant comments about life. The novel shows a noteworthy advance in character portrayal. Particularly effective is the use of a sustained metaphor which dramatically illuminates Mrs. Harrison's relationship with her husband, Munting, and Lathom. Puzzled that Lathom, usually indifferent to food and intolerant of bad painting, nevertheless listens to Harrison's prattle about preparing dishes of edible fungi and feigns admiration for his weak watercolors, Munting suddenly understands: "Mrs. Harrison was the radiant prism for Lathom's brilliance, and Lathom used Harrison in that service as carelessly as in the old days he had used the prefect's toasting forks" (106). The implications of "prism" are deepened by an earlier comment that Mr. Harrison wanted his wife to shine for him alone, yet he checked her demonstrations of affection by such curt rebuffs as "That will do, my dear"; "Pull yourself together, my girl." The author adds: ". . . her radiance sank and was quenched" (76). But she was to blame, also, for she considered her husband's accomplishments too insignificant to merit her praise: ". . . She had no eyes for the half-lights" (105). The image of the prism acquires a cumulative impact: Munting reflects that he does not possess the self-confidence "that would strike the colours from her prism. . . . My diffusion left her dead glass. But in Lathom's concentration she shone. He gave her the colour and the splendour her dramatic soul craved for" (107). Months later, attending the Exhibit to view Lathom's portrait of Mrs. Harrison, Munting sees the painting "blazing out from a wall full of civic worthies" (116); when he meets her in person, "Mrs.

Harrison glowed." For the first time, Munting sees her "in full prismatic loveliness, soaked and vibrating with colour and light" (119).

The metaphor is used again, heightening the tense atmosphere in the laboratory during the test made to determine whether or not synthetic muscarine was added to Harrison's dinner of mushrooms. If the substance is synthetic, it will not rotate a beam of polarized light when viewed through a polariscope. Peering into the instrument, Munting sees only blackness but reflects nervously: "But if the thing had shown all the colours of the rainbow, I should have been in no state to draw any conclusions from it" (281). Later he ponders on Lathom's relationship with Mrs. Harrison: "I want to know whether . . . he had realised that the only real part of her was vulgar and bad, and the rest the brilliant refraction of himself" (283).

Although Miss Sayers feared that the epistolary structure might detract from the novel's popularity, in reality the letters, documents, and reports aided the gradual revelation of character, the analysis of motives, and added to the suspense that builds, not over the crime itself but whether or not the means of perpetrating the murder can be proven. As one critic noted, the letters are "just like genuine ones, but only more so. The letters from a vain, egotistical woman to her lover, hinting that her husband's death would be welcome, are particularly well-done." He calls attention also to the fact that the thought-provoking discussion on the origin of life and death is essential reading, for the author cleverly hid an essential clue to the mystery in Document 52.[24] Although delighted with the story, readers sometimes ask why the author chose the old-fashioned and difficult epistolary style. Undoubtedly she was influenced by her esteem for Wilkie Collins's epistolary masterpiece, *The Moonstone*. In an introductory essay written for the Dent edition of Collins's novel, she states: "Taking everything into consideration, *The Moonstone* is probably the very finest detective story ever written. By comparison with its wide scope, its dovetailed completeness and the marvelous variety and soundness of its characterization, modern mystery books looks thin and mechanical." [25] She had good reason to be aware of the mediocrity of many stories in this genre, for, preparatory to editing volume one of *Great Short Stories of Detection, Mystery and Horror*, she had read countless "moderns" and studied the masters, not only Collins, but the French *roman policier* of Gaboriau and Le Fanu. A. E.

Murch in the *Development of the Detective Novel* notes that, after writing four entertaining but not outstanding novels, she began to take a great interest in the *form* of the detective story.[26] These influences, together with her resolve to bring to the detective story some of the distinctive merits of the novel of manners, had a major impact on her later fiction.

CHAPTER 3

The Later Novels—
Murder and Manners

CONVINCED that, if the detective story were to survive as a significant genre, it must be brought closer to the novel of manners, Miss Sayers decided that she could accomplish this only if she stopped writing about Lord Peter Wimsey and his set. To banish him effectively she planned to write a novel in which he would fall in love, marry, and then drop out of existence, leaving her free to envision new characters in situations which would allow her to make some thought-provoking observations aimed to elicit intelligent responses from her readers. So she settled down to write *Strong Poison*, the novel designed to bring Lord Peter's life to a swift close.

I   Strong Poison

Strong Poison, 1930, opens with the murder trial of Harriet Vane, accused of killing her lover, Philip Boyes, who has died from arsenic poisoning.[1] The judge summarizes the case, reminding the jury of these pertinent facts: Miss Vane, a writer of detective stories, had lived with Boyes as his mistress for almost a year, then left him after a serious quarrel. Later, under assumed names, she bought arsenic in various forms, such as rat poisoning and weed-killer. On three occasions after such purchases, she and Boyes spent some time together; after each visit he suffered an attack of acute gastritis. One evening after dining with his cousin Mr. Urquhart, with whom he was staying, he visited Miss Vane, but as he returned to the Urquhart residence he became so ill that the taxi driver had to assist him into the house. After three days of excruciating suffering, Boyes died. Later, when gossip created a stir, the body was exhumed; analysis revealed that Boyes had consumed a fatal dose of arsenic several days before his death. Mr. Urquhart testified that there was nothing suspicious about the food served at dinner that memorable evening: he, Boyes, and the servants had partaken of each dish. No one except Boyes suffered any ill effects.

Conceding that Miss Vane's literary agent has testified that her forthcoming novel concerns a case of arsenic poisoning, the judge advises the jury: "This woman is charged with having murdered her former lover by arsenic. He undoubtedly did take arsenic, and if you are satisfied that she gave it to him with intent to injure or kill him, and that he died of it, then it is your duty to find her guilty of murder" (34).

The circumstantial evidence fails to convince one jury member, Miss Climpson, who in turn influences others; the trial ends with a hung jury, and a new trial is scheduled for one month later. Having fallen in love with Harriet Vane, Lord Peter is determined to prove her innocence. With the permission of Sir Impey Biggs and Parker, he begins to work on the case. At first he is convinced that Boyes committed suicide; later, assuming that some person, certainly not Harriet, desired Boyes's death, he suspects Mr. Urquhart, who is the trustee to the estate of Mrs. Wrayburn, the invalid aunt of Boyes. When Miss Climpson discovers a will leaving Boyes more than fifty thousand pounds, a motive for the murder is established. At the second trial, Harriet Vane, completely exonerated, is publicly proclaimed innocent of all guilt. How the murder was effected is the mystery that creates suspense.

In evaluating this novel, the author's statement in the essay "Gaudy Night" is revealing: "Let me confess that when I wrote Strong Poison, it was with the infanticidal intention of doing away with Peter; that is, of marrying him off and getting rid of him." [2] Two factors, she admits, kept her from doing this: admirers, uncommunicative up to this time, now wrote to convince her that Lord Peter was too well liked to be banished; then she discovered that, under the circumstances, Harriet could not possibly accept Lord Peter. "When I looked at the situation, I saw that it was in every respect false and degrading; and the puppets had somehow got just so much flesh and blood in them that I could not force them to accept it without shocking myself." She ends with a characteristic comment concerning the integrity of Harriet: "She must come to him as a free agent, if she came at all, and must realize that she was independent of him before she could bring him her dependence." [3]

Harriet is not fully delineated because, when planning the novel, Miss Sayers did not foresee a lengthy existence for her. Although she appears only four times, some significant facts, however, do emerge: orphaned at twenty-three, from then on she earned her own livelihood by writing successful detective stories. She lived with Boyes, although she admits that they were never true friends, for he demanded complete devotion and lied when he claimed that he did not believe in marriage. In reality, the liaison was his test to ascertain that Harriet pleased him; when he found her amusing and compatible, then he proposed marriage. This angered her, for she did not like "having matrimony offered as a bad-conduct prize," and she left him. Very little is told about her personal appearance: Lord Peter finds her deep voice attractive; his mother, present at the trial, comments that Harriet is "perhaps not strictly good-looking, and all the more interesting for that, because good-looking people are so often cows" (37).

One thing is certain: Harriet never indulges in self-pity. Although dubious about the outcome of her trial, she keeps calm, completes a novel, responds to Peter's questions intelligently, copes adroitly with his protestations of love, and captivates him completely when she recognizes and completes his quip from *Kai Lung*. Admitting that she finds him attractive, she confesses that she does not want to rush into love again but offers to live with him for a trial period, so that he may cut loose if he wishes.

This incident allows the author to show Lord Peter's sensitivity to the needs of others. Realizing that Harriet, suffering from feelings of rejection and betrayal, cannot accept his love while burdened with a debt of gratitude to him, Peter reasons that the only way to win her is to submerge his own feelings, allowing her time to regain her self-confidence and personal esteem. Only on terms of such equality can she come to him freely. Here Miss Sayers gives a clue to her own philosophy of individualism: education, wealth, and social position are not the factors that establish equality and mutuality. Harriet, like all genuine persons, must recognize her own merits and defects, accept herself, and respect her own uniqueness; only then can she achieve a satisfying rapport with another.

Frustrated by his inability to assist Harriet's case, Lord Peter relieves his doldrums by helping Parker win the hand of Lady Mary. Parker's reluctance to declare his love is understandable: he is a conservative, middle-class civil servant; Mary, a sophisticated, wealthy aristocrat. Once Peter is convinced that his sister returns Parker's affection, he makes it clear that false ideas about wealth and class should not prevent Parker from proposing. When the aston-

ished Parker asks how he could ever do such a thing, Wimsey
pretends to misunderstand and breezily suggests various methods:
the down-on-the-knees technique, a slangy proposition, a letter,
telegram, or phone call. This pose of anger at Parker's dalliance and
the facetious instructions on ways to propose create comedy, but they
also reveal Lord Peter's growing awareness of, and genuine concern
for, the problems of others.

A charity work, which he jokingly calls "My Cattery," manifests
this also. He helps a group of spinsters, widows, and unemployed
secretaries to earn a respectable living by financing an unique estab-
lishment, a typing service which is also an investigation bureau that
probes questionable advertisements. More than one person advertising in newspapers that he will make money for clients or secure
glamorous positions for young girls, is discreetly investigated by the
"Cattery" and lands in court for attempted procuration or fraud. The
most valued member of the "Cattery," Miss Climpson, plays an
important role in *Strong Poison*, displaying a knowledge of spiritual-
ism and a rare talent for faking mysterious happenings at séances.
Sitting in a darkened room with a metal soapbox strapped to her knee,
she click-clacks the cover of the box, sending impressive raps into the
stillness. By means of long filaments of wire concealed in the folds of
her sleeves, she jerks, rattles, and tilts the séance-table, cleverly
manipulating the Ouija board so that it points to the letter "B,"
supposedly a clue to the whereabouts of the missing will. The letter
"B" gives her the opportunity to search almost every place in the
house: bedrooms, bureaus, bags, boxes, bibelots, and everything
black, brown, and blue, as well as the book-filled library. It is here
that the missing will is discovered. Miss Soloway states that by using
such devices as the séance and Ouija board, the author breaks the
second rule of Ronald A. Knox's "A Detective Story Decalogue":
preternatural agencies must not be utilized to solve crimes; the
detective's wits must suffice.[4] Actually, Miss Sayers does not rely on
preternatural help; it is Miss Climpson who manipulates the devices
and deliberately chooses the letter "B."

Suspense is achieved in a variety of ways, notably by having the
investigation circumscribed by a brief period of four weeks before the
second trial. The reader constantly wonders whether evidence can be
discovered in time to clear Harriet. Tension builds when several
characters take great risks to secure information. Important facts,
hinted at but not disclosed immediately, pique interest. When Lord
Peter, for instance, is called to Scotland Yard, the narrative is inter-

rupted by a chapter detailing Bunter's siege of the Urquhart kitchen; the significance of the Yard visit is not revealed until the next chapter.

The plot is one of Miss Sayers's most ingenious. In a letter to her publisher, Mr. Gollancz, she stated that the idea of building up a tolerance for arsenic by taking small doses over a period of time had tantalized her for about six years, and had started her reading "every detective story about poison, feeling sure that somebody must have hit upon it before I was ready." [5] A session with books about poisons and a study of Housman's poem "Terence, This Is Stupid Stuff," gave her the idea. It is Lord Peter's ingenuity, of course, that discovers how the lethal dose was introduced into the food that poisoned Boyes but did not harm his host. Supported by Yudkin's statement that the method is entirely plausible, Philmore maintained that of the methods of murder described in five thrillers, this is the most perplexing, baffling readers and creating suspense until the very end. [6]

Miss Sayers had an even more baffling problem: according to her own ideas about character portrayal, she could not allow Harriet to accept Lord Peter's offers of marriage, and her readers were clamoring for more stories about Lord Peter. To banish him at this point was unthinkable.

II The Five Red Herrings

Pleased with the increasing popularity of Lord Peter, Miss Sayers finished *The Five Red Herrings*, published in America under the title *Suspicious Characters*, in 1931, just six months after *Strong Poison*. [7] Set in Scotland, the novel concerns characters living in an art colony, Kirkcudbright, and neighboring fishing villages. The territory was familiar to the author, for she and her husband frequently spent their holidays there.

The story opens with a landscape painter, Campbell, quarreling with Waters, an Englishman. Wimsey and several onlookers break up a fistfight between the two in a pub that night. Campbell is found dead about two o'clock the following afternoon. Villagers said that they had seen him painting in the morning and the supposition is that he had fallen into the burn and drowned.

Campbell had bitter enemies; any one of six men in the area might have been responsible for his death. Lord Peter suspects that his death is not accidental. Examining the picture on which the artist was reported to have been working on that morning, Peter notes that the oil paint is not dry. He looks over the oddments in Campbell's satchel; charcoal, sandwiches, cigarettes, chalk, sketchbooks, brushes and paints are all there except one article. "It's not there," he said, "and I don't like the looks of it all, Dalziel" (28). Dalziel is puzzled. Readers will have varied reactions to this ruse: "Here Lord Peter Wimsey told the Sergeant what he was looking for and why, but as the intelligent reader will readily supply these details for himself, they are omitted from this page" (29).

In conference with Constable Ross, Lord Peter reveals the character of the deceased, his unpopularity and quarrelsome disposition, then cites some puzzling details: the rigor of the corpse when it was discovered, the peculiar circumstance of a missing article essential for a painter, and the tar stains in the victim's car. Lord Peter expounds his theory that Campbell was killed the previous evening, his body concealed, placed in his car the next morning when the murderer, wearing the artist's hat and well-known cloak, drove to the site and tumbled the body downhill into the burn. He then set up an easel, sketched a picture in his victim's style, and made a fast getaway, providing himself with an alibi to prove his whereabouts at the time that the death was supposed to have occurred, about 10:30 in the morning.

The list of suspects includes six artists. Waters, who had fought with him on the previous night, was known to have boasted that he could imitate Campbell's customary style of painting. Farren bore him a grudge because of his persistent attentions paid to Mrs. Farren, who, apparently welcoming his frequent calls, refused to obey her husband's orders to discourage these advances. Gowan, Graham, and Strachan had quarreled with the artist in the recent past; Ferguson was furious over a wall knocked down by Campbell's irresponsible driving. No feud seemed an adequate motive for murder, but it was necessary to probe the alibi proffered by each suspect, a task made extremely difficult because five of the six suspects took to their heels.

The movements of each are carefully investigated. Farren is the first, for motives of jealousy and revenge, as well as circumstantial evidence, point to his guilt. The maid asserts that, after a violent quarrel with his wife, he left and has not been home for several nights; Mrs. Farren insists that he has gone on a short fishing trip, but she faints at the hint that Campbell might have been murdered. Then suddenly suspicion points to Waters. If he really went by train to Glasgow to see an art exhibit on the day of the suspected murder, was it likely that he went off in a shabby outfit and took a bicycle? True, he purchased a ticket to Glasgow, but not one passenger remembered seeing him on the train. He talked knowledgeably about the exhibit, mentioning the location and the merits of specific paintings, but he could have gathered that information earlier.

However, his situation does not seem any more incriminating than that of Strachan, whose tale about receiving his black eye on the golf course is obviously a lie. Moreover, his story about night fishing and returning home before midnight contradicts evidence that his car was seen on the road between midnight and 12:30 and that he was seen going into Campbell's home later. Mr. Gowan's alibi sounds water-tight, until Bunter squires a maid from the Gowan household to a cinema and learns that she has seen a ghostly, shrouded figure in a bedroom corridor which she was expressly forbidden to enter that week. Another red herring, another scent to be traced.

One of the intriguing aspects of this story is the way in which various members of the police and detective force work out, each to his own satisfaction, a hypothetical reconstruction of the crime and the suspect's movements to show how he could have perpetrated the murder and yet be protected by his alibi. Sergeant Dalziel, for instance, produces a work of ingenuity: a timetable clocking all of Farren's known movements from six o'clock Monday evening to the mid-afternoon when the corpse was discovered. Those listening immediately find loopholes in his explanation; then Inspector Macpherson gives his theory, reconstructing the crime with Gowan as perpetrator. Others produce timetables and charts to show that they can prove that the murderer is Graham, or Waters, or Ferguson, or Strachan. Finally they turn to Lord Peter to ask which solution is correct. "This," said Lord Peter Wimsey, "is the proudest moment of my life. At last I really feel like Sherlock Holmes. A Chief Constable, a Police Inspector, a Police Sergeant and two constables have appealed to me to decide between their theories, and with my chest puffed like a pouter-pigeon, I can lean back in my chair and say, 'Gentlemen, you are all wrong.' " (300) Later he qualifies his statement: one is less wrong than the others. He then proceeds to solve the puzzle but insists that the entire sequence of events leading up to Campbell's death must be enacted with the suspect taking part in some aspects of the dramatization.

After this is accomplished, Lord Peter is characteristically despondent, for it is through his investigations that the criminal, whom he likes, is apprehended, whereas he thoroughly disliked the victim,

Campbell. When the Chief Constable tries to cheer Wimsey, commenting brusquely, "Murder is murder," he answers, "Not always."
Once again he is correct.

The very qualities that make *The Five Red Herrings* a memorable
thriller for some readers are the traits disliked by others who rate this
novel far below the author's usual standards. Some complained that
the investigation of each alibi with the detailed reconstruction of the
hypothetical actions of the suspects became tediously repetitive;
others felt that the characterization of the six suspects was not distinctive enough to differentiate them fully. Even Lord Peter seems a
rather shadowy figure, revealing little of the jester, aesthete, or
lover. Parker appears briefly, with no mention that he is a prospective
brother-in-law; Harriet is never mentioned. From these facts it might
be conjectured that this was an earlier novel, but it seems more likely
that it was an experiment, a "timetable" mystery, a type that Miss
Sayers did not care to write frequently. She herself expressed slight
misgivings about it, as though she later thought of it as a regression in
her technical development: "It is true that each successive book of
mine worked gradually nearer to the sort of thing I had in view. *The
Documents in the Case* . . . took a jump forward rather out of its due
time; *Five Red Herrings* was a cast back towards the 'time-table'
puzzle-problem." [8]

However, two facts are certain: the novel was a financial success in
England and the United States, and the author took pride in her
workmanship. Her letter to Mr. Gollancz states: "Here is a book in
which nobody falls in love (unless you count Campbell) and every
sentence is necessary to the plot, except a remark or two on Scottish
scenery and the language. I have given up trying to forecast what
anybody will think of anything. . . . I will never write a book which I
know to be careless or meretricious." [9] Her manuscript in the Marion
Wade Collection at Wheaton College shows how carefully details
concerning railroad timetables, baggage checks, ticket punches, and
other pieces of evidence were verified before being woven into the
story. [10] Wisely, she relied not on her own ingenuity but on the aid of
an authority to work out such complexities.

Despite the complaints about the difficulties of keeping the suspects and their complicated alibis clearly in mind as the story
progresses, the book won the approval of many. William Weber in
Saturday Review of Literature stated: "*Suspicious Characters*
[American title] is likely to hold the palm for the best all-round
mystery novel of the year. [11] Barzun praised it as one of the author's
most colorful group studies which improves with each reading: "The

Scottish setting, the artists in the colony, and the train-ticket puzzle, and the final chase place the triumph among the four or five *chefs-d'oeuvre* from her hand." [12]

III   Have His Carcase

Miss Sayers tried once again to solve the vexatious puzzle of the proper way to bring Lord Peter and Harriet together in her next novel, *Have His Carcase*, 1932.[13] Eighteen months after Harriet's trial and acquittal for the murder of her lover, while on a walking tour along the southeast coast of England she saw a man apparently sleeping and attempted to awaken him before he is engulfed by the incoming tide. But then she sees that ". . . the larynx and all the great vessels of the neck had been severed . . . and a frightful stream, bright red and glistening, was running over the surface of the rock . . ." (13–14).

Although Harriet has often described such butchery in her detective stories, she is almost overcome by the sight but she finally becomes calm enough to follow her sleuthing instincts: she photographs the body, studies the footprints in the sand, and discovers an open razor in the water. She hurries to summon the police, but before they arrive the body is submerged under many feet of water. Lord Peter dashes down to Wilvercombe, supposedly to help solve the mystery but in reality to protect her reputation, for ugly rumors are already flying. Although a severe storm prevents the recovery of the body, Harriet's photographs establish its identity as Paul Alexis Goldschmidt, professional dancer and gigolo at the Resplendent, Wilvercombe's largest hotel. Known as Paul Alexis, he had courted Leila Garland until she wearied of his boasts that he is a Russian aristocrat. Rejected by Leila, he woos Mrs. Weldon, a wealthy widow who hoped to marry him in a fortnight.

The police are convinced that Paul Alexis, despondent over his love problems and the insecurity of his way of life, committed suicide, but both Harriet and Lord Peter suspect murder. When they discover that Henry Weldon opposed his mother's marriage, which would most certainly deprive him of a large inheritance needed to extricate him from financial worries, a motive for murder is established. A coded letter, deciphered by Harriet and Lord Peter, discloses that Paul Alexis was lured to a lonely spot on the beach by the promise that he would be given information that might place him on the Russian throne.

The facts that the body was not recovered for several days, that the police discredited all suggestions of murder, that the time of the death was believed to be about two o'clock because the body was oozing blood at the time of its discovery, and that all the suspects seemed to have unbreakable alibis create complications that add suspense. Barzun pointed out that not only are the characters, the ciphers, and the detection topnotch, but here also is the first use of hemophilia as a misleading fact.[14] Commenting on this unusual feature, a reviewer in the *Times Literary Supplement* noted that a story which depends on some peculiar circumstance connected with the crime is usually best, for it provides a "more genuinely intellectual problem than the story in which there are innumerable suspects."[15]

In "Gaudy Night" Miss Sayers states that she wrote *Have His Carcase* to bring Lord Peter and Harriet closer together. Several scenes reveal his deepening love for Harriet and his awareness of her position as a woman accused of murder, acquitted but always held suspect by her peers, tormented by ambivalent feelings of gratitude and resistance toward him. But on several occasions Miss Sayers deliberately shows that Peter is no paragon of virtue; he is human enough to be hurt—and to show it. When he inadvertently reveals that he rushed to Wilvercombe to protect Harriet's reputation, she retorts savagely:

"I suppose you think I haven't been humiliated enough already, without all this parade of chivalry. . . . You think if you go on long enough I ought to be touched and softened. Well, you're mistaken, that's all. I suppose every man thinks he's only got to go on being superior and any woman will come tumbling into his arms. It's disgusting." (120)

Aroused, Peter neither cringes nor cavils under this tirade but protests vehemently:

"Do you think it's pleasant for any man who feels about a woman as I do about you, to have to fight his way along under this detestable burden of gratitude? Damn it, do you think I don't know perfectly well that I'd have a better chance if I was deaf, blind, maimed, starving, drunken or dissolute, so that *you* could have the fun of being magnanimous?" (120–21)

When Harriet murmurs that she realizes that she is ungrateful, he expostulates: "Grateful! Good God! Am I never to get away from the bleat of that filthy adjective? I don't want gratitude. I don't want kindness. I don't want sentimentality. . . . I want common honesty" (121).

Miss Sayers gives many hints that Harriet, in spite of herself, is falling in love with Lord Peter Wimsey. When she discovers the corpse, for instance, she wonders what Lord Peter's reactions would be, then resolutely focuses on the probable actions of her own literary creation, Detective Templeton. At times she ponders what it would be like to be married to a lord. She has always considered her suitor, "intelligent, clean, courteous, wealthy, well-read, amusing and enamoured. . . ." but suddenly she realizes that there is "something godlike about him" (146). Although she lacks his aristocratic heritage, wealth, and sophistication, she values her own accomplishments: she, too, is an Oxford graduate and has used her talents wisely, achieving an enviable reputation as a novelist. Nevertheless, at times she feels inferior to him, a conflict that she alone can resolve.

Puns, parody, and literary quotations are not scintillating, but they provide mild humor. Miss Sayers continues to sketch minor characters by listing details of dress and mannerisms of speech. The landlady of Paul Alexis is "an ample personage with brazen hair, who was dressed in a pink wrapper, much-laddered artificial silk stockings and green velvet mules, and wore about her heavily powdered neck a string of synthetic amber beads like pigeon's eggs" (135).

While making Lord Peter less aristocratic and overbearing, Miss Sayers obliquely criticizes those who obsequiously cater to the upper class. When Lord Peter purchases some choice ham from a fashionable shop, she mockingly describes each act of the fawning clerks who swathe the delicacy in special paper, cord it with the best quality string, and handle it "like a nurse with a swaddled princeling." Lord Peter departs but not alone: "A little ritual procession streamed out into Jermyn Street, comprising: the Assistant, carrying the ham; Lord Peter, drawing on his driving-gloves; the Manager, murmuring a ceremonial formula; the Second Assistant, opening the door and emerging from behind it to bow upon the threshold; and eventually the car glided away amid the reverent murmurings of a congregation of persons gathered in the street . . ."(53).

When Mr. Gollancz complimented Miss Sayers on *Have His Carcase*, assuring her that it was "a real triumph," she answered that the novel had given her so much trouble that she had begun to fear that it was almost hopeless, despite the ruse of making the time of the gigolo's death uncertain because of his hemophiliac condition. She added: "The one fairly original thing in the book is, I think, the murderers laboriously preparing an alibi and then realising with bewilderment that nobody is bothering about the *time* of the alibis and so finding the alibis a suspicious nuisance." [16]

IV   Murder Must Advertise

Murder Must Advertise, 1933, begins with the staff of an advertising agency, Pym's Publicity, being introduced to a new copywriter, Death Bredon, hired to replace Victor Dean, who died after a fall down the spiral staircase at Pym's.[17] The staff is unaware that the new man has been hired as a private detective to discover if there is any truth in Dean's allegations made privately to Mr. Pym that something suspicious is going on at the agency; Mr. Pym is unaware that he has gained the services of the ineluctable Lord Peter Death Bredon Wimsey, who is using his middle name to hide his identity.

Death Bredon joins in all the activities at Pym's. He gossips and squabbles with the staff, contributes to the collections for wedding gifts and betting pools, enjoys the camaraderie and rivalries of the various departments, turns out clever advertisements, and wins respect for his affability and imagination. After a very short time, he is convinced that Dean's death was not accidental and that Tallboy, another copywriter, was somehow involved. Interrogating Dean's sister, he learns that her brother had become involved with Dian de Momerie and her set and for months before his death had been "sinning above his station in life" (79).

To secure more information, Lord Peter as Death Bredon joins the de Momerie group, spending evenings with this glittering, pseudo-sophisticated crowd. His suspects that Milligan, a friend of Dian's, has something to do with the advertisement composed at Pym's giving dope-dealers the clue to the place where the next week's supply can be picked up. He surmises too that Milligan is connected with the narcotic distributors whom his brother-in-law has been trying to trace for some time. When Parker and Lord Peter join forces, the mystery of the tell-tale advertisement is solved and the distributors are apprehended, but not before Dian and Milligan are murdered by the gang, who suspect them of betrayal.

In *Murder Must Advertise*, Miss Sayers came close to her ambition of fusing the novel of manners with the detective novel. In "Gaudy Night" she stated that in this work for "the first time, the criticism of life was not relegated to incidental observation and character sketches, but was actually part of the plot, as it ought to be." [18] The busy, competitive world of Pym's was not difficult for her to portray realistically for she had been a copywriter for ten years in a similar London advertising agency, Messrs. S. H. Benson. The plot involving drug traffic, her intimate knowledge of the advertising world, coupled with themes of grave concern to her—the morality of production and the integrity of work—make this novel more than just an amusing detective story; it is a mystery novel that makes trenchant observations on current problems of society.

Through Lord Peter, Miss Sayers expresses her concern about the lack of ethics in advertising. After a week at Pym's, he voices his doubts about the honesty of the reams of copy written to lure some poorly paid typist to spend her pennies on Muggin's Magnolia Face Cream in the hopes that her complexion will capture the affections of some Prince Charming. Lord Peter ponders: "If all the advertising in the world were to shut down tomorrow, would people still go on buying more soap, eating more apples, giving their children more vitamins, roughage, milk, olive oil, scooters and laxatives. . . . Or would the whole desperate whirligig slow down, and the exhausted public relapse upon plain grub and elbow-grease?" (187). After two weeks at Pym's, Lord Peter is aware of the dichotomies that exist there and every place where morality is ignored: "In this place . . . the spiritual atmosphere was clamorous with financial storm, intrigue, dissension, indigestion and marital infidelity. And with worse things—with murder wholesale and retail, of soul and body. . . . These things did not advertise, or, if they did, they called themselves by other names" (289).

Miss Sayers blames advertisers for invading areas that should be personal and private, but she also castigates the public which, indifferent to blatantly prying advertisements, willingly purchases products, no matter how offensively these are promoted. Her thoughts are expressed by Ingleby: "How should anything be sacred to an advertiser. . . . We spend our whole time asking intimate questions to perfect strangers,' . . . Mother, has your Child Learnt Regular Habits?' 'Are you Troubled with Fullness after Eating?' . . . Upon my soul, I sometimes wonder why the long-suffering public doesn't rise up and slay us" (69).

Some critics objected to the amount of space given to the advertising campaigns and the emphasis placed on unethical advertising practices, particularly the crass materialism behind the exploitation of some products, but by this detailed exposé Miss Sayers highlights her primary theme: the culpability of those who produce and promote the sale of shoddy, unnecessary commodities, and the folly of those who are gullible enough to be hoodwinked into spending their money. Few critics commented on her second theme: the appalling evils resulting from drug abuse and the attitude of the law toward those who traffic in narcotics. Parker states the case succinctly: "Dope-runners are murderers, fifty times over. They slay hundreds of people, soul and body, besides indirectly causing all sorts of crimes among the victims. Compared with that, slugging one inconsiderable pip-squeak over the head is almost meritorious" (250). Although Wimsey twits Parker for uttering such an irreligious thought, he agrees that the law takes just such a view—hanging the murderer and giving the dope-dealer a few weeks in jail.

Miss Sayers integrated themes, plot, and setting with true crafts-manship. Although the advertising milieu offers Lord Peter few opportunities to exchange literary gems, pages sparkle with puns, alliterative flights of fancy, and witty, sometimes slightly coarse ripostes, which he enjoys. Surprisingly enough, no critic expressed concern or disbelief that Wimsey, lover of incunabula, music, and literature, seemed content to write advertisements for such commod-ities as bathroom antiseptics.

Dian de Momerie's world provides a sharp contrast. At a housepar-ty, drunken couples take their pleasure in "sinister little cubi-cles . . . each heavily curtained and furnished with a couch and mirror" (75). At one such party, Lord Peter, in a black and white harlequin costume, dives into the swimming pool, emerges with Dian over his shoulder, and bids her to follow him. He recklessly races his car against hers. The chase ends in a woods where he vanishes, piping a penny whistle and singing derisively: "Tom, Tom, the Piper's son. . . ." Exhausted and frightened, Dian searches through thickets and briars, only to discover that Wimsey is high in the treetops. In the lengthy cross-questioning that follows, Dian answers submissively, telling about Dean and her subjection to Milli-gan. Helpful though her confession is for the purposes of plot, yet the mental picture of Lord Peter in the treetops and Dian huddled on the grass in the darkness makes the scene grotesquely unreal.

Indefatigable though Lord Peter has been in past novels, yet it is almost beyond credulity that his physical stamina is so boundless that after indulging in midnight races and playing "Follow the Leader" through the treetops, he can report jauntily at Pym's at nine o'clock, toil all day, and produce witty, acceptable advertising copy. His talents seem endless; he is endowed with such charisma that every woman is attracted to him. The *Times Literary Supplement* com-mented that Wimsey "is now becoming almost too much of a univer-sal genius. . . . Miss Sayers will find it necessary soon to consider whether he should not succeed his brother and retire into ducal ease or find some more sudden form of withdrawal." [19] However, instead of vanishing, he becomes more real, with an entry in *Who's Who*, a fact discovered by Miss Meteyard, who has long suspected that her office-mate is more than what he pretends to be.

In attempting to humanize Lord Peter so that Harriet will finally consent to marry him, Miss Sayers unwittingly endowed him with more character than she had intended: Lord Peter Wimsey is no puppet to be summarily vanquished. His bonhomie at Pym's, his growing awareness of the problems of other people, his distaste for the superficiality of Dian de Momerie's set, his affability, revealed in the domestic vignettes at the home of Mary and Parker, where he resides while posing as Death Bredon, charmed readers, new and old, who did not hesitate to voice their dismay over the rumor that their favorite sleuth was to disappear in the near future.

The novel does nothing to further the romance between Lord Peter and Harriet. Bunter appears infrequently because his services are not required while Lord Peter resides with Lady Mary and Parker. The story proceeds in a more leisurely fashion than is customary in this series, yet readers did not object to the detailed descriptions of the advertising milieu or the whirligig world of the de Momerie set. Readers and critics regarded the novel highly, despite the author's frank criticism: "It was not quite successful; the idea of symbolically opposing two cardboard worlds—that of the advertiser and the drug-taker—was all right; and it was suitable that Peter, who stands for reality, should never appear in either except disguised; but the working-out was a little too melodramatic, and the handling rather uneven." [20] Her public did not agree; like Howard Haycraft, many placed *Murder Must Advertise* among her top three: others approved of Sutherland Scott's estimate: "Although many regard *Gaudy Night*, *The Five Red Herrings* and *The Nine Tailors* as Miss Sayers' best novels, I would accord pride of place to *Murder Must Advertise* because of its superbly authentic background. Indeed, I would class *Murder Must Advertise* as one of the greatest, most satisfying mystery novels of the past twenty years." [21]

V   The Nine Tailors

The Nine Tailors, 1934, opens with Lord Peter driving across the Fens in a heavy snowstorm with Bunter on New Year's Eve. [22] Veering too sharply, Lord Peter runs his Daimler into a ditch. Fortunately, in the village of Fenchurch St. Paul, an amiable rector, Mr.

Venables, invites them to spend the night at his home. For Peter, it is not a night of rest. Discovering that his guest is familiar with the art of change ringing, the rector coaxes him to take the place of a bell ringer sick with influenza so that the cherished plan of ringing in the New Year can be accomplished.

The project is an extremely ambitious one, for the peal is the Kent Treble Bob Major, requiring 15,840 changes to be rung over a period of nine hours, each stroke demanding strenuous energy, concentration, and consummate skill. Exhausted by the performance, Lord Peter revives after breakfast, grateful that he does not have the responsibilities of Mr. Venables, who is called away to assist at the deathbed of a parishioner, Lady Thorpe. During his stay at the rectory, Lord Peter is intrigued by Mr. Venables's account of an unsolved mystery: the theft of a valuable emerald necklace taken from the Thorpe household some twenty years ago.

Several months later, Lord Peter receives a letter from Mr. Venables, telling of an incident that has shocked the parish almost as much as the emerald robbery. When Sir Henry Thorpe died suddenly, the grave of his wife was opened so that his remains could be placed near hers. To the astonishment of everyone, a corpse was discovered there, with hands severed and face badly beaten. Because Lord Peter was at the rectory when Lady Thorpe died, Mr. Venables thought that this strange situation would interest him. It did, indeed. He returns to the village in time to hear the inquest proceedings and the tentative identification of the body as that of an itinerant garage mechanic. Later, it is suspected that it is Cranton, the London thief convicted of involvement in the emerald robbery. Clues are few and perplexing; the police are baffled. By a bit of clever trickery, Lord Peter and Bunter obtain from the post office a letter mailed from France addressed to Paul Taylor. There is no person by that name in the parish, but Wimsey recalls that Tailor Paul is the name of the old church bell that tolls to announce a death: nine teller strokes for a man, six for a woman, three for a child. The letter was written by the wife of Jean Legros, who is actually Geoffrey Deacon, an accomplice in the jewel robbery. Returning to England to secure the emeralds secreted in the church, Deacon is recognized by Will Thoday, happily married to Deacon's supposed widow. Distraught over the scandal that will destroy his marriage if any parishioner sees Deacon, Will forces him into a remote hiding place, intending to release him the next day, but illness prevents him from carrying out his plans. His brother Jim discovers the corpse the day after the ringing of the Kent

Treble Bob Major. Circumstantial evidence points to the guilt of the Thoday brothers until Lord Peter discovers how Deacon was killed.

Determined to solve the other mystery, that of the missing emeralds, Peter and the rector toil for hours deciphering a complicated cryptogram that taxes their very specialized knowledge of the art of bell ringing, but the final results are disappointing. When deciphered, the coded message reveals no specific hiding place but gives only a jumble of biblical phrases. During a Sunday service, while admiring the roof beams decorated with gilded angel heads, Lord Peter suddenly guesses the significance of the phrases and deduces the hiding place of the jewels.

Although these mysteries are solved, suspense continues, for the last section of the novel describes the devastation of the flood that breaks through dykes and barriers, engulfing the land, obliterating even the river. After two weeks of suffering, the parishioners rejoice to hear the bells ring out the good tidings that the waters are receding, but this occurs only after Will Thoday drowns, attempting to rescue a flood victim. That Will in the plan of Divine Providence has offered retribution for his past is implied in Mr. Venables's comment: "Poor Will, he died finely and his sins died with him."

Miss Sayers's power of characterization is notable in this novel. Among the most memorable figures is the genial Mr. Venables, who, no doubt, bears some resemblance to her own father. Scholarly but absent-minded, the rector forgets where he left the keys to the church of which he is so justly proud and strays from the topic of conversation just when Lord Peter hopes to hear some significant information. The rector's most endearing quality, his trust in Divine Providence, is evident in his reply to the message that the sluice gates are breaking: "Yes, yes. The first thing to do is to ring the alarm. They know what that means, thank God. They learnt it during the War. I never thought I should thank God for the War, but He moves in mysterious ways" (335). Watching Mr. Venables direct procedures, Lord Peter comments: "Good Lord, sir . . . anybody would think you'd done this all your life." The rector's response typifies his faith and humility: "I have devoted much prayer and thought to the situation in the last few weeks. . . . But my wife is the real manager. . . . Alf! Alf Donnington! What about that beer?" (337). When Lord Peter suffers remorse for having exposed the guilty, the rector counsels: "My dear boy, it does not do for us to take too much thought for the morrow. It is better to follow the truth and leave the result in the hand of God. He can foresee where we cannot, because He knows all the facts" (271).

Potty Peake, another well-drawn character, is a kind-hearted, half-witted creature, a "natural" who pops up behind church walls and tombstones, interrupting Superintendent Blundell's conferences with Lord Peter. Potty prattles about bells, ropes, strange men, and hangings in the belfry but Blundell assures Lord Peter that old Potty has had a fixation about hangings ever since, as a child, he found his mother hanging in a cowshed. Lord Peter, however, listens attentively, particularly to Potty's tale about a black-bearded stranger in church. Questioned when this occurred, Potty only knows that it was the day the rector preached about thankfulness: "Be thankful for Christmas, he says. There was roast fowl Christmas Day and boiled pork and greens Sunday. . . . So Potty slips out at night, for to be thankful again. You got to go to church to be thankful proper, ain't you, sir?" (204). Miss Sayers intimates that it is not only Wimsey's detective instincts that make him pay attention to Potty's ramblings but also his belief in the inherent dignity of every person, even a "natural." The Superintendent lacks this awareness; the minute that he shows his disdain for Potty, the poor fellow sullenly mutters: "You lemme go, mister, I gotter feed my pigs" (205). Humorous at times, frequently pathetic, Potty adds a note of sinister suspense whenever he appears. The author delineates him vividly, avoiding caricature and sentimentality.

Harriet does not appear in this novel, but Miss Sayers continues her efforts to make Lord Peter more human and endearing. Still excited by baffling mysteries, suffering scruples and remorse after bringing a criminal to justice, nevertheless Lord Peter is less concerned about his creature comforts and far more interested now in the welfare of others. This is very evident in the ordeal of the flood. However, he is still arrogant. When Jack Godfrey comments that the bell rope will have to be let down considerably because the new substitute is so much shorter than the regular ringer, Peter retorts: "Never you mind. In the words of the old bell motto: 'I'll have it understood that though I'm little, yet I'm good'" (27).

Despite the repeated requests of friends, the author steadfastly refused to transform Lord Peter into a religious person, although she makes the teachings and the traditions of the Anglican church a part of his background. At times he seems a curiously devout humanist. Deeply moved by the beauty of Fenchurch St. Paul, he gapes at the roof where with "bright hair and gilded outspread wings, soared the ranked angels, cherubim and seraphim, choir after choir. . . ." Oblivious to the congregation, he murmurs: "He rode upon the cherubims and did fly; He came flying upon the wings of the wind" (36). In *The Mind of the Maker*, Miss Sayers explains that, while writing this episode, her imagination was stirred by memories of passages from a wide variety of sources dear to her: the Psalms of David, the Book of Job, favorite lines from Milton, Keats, Tennyson, Browning, T. S. Eliot, and others; the creative power of their words inspired her creativity.

In a letter to Mr. Gollancz, Miss Sayers apologized for the delay in finishing *The Nine Tailors*, explaining that she had had to spend a considerable amount of time studying the technique of bell-ringing. When she started to plan the novel, she knew nothing about campanology, but, chancing upon a copy of A. W. Troyte's *Change Ringing* (1880), she began to study the matter seriously and decided to make the bells an essential part of the plot. Despite minor errors, such as giving Lord Peter a rest during the ringing of the New Year's Eve peal, the explanations are competently handled and skillfully woven into the narrative. She endows the bells with almost human characteristics, allowing them to serve as instruments of Providence. When the mystery of Deacon's death is finally solved, the rector murmurs that one bell, old Batty Thomas, has been the cause of two other deaths, adding thoughtfully: ". . . the bells are said to be jealous of the presence of evil. Perhaps God speaks through those mouths of inarticulate metal. He is a righteous judge, strong and patient, and is provoked every day" (350). Chapter headings come from some facet of campanology. Defining bell-ringing as "not so much a brand of music as mathematics athletically applied to the making of a merry noise," *The Oxford Companion to Music* ends a lengthy article on the subject with the comment: "Sayers' novel, *The Nine Tailors*, gives an admirable description of English bell-ringing."

In *Adventure, Mystery, and Romance*, John Cawelti deals with aspects of this novel in the chapter on the art of the classical detective story. Claiming that the heart of the classical detective story is the examination of clues and the questioning of suspects, he shows that Miss Sayers combines "pure ingenuity of ratiocination and mystification with other narrative interests—character, setting, theme—completely subordinated to their role in this structure. . . ." [23] (Miss Sayers, like Miss Climpson, keeps things in the right proportion.) His shrewd analysis of the structure of this work and its relationship to great novels dealing with religious aspects of murder, such as *Crime and Punishment*, is worthy of close study.

Edmund Wilson denounced *The Nine Tailors* as one of the dullest books that he had ever encountered, adding: "The first part of it is all about bell-ringing and contains a lot of information of the kind that you might expect to find in an encyclopedia article. . . . I skipped a great deal of this. . . ." [24] Some readers found the explanatory material about change ringing tedious; others were not interested in spending time on the puzzling cryptogram, obviously the work of an experienced change-ringer, but it is doubtful that any reader skipped the dramatic account of Lord Peter's experience in the bell-chamber when the clanging fury of the bells fell upon his ears like a thousand beating hammers: "Through the brazen crash and clatter there went one high note, shrill and sustained, that was like a sword in the brain. . . . He released his hold of the ladder and tried to shut out the uproar with his fingers, but such a sick giddiness overcame him that he swayed, ready to fall. It was not noise—it was brute pain, a grinding, bludgeoning, ran-dan, crazy, intolerable torment. . . . His ear-drums were cracking; his senses swam away" (344).

Equally important is the setting, the wind-swept, dyke-riven, sparsely populated countryside where seagulls swoop and ravens scream. In "Fen Floods: Fiction and Fact" Miss Sayers recalls childhood memories of the East Anglian floods which receded in spring, leaving spears of green wheat to flourish, and flooded fields in September, leaving sodden ricks and rotting corn instead of the hoped for harvest. She explains that the flood in this novel was based on an actual occurrence: "So, for a parallel to the disaster imagined . . . I turned to the records of 1713, and tried to reproduce in miniature, what happened when the great sluice burst at Denver. (This seemed more appropriate since I had borrowed for the head of my hero's illustrious house, a title of nobility taken from that very same sluice and village). . . . I borrowed the framework, doing it on a more modest scale, allowing a mild flood of a fortnight or so and drowning only a few isolated parishes." [25]

Although Miss Sayers regarded her next novel, *Gaudy Night*, her best work in fiction, many readers and critics accord this honor to *The Nine Tailors* because theme, setting, and plot are so perfectly integrated: the bleak lowlands of the East Anglian fens, the imposing church built on the remains of the old Norman Abbey, and the magnificent bells that announced the news of death and danger as well as glad tidings of births, marriages, and good fortune. "When

properly employed," Haycraft points out, "the specialized background can be a pleasant variation and a restorer of jaded plots and
situations. It is at its best when crime and solution can be conclusively
correlated with it (the perfect example, of course, is Dorothy Sayers'
The Nine Tailors)." [26]

VI Gaudy Night

In *Gaudy Night*, 1936, it is not a murder nor an unidentified corpse
that disturbs the scholastic calm of Shrewsbury, a woman's college at
Oxford, but the malicious activities of a poltergeist whose nocturnal
perambulations result in ink-bespattered walls, smashed crockery,
and black-robed effigies stabbed with butcher knives. [27] Harriet Vane
comes on the scene when she reluctantly accepts an invitation to
attend an alumnae reunion, a Gaudy Weekend at Shrewsbury. It is
ten years since she took her First in English Literature there, and she
ruefully reflects that since then she has broken old ties and half the
commandments, as well. While chatting with former classmates and
tutors, Harriet is aware that they are deliberately avoiding any reference to her involvement in a sensational murder trial, recalling
instead her success as a writer of mystery fiction. Mistakes of the past
are obviously forgiven and forgotten.

During the visit, Harriet has two surprises. The first concerns Lord
Peter. She knew, of course, that he was a Balliol man but never
suspected that he was such a source of interest to her friends, who
plague her with questions about him. When a former classmate asks if
it is exciting to work with him on a case, Harriet answers caustically:
"Seeing . . . that he got me out of prison and possibly saved me from
being hanged, I am naturally bound to find him delightful" (32). Later
she wonders why she is so disagreeable every time his name is
mentioned. The second surprise is more annoying. Picking up a sheet
of paper blowing in the quad, she discovers an obscene drawing, a
childish picture of a naked female figure inflicting savage outrage on a
figure clad in cap and gown. Homeward bound for London, she finds
in the sleeve of her academic gown another crumpled paper with a
scrawled message: "You Dirty Murderess, aren't you ashamed to
show your face?" (51).

Months later, Harriet is urged by the Dean, Miss Martin, to return
to Oxford to help solve the mystery of the malefactor, now wantonly
destroying property. The latest outrage, the destruction of sections of
Miss Lydgate's monumental study of English Prosody, is, the Dean

confides, more than a prank; it is a truly "horrid act of pottiness" (65). Harriet goes to Oxford and, on the pretext of doing research on Sheridan Le Fanu, she resides at Shrewsbury, carefully investigating the situations that occur with alarming frequency. With the precision to be expected of a detective novelist, she collects data, examines alibis, and studies the obscene drawings and notes that appear mysteriously.

The last week in Hilary term proves eventful. The poltergeist raids three residence halls, wrenching open fuse boxes, pulling out the main fuse, leaving behind Stygian blackness and a trail of damages. Tension and suspicion mount among the faculty; students are notably more uneasy. The summer term is quiet, but when faculty and students return, harassments resume. Anonymous letters plague the faculty; Third Year students facing examinations receive dire prognostications of failure which increase their nervousness. After a student, a victim of thirty poison-pen notes, attempts suicide, the Dean and the Warden agree with Harriet that outside help must be summoned; at Harriet's request, Lord Peter comes.

After studying the dossier of the case, Lord Peter views the situation objectively. One evening when he is in the Senior Common Room talking with the dons, a heated discussion takes place about the importance of intellectual integrity. Miss De Vine tells of a situation in which a man deliberately suppressed information that invalidated his research and the main argument of his thesis. Pressed for more details, she explains that the man had discovered this information in a letter in an obscure European library when his thesis was almost written and he had no time to rewrite it. Besides, he had grown so convinced of the validity of his own theory that he could not bear to admit that it was inaccurate, so he hid the letter. When his dishonesty was exposed, he lost his professorship and his M.A. degree. After much discussion about the necessity of maintaining intellectual honesty even when it conflicts with one's personal needs and ambitions, Lord Peter asserts that the world would be completely changed if the time ever comes when people learn "to value the honour of the mind equally with the honour of the body." Alerted by Miss De Vine's story, Lord Peter soon identifies the Shrewsbury marauder, who admits that by her mischief she hoped to avenge the disgrace and consequent suicide of her husband, who was the dishonest M.A. candidate.

Intellectual honesty was a theme of vital importance to Miss Sayers. Invited to give a toast at a Gaudy dinner at Somerville

College, she thought deeply about the value of a university education, and decided that, before everything else, such an education forms "that habit of *intellectual integrity* which is at once the foundation and the result of scholarship." This idea became the solution to the vexing problem of placing Harriet on an equal footing with Lord Peter. "On the intellectual platform . . . Harriet could stand free and equal with Peter, since in that sphere she had never been false to her own standards. By choosing a plot that should exhibit intellectual integrity as the one great permanent value in an emotionally unstable world I should be saying the thing that, in a confused way, I had been wanting to say all my life. Finally, I should have found a universal theme which could be made integral both to the detective plot and to the 'love interest' which I had, somehow or other, to unite with it." [28]

To develop the love interest, Miss Sayers shows Harriet, now in her early thirties, attempting to analyze her emotional and intellectual involvements with objective candor. Still suffering from misadventures in love, attracted to Lord Peter but unwilling to accept his love while indebted to him, she fears that she will never feel that she is his equal. Finding some peace in the scholastic life at Oxford, she toys with the idea of giving up her career and retiring there to do research and scholarly writing, but she realizes that this is only an escape, a way of avoiding her problems. Since Miss Sayers planned this novel with the express purpose of bringing about Harriet's acceptance of Lord Peter, his faults are emphasized so that Harriet can see him in a new light. Accustomed to thinking of him as a person always in complete control of his emotions, she is first surprised and then amused that he is jealous of his nephew, a student at Oxford. Resentful of the boy's youthful vigor, insouciance, and camaraderie with Harriet, Lord Peter treats him with scornful condescension.

The first hint of Harriet's changing attitude toward her lover occurs when, engaged in the dangerous pursuit of tracking down the mysterious mischief-maker at Shrewsbury, she is cautioned by Lord Peter that despite the hazards she must not turn away from the task. Surprised, she concedes to herself that most males would have given the opposite advice, insisting on proffering assistance; only one in ten thousand would have shown such trust, which she sees as an unexpected admission of equality. She reflects seriously: "If he conceived *of marriage* along these lines, then the whole problem would have to be reviewed in that new light . . ." (230). She is further surprised by his great esteem for all that Oxford represents. His rueful admission, "Here's where the real things are done, Harriet," and his denuncia-

tion of the self-aggrandisement, haste, violence, and slippery clever-
ness of his worldly milieu strips away his mask of self-complacency.
Dropping his facetious manner, he reveals his deep love for his family
heritage and confesses that he has "a cursed hankering for musty old
values." It is then that Harriet realizes that during the five years that
she has held out against him, she has seen only his aristocratic
certitude, his erudition, and sophisticated aplomb; within an hour
she discovers his weaknesses and fears, his concerns and loyalties.
Aware of his vulnerability and his willingness to free her, despite
potential dangers, from all obligations of gratitude to him, she begins
to understand his true nature. Miss Sayers explains: ". . . I had made
Harriet's surrender easier by letting her see Peter's weaknesses
instead of (as hitherto) his strength: his jealous irritation at the mis-
deeds of a prodigal nephew; his personal vanities, his carefully concealed sentimentalities, his resentment of his own small stature and
its compensating outbursts of childish exhibitionism . . . and had
further enhanced his attractions by making somebody else fall in love
with him. . . . Thus the train was laid for the overthrow of Harriet's
defences. . . ." [29] And accept him she finally does, in a manner in
keeping with her character—and his:

. . . She searched for the word that should carry her over the last difficult
breach.
   It was he who found it for her. With a gesture of submission he bared his
head and stood gravely, the square cap dangling in his hand.
   "*Placetne, magistra?*"
   "*Placet.*" (482)

Miss Sayers creates humor in *Gaudy Night* by wittily limning the
personalities and foibles of the dons. With gentle raillery she associates each with a special area of knowledge, detailing with comic
exaggeration the intense preoccupation with which each views her
own specific interest: Miss Flackett's knowledge of the life history of
the liver-fluke; Miss Schuster-Slatt's *idée fixe*: the necessity of ster-
ilizing the unfit; Miss Fitt's learned discourses on the tumulus at
Halos; and Miss Lydgate's work on English verse from Beowulf to
Bridges. Admiring the author's skill in capturing nuances of tone and
tempers, the *Spectator* critic commented that Miss Sayers achieved
just the right "mixture of highmindedness, jealousy, learning and
frivolity . . . ludicrously similar to that of their male counterparts." [30]
Humorous, too, are the alumnae returning for Gaudy weekend.
Viewing them, Harriet wonders if one of them might be the myste-

rious prankster, perhaps the "curly-headed person in tweeds, with a masculine-looking waistcoat and the face like the back of the cab? Or the tightly-corseted peroxide of sixty, whose hat would better have suited an eighteen-year-old débutante at Ascot. . . . Or that curious little creature dressed in unbecoming pink, who looked as though she had been carelessly packed away in a drawer all winter and put into circulation again without being ironed . . ." (55–56).

Neither Bunter nor Miss Climpson is significant; Freddy Arbuthnot appears briefly, furnishing information about Lord Peter. Dean Martin, the dons, a few students, and Annie Wilson, a scout at Shrewsbury, are developed to the extent needed for their roles in the plot and theme, which, Miss Sayers states, are one and the same: "Namely, that the same intellectual honesty that is essential to scholarship is essential also to the conduct of life." [31]

The novel furnished the author with unparalleled opportunities to indulge her gift for literary quotations, quips, and puns. The conversational stamina of the dons and guests never flags: learned discourses highlight exchanges in the Senior Common Room, at High Table, and even during boating parties. Edith Hamilton advises readers to get out their Bartlett to help them decide whether Lord Peter's ripostes are original or from the masters, for "quotation marks are not in order. Oxonians do not need such guide posts." Guests, asked their views of Platonic philosophy, answer with "an airy quip from Aristotle—in Greek, which the company welcomes as a familiar friend." [32] However, all conversation is not that erudite. The Dean, for instance, talks with breezy informality. Annoyed over the mischief-maker's fleet get-away after hours of devastation, she blames the dons for their heedless reactions: "The silly cuckoos! If they'd *only* sat tight on their little behinds last night, we could have cleared the whole business up" (210).

The chapter headings in *Gaudy Night* are notable for the variety of authors quoted: Bacon, Drayton, Dekker, Herrick, Spenser, Shakespeare, Queen Elizabeth, Sidney, and others. The selections are unusually long, with a prevailing somberness, excoriating conceit and folly, and counseling goodness: "Think not that the nobilitie of your Ancestors doth free you to doe all that you list, contrary-wise, it bindeth you more to follow vertue."

Many points of style were censured in *Scrutiny* by Q. D. Leavis who placed the author on the level of such sensational writers as Ouida, Marie Corelli, and Baron Corvo. Accusing Miss Sayers of giving "a peepshow of the senior university world, especially of the women's college," the critic continued: "It is a vicious presentation because it is popular and romantic while pretending to realism." She castigated the reading public for accepting Miss Sayers's "literary glibness and spiritual illiteracy," hinting that those who have canonized her as a literary stylist reveal their own lack of perception and good taste.[33] Few critics were that severe, although many noted that, as a detective story, it lacked excitement; there was not even one murder. Miss Sayers explains: "Murder meant publicity and the police, and I wanted to keep my action within the control of the Senior Common Room. There was one crime which could readily be dealt with by academic authorities, and which they would be particularly anxious to screen from publicity, and that was the crime of disseminating obscene libels, and committing malicious damage." [34]

Readers and critics found the mystery, theme, and portrayal of life at Oxford sufficiently interesting without a murder or corpse: mischief and mayhem create and sustain suspense. Haycraft, however, expressed some misgivings: ". . . The author in her frank and laudable experimentation intruded unwittingly on the dangerous no-man's-land which is neither good detection nor good legitimate fiction." [35] From his viewpoint as a critic of detective stories, his reaction is understandable, but did his verdict take into consideration Miss Sayers's expressed aims? She felt that she had achieved three goals: by bringing about Harriet's unreserved acceptance of Lord Peter, the couple could be united and banished, leaving the author free to pursue other aspects of creativity; moreover, she had succeeded—to her satisfaction, at least—in combining the detective story with the novel of manners, and in doing so, made a statement of profound concern to her: the value of intellectual integrity.

VII Busman's Honeymoon

Last in the series of the Lord Peter Wimsey novels, *Busman's Honeymoon*, 1937, is subtitled "A Love Story with Detective Interruptions." [36] Affirming her belief that any love interest in a detective story is an intrusion, Miss Sayers nevertheless justified it here because it answers so many questions about the couple and their adjustments to married life. She adds: "If there is but a ha'porth of detection to an intolerable deal of saccharine. let the occasion be the excuse." [37]

When Lord Peter, Harriet, and Bunter arrive at the honeymoon hideaway, they are chagrined because the house is dark and locked. The former owner, Mr. Noakes, has not followed their directions about preparations for their arrival; he is not even present to welcome them. A sign, "No Bread and Milk till Further Notise [sic]," confirms a neighbor's protests that "no lords or ladies were expected." The following morning Bunter discovers the body of Mr. Noakes in the cellar. When the official report confirms that he died from a heavy blow on the head, suspicion falls on Miss Twitterton, Noakes's niece; Joe Sellon, a young police officer; and Frank Crutchley, the gardener. Each had a reason to loathe Noakes and more than one opportunity to do away with him.

The plot of the novel was familiar to many, for a stage version, written at the suggestion of and in collaboration with Miss Sayers's close friend Muriel St. Clare Byrne had appeared earlier, running for several months at a London theater, but this did not detract from the book's popularity or sales.[38] Two weaknesses, less evident on the stage, mar the novel. Raymond Chandler commented caustically on the first: ". . . a man is murdered alone at night in his house by a mechanically released weight which works because he always turns the radio on at just such a moment, always stands in just such a position in front of it, and always bends over just so far. A couple of inches either way and the customer would get a rain check. This is what is vulgarly known as having God sit in your lap; a murderer who needs that much help from Providence must be in the wrong business."[39]

The second flaw concerns the motivation for the murder. Crutchley, convinced that Noakes will never repay the sum of forty pounds which he promised to invest, carefully plans and executes this drastic revenge against his employer. Robert Philmore stated that the murder might have seemed more plausible if Crutchley had been portrayed not as a rather ordinary working-class fellow, but as an abnormal individual, a psychopathic case or a sadist.[40] The stage production gave more opportunity to highlight Crutchley's vindictiveness: in love with pretty Polly Mason, he is in the galling position of being shackled to Noakes's ageing niece, whose spinsterish ways provoke him.

More a novel of manners than a detective story, *Busman's Honeymoon* has many comic episodes, some farcical, some tinged with pathos. Several were more effective on the stage than in the novel. When Mr. Puffett, for instance, fails to rid the clogged chimney of soot, the vicar, Mr. Goodacre, undertakes the task by firing his shotgun up the flue. Bowled over by the blast, he falls, enveloped in the chimney drape and by cascades of soot, masonry, and other rubble. Peter is speechless with laughter at the sight of the shrouded vicar and the vision of Bunter, "snorting and blind, and black as any Nubian Venus . . ." (122). The visual effect is mirth-provoking and the timing exactly right, for a scene of tension follows: Bunter announces that he has found a week-old corpse in the basement.

Miss Twitterton's manners and habits provide comedy and pathos. Asked where she keeps her uncle's keys when he is away, she answers: "*Always* in my bedroom. The keys, and dear Mother's silver tea-pot and Aunt Sophy's cruet that was a wedding present . . . I take them up with me *every* night and put them on the little table by my bed, with the dinner-bell handy in case of fire" (188). When Crutchley learns that she will not inherit her uncle's savings, he breaks the engagement with the sneering comment: "A man that's starting in life wants a wife, see? A nice little bit to come 'ome to. Some 'un he can cuddle—not a skinny old hen. . . . You'd like to take me up to bed like the silver tea-pot and a silver tea-pot 'ud be about as much use to you, I reckon" (318).

After hearing about the spinster's involvement with Crutchley, Harriet begs her husband not to reveal to the police that Miss Twitterton had both the opportunity and motive to murder her uncle, but he refuses to hide any facts. Shortly before this, he has wrestled with his own conscience, for he was reluctant to tell the authorities that Joe Sellon had lied, but the truth must be revealed and Lord Peter does so. After a long, serious discussion about the inviolability of conscience, the newlyweds solemnly promise that they will never allow their emotions to swerve them from the way of truth and justice: affection for one another must never corrupt their judgment or conscience. With shrewd discernment, Miss Sayers moves from comedy to pathos to a scene of moral commitment. As in *The Documents in the Case* and *Unnatural Death*, she states that the integrity of an individual must not be perverted by bonds of affection or false loyalties to another person.

Lord Peter's wit and antics have the zany touch notable in the early novels. He exchanges literary gems and jests not only with Harriet but with Superintendent Kirk, who delights in identifying every quotation. When Bunter is acclaimed "sea-green incorruptible," Kirk responds: "Carlyle—*French Revolution*." When he is about to sit in Noakes's chair, to Peter's comment, "Galahad will sit down in Merlin's seat," Kirk answers: "Alfred—Lord Tennyson." He recognizes Dickens's "Artful Dodger" but misquotes Pope, meriting Wimsey's correction—"Not knowledge—learning! A little learning!" Q. D. Leavis commented acidulously: "Literature gets heavily drawn upon in Miss Sayers's writings, and her attitude is revealing. She displays knowingness about literature without any sensitiveness to it or any feeling for quality—i.e. she has an academic literary taste over and above no general taste at all. . . . " [41]

In the interval after Crutchley's trial and before his execution, Lord Peter's nerves are in such a terrible condition that Harriet seeks advice from his mother, who promptly invites them to visit Denver Place while the Duke and Helen are away. The grounds, house, furnishings, servants, relatives, and even some stray ghosts are described in detail, providing a change of pace and light humor, but when the couple return, tension mounts: the condemned Crutchley refuses to make his peace with Lord Peter or to repent. If some readers had misgivings about the future happiness of the honeymooners, the last chapter must have quelled all doubts. Harriet, realizing that she cannot dispel the black despair that engulfs her husband, waits with inner turmoil but resolute steadfastness until Peter, recognizing his need, comes to her for support and solace.

Despite its subtitle, *Busman's Honeymoon* is neither a satisfactory detective tale nor an absorbing romance; practically its only virtue is that it serves to unite Harriet and Lord Peter. Asserting that her earnings from her novels had made her sufficiently independent so that she could devote her time to other types of creative writing, Miss Sayers announced that there would be no more Wimsey novels. Despite this avowal, she began work in the 1940s on a novel tentatively named *Thrones, Dominations*, in which Uncle Paul Delagardie recounts to Harriet some of her husband's youthful involvements. Five chapters in longhand, with pages of revisions, now in the Marion E. Wade Collection, Wheaton College, prove that Miss Sayers had not utterly banished Lord Peter Wimsey.

VIII   *Mistress of Mystery*

During her lifetime, Miss Sayers earned an enviable reputation as a gifted writer of detective novels. A cool-headed constructionist, she planned each novel meticulously, organized the plot carefully, made the method and the means of murder mystifying but plausible, and worked out all details accurately. In the Marion E. Wade Collection, notes and charts show that, while planning *Have His Carcase*, she carefully calculated the times and depths of tides and the minutes required to traverse on foot and by horseback a stretch of sandy beach. Numerous handwritten exercises in intricate types of peals fill pages of a copybook, proving how industriously she studied the techniques of change ringing after she decided to make campanology an important feature in *The Nine Tailors*. She did not hesitate, however, to seek assistance, calling on a friend, for instance, to help her with supporting details necessary for *The Five Red Herrings*. She planted clues for the alert, rational mind to see and to draw from them the right, inevitable conclusions.

In her early novels she adhered to the rules of fair play; she rarely concealed a vital clue and did not overuse coincidence or allow it to explain a mystery. She hesitated to introduce characters that were too human, for fear of lessening the suspense, allowed no love interest, and deplored detectives who became romantic about young ladies. Unlike Agatha Christie, she did not think that it was absolutely necessary to conceal the identity of the murderer until the last pages, for she thought that the *Why* and *How* were just as mystifying as *Who*. Lord Peter Death Bredon Wimsey passed the qualifications set by S. S. Van Dine, who declared that a detective must be a character of high and fascinating attainments, human, unusual, colorful, and gifted.

After years of studying examples of this genre, the classics, pulps, and the in-betweens, she decided that Dickens, Le Fanu, Wilkie Collins, and the French author Gaboriau wrote better than the modern practitioner, for their novels had not only mystery, suspense, and intricate problems to be solved but also characters of some psychological depth, involved in perplexing situations that were more than mere puzzle plots. Realizing that the rules for the detective novel had become too restricted, she broke with tradition: she introduced love interests, specialized knowledge, and unusual backgrounds fundamental to the plot. She experimented, attempting to give the novel some of the literary merits and characteristics of the novel of manners; themes of significance were woven into the plot; perceptive comments exposed some of the follies and foibles of the times. Although *Murder Must Advertise*, *The Nine Tailors*, and *Gaudy Night* brought her nearer to her goal, she was not satisfied.

In a little-known essay, the introduction to an anthology, *Tales of Detection*, she claimed that although experimentation with the form had brought it closer to the achievements of Dickens, Collins, Le Fanu, and Gaboriau, and that present novelists handled the elements of plot with ease, yet they did not know how to combine these with an artistic treatment of the psychological elements.[42] She stated that in 1936; in 1937, she announced that she intended to write no more novels of detection. Evidently she had decided that it was not worthwhile to continue.

In the distinguished company of Agatha Christie and Margery Allingham, she was recognized in her lifetime and is noted today as one of the gifted mistresses of suspense and mystery. In the literary history of the development of the detective novel, Dorothy L. Sayers will be remembered as one who raised the standards of this genre during its Golden Age.

CHAPTER 4

The Stories—Short but Sinister

MISS Sayer's first collection of short stories, *Lord Peter Views the Body*, 1927, features Wimsey in twelve stories.[1] Not all are of equal merit. "The Entertaining Episode of the Article in Question," "The Fantastic Horror of the Cat in the Bag," and "The Unprincipled Affair of the Practical Joker" are entertaining but slight works. For genuine mystery, original plot, and startling denouement four rank among the best: "The Abominable History of the Man with Copper Fingers," "The Undignified Melodrama of the Bone of Contention," "The Adventurous Exploit of the Cave of Ali Baba," and "The Learned Adventure of the Dragon's Head."

"The Abominable History of the Man with Copper Fingers" begins in a secluded smoking room of an exclusive club in London where members are exchanging tales one evening. Varden, an actor, tells of a strange experience that occurred in America when he was visiting Loder, a sculptor. Previous visits had been delightful, but on this occasion, despite the fact that his host had repeatedly urged, indeed, had insisted on this visit, Varden was uneasy, for he sensed that his host was hostile, almost malignant toward him at times. He noted that Loder's most recent artworks showed signs of psychotic stress—the settee in the living room, for instance. There was nothing very unusual about the base, but the couch itself was strange: the actual seat, almost a throne, was in the shape of a fleshy nude, closely resembling the artist's mistress, who had recently deserted him.

When a stranger breaks into Varden's room at midnight and arouses him, telling him that he must leave Loder's place at once, for his life is in danger, the situation seems ridiculous until the intruder draws Varden into the living room, approaches the settee, cracks open the silver arm of the reclining figure, and draws from its recesses a long, dry arm-bone. Varden bolts for his life. His macabre tale is completed in the club room by the mysterious intruder, Lord Peter, who describes Loder's last moments twitching in a vat of copper sulphate and cyanide while his graphite-blackened hands are slowly copper-coated.

The story is typical of Miss Sayers's artistry. Carefully developed details aid the plot: the unusual feature that Maria's second toe on the left foot is shorter than the one on the right; Wimsey's discovery of the electro-type of the American consular seal made by Loder for his passport; Wimsey's flash of intuition that the criminal's plans hinge on three things, which, of course, are figured out in time to save Varden. The viewpoint is handled deftly: Varden recounts his experiences up to his hasty exit from Loder's apartments; slipping into the group of listeners, Lord Peter finishes the story down to the last detail, the disposal of Maria's Sheffield-plated body in a remote corner of a Catholic cemetery.

The longest story and one of the cleverest is "The Undignified Melodrama of the Bone of Contention," which concerns the missing will of Mr. Burdock, a "spiteful, badtempered, dirty-living old blackguard." Despite this reputation, after his death he is given all the honors usually accorded to the most devout parishioner: he is laid out in the Lady Chapel; candles burn around his coffin; eight men keep a night vigil. But before the funeral takes place, strange stories begin to circulate about a mysterious apparition: a shining white death-coach, a headless driver, and four white horses have been seen speeding down a country lane. The mystery of the missing will, the complications concerning the rightful heir, and the disposal of the corpse create a story rich in humor, suspense, and surprise. The descriptions of the death-coach, the gloomy chapel, and the old library add immeasurably to the eerie atmosphere. Imaginative resourcefulness helps Lord Peter to outwit fraud and conspiracy, making this a tale not to be missed; mood, setting, and characterization are brilliantly handled.

More melodramatic, "The Adventurous Exploit of the Cave of Ali Baba" opens with a newspaper account of the death of Lord Peter and details about his will. Rogers, known as an ex-footman, reads the article, leaves his Lambeth flat, and goes to a pub where he makes some sinister contacts. Later he joins other members of a secret society in a sequestered house on Hampstead Heath. Here masked strangers learn with fear and horror that a spy has infiltrated the group. Reminding them that several plans have gone awry recently, their leader demands that the informer, Number Twenty-one, step forward. Questioned, Rogers admits that he is Lord Peter Wimsey. Suspense mounts. Will he be killed for his betrayal? Will he be saved by his threat that in a vault at 110 Piccadilly is a ledger containing information which will endanger each member if it falls into the hands of the police, who are already alerted? The hysteria of the ringleaders, the suspense concerning who will be the first to arrive at the vault to manipulate the electronic device adjusted to respond to Wimsey's voice only, are all done in Miss Sayers's best style. She included this in her anthology *The Second Omnibus*; it also appears in Richardson's *Best Mystery Stories*, one of which it surely is, although some critics prefer to think that it is a clever spoof of the terror tale retold weekly in the pulps.

"The Learned Adventure of the Dragon's Head" has two mysteries and a paradox: a perplexing will, a buried treasure, and Lord Peter in the role of a benevolent uncle temporarily in charge of nephew Jerrykins or "Pickled Gherkins." Fascinated by a worn copy of Munster's *Cosmographia Universalis*, Jerrykins lays out all his pocket money for the volume. After a stranger attempts to buy the book and, rebuffed, resorts to more aggressive action, Lord Peter and his nephew visit the former owner of the volume, a Dr. Conyers, who recounts a strange tale of an ancestor's mysterious will stating that his pirate gold is buried in Munster. But which Munster? Ireland? Germany? Lord Peter's special knowledge—in this case astrology, Latin, cartography, and handwriting peculiar to the 1700s—leads him to the solution. Unforgettable is the picture of Lord Peter urbanely instructing his nephew on the proper method of extracting a pistol from the burglar's pocket and carrying it to safety. Miss Sayers has a bit of fun satirizing poor taste: the old sea-lord's ancient mansion, Yelsall Manor, is a Tudor house with Italian embellishments, with grounds laid out so that grove nods to grove; later additions include a Chinese pagoda and lakes dotted with islands, replete with temples, tea-houses, grottoes, and bridges.

Two stories are more amusing than mysterious; each involves a bizarre situation. "The Piscatorial Farce of the Stolen Stomach" concerns the peculiar legacy left by Scotsman Ferguson, whose will directs that "after my death, the alimentary organs be removed entire with their contents from my body, commencing with the oesophagus and ending with the anal canal, and that they be properly secured at both ends . . . and be enclosed in a proper preservative medium in a glass vessel and given to my nephew . . . now studying medicine" (290). How these organs, which served the old man so well for ninety-five years, can possibly help the young medic will puzzle the reader as much as it did the heir, but the solution is satisfactory, except perhaps to the squeamish.

Another story of a hidden will, "The Fascinating Problem of Uncle Meleager's Will," involves a mysterious crossword puzzle that is worked out, not on shiny squares of glossy paper or newsprint, but on the red, white, and black marble tiles of a small pool, part of an old Roman villa built by an eccentric gentleman in Dorking. When Lord Peter falls into the pool, he is not too wet to see that a clue is hidden in the couplet: "Truth, poor girl, was nobody's daughter; She took off her clothes and jumped into the water." The crossword puzzle is complex enough to please the devotee; for others, the solution is given at the end of the volume.

While listening to his host proclaim the benefits of Vitamin B, Lord Peter also hears reverberating footsteps emanating from rooms upstairs, deduces several truths about the occupants, and, minutes after shrieks resound, traps a murderer. Modestly admitting that he was born noticing things and has improved the trait by practice, Wimsey reveals the secret of his successful sleuthing: he notes when something is wrong, perhaps just a common object out of place; an impression is left on his eye; the subconscious registers it; his brain starts working . . . and it all comes back. A hunch or a flash of intuition helps, but it all starts with the eye, the discerning sense that something is "out of place or awry." "The Footsteps That Ran" is a model of deductive reasoning as sharp as the skewer rescued in time to prove murder has been committed.

For readers interested in Miss Sayers's development of the character and personality of Lord Peter, several stories will have a special appeal. "The Bibulous Business of a Matter of Taste" demonstrates that his palate for fine wines is as exceptional as has been implied in many novels; his sharp ear for inaccuracies in grammar leads to the capture of a jewel thief who, while impersonating a female, carelessly uses the masculine article, "un," when referring to himself. "The Entertaining Episode of the Article in Question" turns on that simple point. In "The Unsolved Puzzle of the Man with No Face," Wimsey comments on attitudes toward work, particularly an artist's feelings toward his own creativity, a theme of concern to Miss Sayers.

The stories in *Lord Peter Views the Body*, not all of which have been mentioned here, range from the macabre and grotesque to the mildly entertaining. Each reveals the author's power to create believable situations, unusual settings that add to the atmosphere, and interesting characters, developed to the extent usual in this genre. Flashes of intuition and clever reasoning help Lord Peter solve the most perplexing mysteries. How he happens to drop into a certain office, be present on a railroad platform at a significant moment, or be cantering at midnight along a road where headless horses draw an eerie coach, is, of course, a question that only Miss Sayers could answer. Although Barzun calls this her "prime collection," praising it for its variety, balance, picturesqueness, and ingenuity of plot, yet there is an unevenness in the stories.[2] Some are entertaining for the first reading only; others, particularly "The Learned Adventure of the Dragon's Head" and "The . . . Man with Copper Fingers," are amusing after several encounters.

In the introductory essay written for volume two of *Great Short Stories of Detection, Mystery, and Horror*, 1931, Miss Sayers forecast a gloomy outlook for the future of the well-written detective short story which, she felt, was in the precarious position of a city built between the sea and a precipice: constantly undermined on one side, with no opportunity for expansion on the other. Editorial rules severely restricted subject matter and tone, as well as length, trimmed down to a mere 6,000 words usually. To add to the difficulties, readers knew most of the tricks of the trade: forged fingerprints, the put-back clock, the trick flask, the substituted corpse, and the gramophone alibi which, she asserted, should be given a long, long rest. She had even less esteem for the detective problem in which the crime and all the clues are flatly given so that the reader can play "Guess Who?".[3] Despite her complaint that it no longer seemed worthwhile to invent an agreeable murder, a suitable detective, add a bit of human interest, then attempt to compress all this into the limited space of a short story, she accomplished this feat in her next volume.

I   Hangman's Holiday

Six of the twelve stories in *Hangman's Holiday*, 1933, feature Montague Egg, a traveling salesman for Plummet & Rose, Wines and Spirits, Piccadilly.[4] Less sophisticated and erudite than Lord Peter Wimsey, Monty is equally astute in solving puzzling mysteries. Asked about his success in such matters, he answers modestly: "I'm not a brainy man, but in my line one learns to size up a party pretty quickly." Miss Sayers adroitly emphasizes his unassuming manner, middle-class lifestyle, and amiable temperament, showing him at ease with his fellow salesmen at the Pig and Whistle or the seedy Green Man, enjoying meeting old customers and potential buyers.

Pleased by the favorable reception of the Montague Egg stories in various magazines, Miss Sayers accepted Mr. Gollancz's suggestion that these be included in a new anthology of short stories: "I'm glad you find Monty publishable," she wrote. "Of course, he is only Passing Show stuff and rather lacking in literary distinction. . . ." [5] Readers found him amusing, a welcome contrast to the flamboyant personality of Wimsey. Like him, Monty has a penchant for quoting favorite lines but these are not culled from Shakespeare, Donne, or Beddoes but come straight out of the *Salesman's Handbook*, a compendium of sophomoric wisdom phrased in banal couplets: "The good will of the maid / Is nine-tenths of the trade"; "Don't let a sudden question rout you, / But always keep your wits about you." Serious, sober, and shrewd, Monty is able to solve perplexing puzzles and to quote a saying appropriate for the most trying circumstance.

"The Poisoned Dow '08" opens with Monty being confronted by a policeman who informs him that his customer Lord Borrodale is dead, poisoned by port wine, Dow '08, sold by Monty himself. With the permission of the authorities, Monty visits the wine cellar where he examines the bottles, the unopened and the empties. "The salesman with the open eye sees commissions mount up high" is one of Monty's favorite gems, but in this case he is on the lookout for something more important than sales. He discovers some interesting facts, interrogates the butler, then makes a trip to the furnace room. When asked what led him to suspect the identity of the murderer, Monty admits that it was not circumstantial evidence but a change in the tone and manner of the culprit when accosted. After all, the *Salesman's Handbook* says: "Whether you're wrong or whether you're right, it's always better to be polite" (77).

Monty's shrewd appraisal of human reactions, his fund of arcane information, and his sharp intuition aid him. In "Sleuths on the Scent," the telltale way a man removes a glass stopper from a bottle labels him a chemist—and a murderer. "One Too Many" concerns the disappearance of Simon Grant from a first-class railroad carriage. He was seen there by many people; where did he go and when? No one saw him leave although a few personal articles are found along the tracks. Unabashedly, Monty tells how it is possible to elude the watchful ticket collector at the barrier and "pass through" without surrendering one's ticket or paying for the ride. His explanation solves the mystery but merits him a rebuke from railroad officials who frown at his bromide: "Speak the truth with cheerful ease, if you would both convince and please." The ingenious solution, humor, and characterization are all convincing. Less successful is "Murder in the Morning," in which Monty shows that some clocks tell actual time and some just "lighting-up" time, to the confusion of a murderer. "Murder at Pentecost" is remarkable for only one feature: Pentecost College, Oxford University, and the inner sanctum of the Bodleian are the most unlikely settings that one can imagine for Monty's sleuthing. "Maher-shalal-hashbaz" is a horror story that starts out pleasantly enough with Monty befriending a child delivering some cats to strangers, but it ends with him envisioning paramount cruelty: an old man clawed, scratched, terrorized in the dark of night by leaping figures, black, tabby, and ginger.

Lord Peter appears in only four stories. "The Image in the Mirror," a slight tale, involves identical twins, one of whom is a killer and the other, a shell-shocked somnambulist. Lord Peter does not make his appearance in "The Incredible Elopement of Lord Peter Wimsey" until after Mr. Langley, traveling in the Pyreenes, has the upsetting experience of meeting Doctor Wetherall and his wife, whom Langley remembers as a beautiful, golden-haired girl. When her husband orders her to greet her old admirer, Langley is stunned: "Something shuffled and whimpered. . . . It was dressed in a rich gown . . . that hung rucked and crumpled upon the thick and slouching body. The face was white and puffy, the eyes vacant, the mouth drooled open, with little trickles of saliva running from the loose corners. A dry fringe of rusty hair clung to the half-bald scalp, like the dead wisps on the head of a mummy" (38).

To rescue the lady in distress, Lord Peter, assisted by a Spanish conjuror, plays upon the superstitions of the servants who are captivated by seven white cats, a talking parrot, and a leaping lemur performing in the gloom-shrouded room while a wizard, chanting what sounds suspiciously like Homer's Catalogue of Ships, produces from mid-air a metal casket filled with enchanted wafers for their mistress. These bizarre performances continue for several weeks while the husband is away; when he returns, his lady, servants, familiars—all have disappeared, and Lord Peter's elopement, "in a purely Pickwickian sense," as he carefully explains, is over, too. A blend of black magic and fantasy, the tale has interesting medical information which gives a special turn to the plot.

"The Queen's Square" concerns a murder that occurs at an elaborate ball where the guests are costumed to represent games. Miss Sayers's wit and imagination enliven the scene: Lord Peter is a colorful Jack of Diamonds; the host, as "Emperor of the great Mah-jongg dynasty," is resplendent in a "Chinese costume patterned with red and green dragons . . . carrying on his shoulder a stuffed bird with an enormous tail." Mrs. Wrayburn, in a gown boldly outlined in the red and black points of a backgammon board, comments caustically on the outfit of another guest: "Water-polo—so sensible, just a bathing dress and a ball; though I must say it would look better on a less *Restoration* figure!"

Obedient to their host's commands, the guests twirl and caper through the intricate steps of a country dance until halted by a shrill cry: "Charmain . . . in the tapestry room . . . dead . . . strangled." To help solve the mystery, readers are provided with a detailed map showing the location of the library, ballroom, tapestry room, the musician's gallery, and the garden. The story gives accurate explanations of the guests' movements during the fatal hour, but so much attention is given to the descriptions of the ball, the costumes, and the zeal of the host to create the spirit of medieval jollity that there is little room to develop characterization and motivation. It is one of the few times that Miss Sayers allows extraneous features in a short story to get out of control. Even the plot is thin; the trick of lighting on which it hinges is too implausible.

If "The Queen's Square" errs in revealing too much that is inconsequential and too little that is significant, "The Necklace of Pearls" has no such flaws. In *Crime in Good Company*, L. A. Strong praised Miss Sayers not only for the "resplendent idea of a hiding place" but also the manner in which she played it down "by skillful timing and making it appear just another of the story's virtues, instead of the centre around which the whole thing grew."[6] Characters, plot, motivation, and the hiding place are all in proportion and completely believable.

"The Fountain Plays," one of two stories without a detective, shows an artistic balance between what is revealed and what is hidden, what is told and what is implied. Characterization and suspense are well handled. Miss Digby, a young widow, finds Mr. Spiller, a widower—and his villa—very attractive except for one jarring note: the frequent visitor, Mr. Gooch, who drinks too much, stays too long, and treats his host with scarcely veiled insolence. Mrs. Digby resolves that if the time ever comes when she is mistress of "The Pleasaunce," her first move will be to oust this boor. But burdens do not vanish so easily. When Mr. Spiller is free of one specter, another invidiously appears, more frightening than the first, boding ill for Mrs. Digby's hopes and Mr. Spiller's peace of mind. Although a murder occurs in "The Man Who Knew How," no detective traces the criminal. Interest centers on Pender, who becomes increasingly irritated by the probing gaze and sardonic smile of a stranger staring at him in the train compartment. Finally silence is broken and the conversation veers toward detective stories, particularly murder mysteries. The stranger tells how he would perpetrate a murder that could not possibly be detected. From that moment on, poor Pender is a victim of fears and curiosity: at the end, his surprise will jolt the reader, too. "It is not exactly a detective story," Miss Sayers wrote to Mr. Gollancz, "but it is one of the best shorts I've done."

The selections in *Hangman's Holiday* are pleasantly varied, ranging from slight tales of whimsical humor to the complex and macabre. The ingenious situations demand "a certain amount of elbow room in order to reach a satisfying conclusion," [7] but setting, mood, and characterization are, for the most part, kept in harmonious proportions. Yet it is obvious that the limitations of the detective short story circumscribe Miss Sayers's fictional creativity.

II   In the Teeth of the Evidence

In the Teeth of the Evidence, 1939, has only two Lord Peter stories; five feature Montague Egg. In the remaining ten, no detective appears, although there are many sinister events and mysteries, solved and unsolved.[8] In the story from which the collection takes its name, Lord Peter, seated in the "green velvet torture chair," is so intrigued by his dentist's tale of a corpse found in a burning garage that he accompanies Mr. Lamplough to the mortuary and watches while an examination is made of the dental work of the corpse. This establishes the identity of the victim to the satisfaction of those concerned, but Lord Peter questions: Was the death an accident, a suicide, or a suicide made to look like an accident? It was none of these but murder, arson, and fraud. The other Wimsey story, "Absolutely Everywhere," involves a murder, but neither of these stories is as clever as the Wimsey tales in the earlier anthologies.

The Montague Egg stories, "A Shot at Goal," "Dirt Cheap," "Bitter Almonds," and "False Weight," hold the reader's interest, but "The Professor's Manuscript" is the most intriguing. Hearing that a newcomer, a "funny old bird, Professor Pindar," might be a potential customer, Monty makes a business call, secures an order for wines, but leaves with several vexing questions. If it is really true, as the gossips insist, that the old man orders the best chops and steaks from the butcher, how does it happen that the professor's dental plate is so "wonky" that Monty suspects that to chew scrambled eggs would be difficult? Three peculiar conditions in the library start Monty off on a chase that discloses the true identity of the professor and why he needed protective coloring.

"Bitter Almonds" begins with Monty mourning: "There's another perfectly good customer gone west." His chagrin is even greater when he discovers that his client, Mr. Whipley, died after sharing with his son an after-dinner liqueur of crème de menthe supplied by Monty's firm. When drops of prussic acid are discovered in the old man's glass, the situation looks grim for his son. After examining a lead-foil capsule found in the library grate, Monty makes a phone call to his firm, receives information that confirms his suspicions, and goes off to see the coroner. Monty's esoteric knowledge or, as he terms it, a "dim recollection of something read long ago," alerts him to the fact that Noyeau, a liqueur flavored with bitter almonds, could accumulate over a period of years an oil containing prussic acid, fatal if not drained from the bottle. What made Monty investigate the situation in the first place, since everyone else suspected murder? He answers that his customer never drank crème de menthe; he kept it for the ladies.

Sinister intrigue and hints of the preternatural appear in "The Leopard Lady." Did Tressider actually hear, or did he only imagine that he heard the whispered message: "If the boy is in your way, ask at Rapollo's for Smith and Smith"? At Rapollo's, he meets a stranger, Mr. Smith, who not only knows about his financial losses but also his vague desire to rid himself of the care of his wealthy ward and nephew, six-year-old Cyril. Listening to Smith's insidious suggestions, Tressider is almost overcome with terror, but, after sipping a strange drink, peace surges over him; then suddenly he is out in the country, approaching a poplar-lined avenue leading to a low gray house: Smith & Smith—Removals.

When Cyril announces that he is no longer lonely, for he has found in a neighboring garden two leopards and a fairy lady with golden eyes, Mrs. Tressider is annoyed; later, when he is ill, she reminds him that little boys who tell tales are usually punished. Of course, she knows nothing about a check for two thousand pounds made out to Smith & Smith—Removals. After the child's death, Tressider wonders if he really visited such a firm. Was there a gray house and in it, four men and a girl with golden eyes? Was it an hallucination? Something diabolical? A wish fulfillment of his own diseased self, envious and grasping for wealth not his? Surrealist in mood and action, the story raises more questions than it answers.

"The Cyprian Cat," "Scrawns," "The Milk-Bottles," and "Dilemma" are interesting but too brief to create tension or to delineate memorable characters. "Nebuchadnezzar" is an absorbing study of the agony of a man who, watching his guests act out, charade-fashion, the story of Jael, believes that they are pantomiming his own actions, the poisoning of his wife. Distraught with guilt and fear, he shrieks out his confession. Slightly akin to "The Leopard Lady" and "Blood-Sacrifice" in portraying a disturbed conscience, this places more emphasis on the inner turmoil, the tumult in the brain as fear of exposure mounts. Such a psychological study is unusual in this genre. To offset the horror, Miss Sayers works out details of costume and movement that are hilariously funny. In "Suspicion," Mr. Mummery, suffering for the past weeks from attacks of dyspepsia, discovers that a can of weed-killer, sealed months ago, has been opened recently. Uneasily he recalls stories about the arsenic-maniac who has murdered several people in the area but has not been apprehended by the police. He becomes suspicious, then fearful for the safety of his young wife—and himself. Was it not just a month ago that they had hired a new cook, a stranger without credentials? His fears deepen into terror, but, until the last sentence, readers will not guess his horrifying discovery.

"Blood-Sacrifice" has a significant theme: the integrity of the writer. Despite the box-office success of his first drama, *Bitter Laurel*, Scales is unhappy. In response to his friends' taunts that he has prostituted his talents, he protests that the plot, theme, and characterization of his play were all changed drastically during rehearsals, reshaped into a sentimental, saccharine vehicle to display the histrionic talents of Mr. Garrick Drury. Scales disconsolately pockets a considerable sum each week, but the money does not compensate for the loss of friends, sneers of the critics, and his own guilt for having betrayed his artistic ideals: he did rewrite scenes to please Drury.

Suddenly an accident occurs; Drury is struck down. Scenes of tension build suspense, speculation, bafflement. Will Scales voice his suspicion that amid the bustle and confusion of the dressing room, hastily transformed into an operating laboratory, a strange mix-up occurred? Or had it? Perhaps he had imagined it. Had any one else seen the exchange? Could the accidental mix-up be discovered later? Would he be to blame if—? Scales was not certain himself—"except in the hidden chambers of his heart."

But concerning one situation, Scales has no doubts; he realizes that it will torment him all his life, for he knows that, in succumbing to Drury's blandishments to write scenes of inferior quality, he sacrificed his own integrity. Deftly woven into the plot, these oblique observations about the duty of the creator to safeguard his work from corruption add to the significance of the story.

III Striding Folly

The last Lord Peter stories appeared in a posthumous collection, *Striding Folly*, in 1972.[9] The title story and "The Haunted Policeman" were first published in *Detection Medley* as early as 1939, but the third story, "Talboys," written in 1942, was not published previously. Undoubtedly Miss Sayers did not regard the latter tale very highly, nor did Miss Olivia Gollancz, who some years ago declined to publish it, stating that the portrayal of Lord Peter as a doting, indulgent father would embarrass rather than please his admirers. The story opens with young Bredon confessing to his father, Lord Peter, the theft of Mr. Puffett's prize peaches. While Lord Peter administers a caning to the culprit in private, Harriet is obliged to listen to the remonstrances of their house guest, Miss Quirk, who insists that such punishments can ruin a lad's character by arousing resentments that may lead to greater calamities. The mystery of the orchard-thief is solved, but a greater puzzle remains: could Wimsey really bring himself to play such a vulgar, crude prank on Miss Quirk? Except for the information that Lord Peter, now fifty-two, is the father of three boys, Bredon, Roger, and Paul, the story offers little to amuse readers who cherish a younger Wimsey, witty, shrewd, and always a gentleman.

Although he appears only briefly in "Striding Folly, he solves the strange case of Mellilow, accused of murdering his neighbor and chess partner Creech, who during their last game announced that, having bought up all the available Striding property, he has sold it to an electrical company. Within weeks, a power plant will be erected; the whole face of the countryside will be changed. When the murdered body of Creech is found the next day, few believe

Mellilow's story that he was at home, playing chess with an unknown, uninvited passerby who wanted to play a game. Ominous silence greets the news that there are no fingerprints on the chess figures; the mystery man wore a glove on his right hand. Lord Peter is more interested in the suspect's horrible nightmare than in the stranger. When Mellilow tells of his dream of lost galoshes, vanishing bridges, a moving tower, and an outstretched corpse, Lord Peter concentrates not on chess moves but on footsteps, to and fro. Mood, mystification, setting, and characterization make "Striding Folly" an elusive, satisfying tale.

The beginning of "The Haunted Policeman" is marred by inanities uttered by Lord Peter when the nurse shows him his first-born, a son. Relieved that the event is over, Lord Peter takes a stroll, invites a befuddled policeman going off duty to stop in to the library for a toast, then pours glass after glass while his guest tells a strange tale about looking through a letter-box opening, seeing a body of a woman stretched out on the black and white tile hallway, the corpse of a man with a dagger in his back behind her. All this was supposed to have been seen at house number 13, but when he summons his fellow officer on the beat, they discover there is no house of that number; nowhere is there evidence of foul play. After securing some information about the appearance of the hallway, and a visit to a certain house on the block, Lord Peter solves the mystery. His shrewd deductions may send some inquisitive readers to the National Art Gallery or their local art museum.

IV   Lord Peter: A Collection of All the
Lord Peter Wimsey Stories

In 1972 the Wimsey stories, twenty-one in all, appeared in the anthology *Lord Peter*, compiled by James Sandoe.[10] His introduction, sketching the chronological development of Miss Sayers's novels, short stories, and some of her other writings, notably her translation of Dante's *Divine Comedy* and her two volumes of Dante studies, serves as a reminder that although her career included much more than the works devoted to Lord Peter, she wrote with "as deep a responsibility to the tale of detection as she brought to the tale of salvation while translating Dante."[11] The volume includes Carolyn Heilbrun's valuable essay "Sayers, Lord Peter and God," which first appeared in the *American Scholar* in 1968, and the witty parody "Greedy Night," by E. C. Bentley, British poet and novelist, known to detective-story readers as the author of *Trent's Last Case.*

In the essay "The Eighth Bolgia," Miss Sayers states that the good storyteller is born, not made; those who do not have the gift cannot acquire it, but those who do possess it can improve it by pains and practice.[12] Her best stories in the first three volumes, *Lord Peter Views the Body*, *Hangman's Holiday*, and *In the Teeth of the Evidence*, reveal her skill in the art of constructing short works of detection. In "The Sport of Noble Minds," an essay on the art of detective fiction, she ruefully admits that there are not more than half a dozen deceptions in the mystery-monger's bag of tricks, all too quickly learned by the reader, who then starts watching the writer instead of the detective.[13] A limited number of tricks there may be, but techniques and talents are another matter. A born storyteller, Miss Sayers has many. Her best short stories, almost half of those that she has written, reveal that she plots complex but plausible crimes, particularly intricate methods of murder, leaves clues for intuitional and ratiocinative minds to discover, builds settings and atmosphere by selecting meaningful details, utilizes specialized, sometimes arcane knowledge to confound and mystify, creates characters by utilizing significant actions and brisk dialogue, and mingles humor, pathos, comedy, and irony to reveal the human condition.

V *The Detective Club Collaborations*

Always keen to participate in the activities of the Detection Club, Miss Sayers joined in the fun of producing novels with individual chapters written by certain members. The first, *The Floating Admiral*, 1931, has chapters written by G. K. Chesterton, Agatha Christie, Ronald A. Knox, Freeman Wills Croft, Anthony Berkeley, Miss Sayers, and several others.[14] She contributed the Introduction, Chapter VII, "Shocks for the Inspector," and her solution to the crime. G. K. Chesterton admits that only the "gang of criminals" who wrote the novel could really understand it. Many enjoyed it but did not know the inside joke which, Chesterton reveals, is the fact that every chapter contributed by one of the writers is, in reality, a satire on the personal peculiarities of the last author. (He also tells that with the profits from successful sales, they hired a garret for a Club Room. On the first night that the members received their keys, the premises were burglarized; he adds: Shades

of Lord Peter, Father Brown, and Monsieur Poirot!) [15] Six collabo-
rators produced *Ask a Policeman*, 1933. Miss Sayers contributed
"The Conclusions of Mr. Roger Sheringham." *Double Death: A
Murder Story*, 1939, was the last effort. [16] Critics judge that the last
two works have more of the characteristics of the "long" short story
than that of the detective novel. All three are out of print at this
time.

VI   *The Anthologies*

In addition to becoming one of England's most popular writers of
detective novels and short stories during the 1920s and 1930s, Miss
Sayers earned an enviable reputation as an anthologist. Her first
volume, *Great Short Stories of Detection, Mystery and Horror*,
1928, published in America as the first *Omnibus of Crime*, has a
scholarly introduction tracing the rise and development of detective
fiction, and its counterpart, stories of mystery and horror. [17]
Developing at length a study of the contributions of E. A. Poe, she
credits him not only with inventing the formula of the eccentric but
brilliant detective whose doings are chronicled by a slow-witted but
admiring friend, but also with developing new techniques of plot
still in use today: the wrong suspect or "red herring" technique, the
sealed death-chamber, psychological deduction, the "most unlikely" person, and the cipher plot. From Poe, she asserts, came the
two great lines of development: the Romantic and the Classical, or,
more accurately, "the purely sensational and the purely intellectual" (19).

Under the heading of the "Pre-Doyle" period, she evaluates the
techniques and contributions of such notable figures as Wilkie
Collins, Mrs. Henry Wood, and Sheridan Le Fanu. After presenting the influences of Conan Doyle's Sherlock Holmes stories, she
discusses a variety of topics: an analysis of the "fair-play" method,
variations in handling point of view, the artistic status of the
detective story, and a brief survey of changing techniques notable in
stories of mystery and horror. Haycraft ranked this essay as one of
the finest studies on the subject of the development of detective
fiction. [18]

The anthology of stories is divided into two sections: Detection and
Mystery, and Mystery and Horror. Under the heading "The Modern
Detective Story," are twenty-three tales, ranging from the sensation-
alism of Mrs. Wood's "The Ebony Box" to an interpretation of real life

in Aldous Huxley's "The Gioconda Smile." A number of stories are grouped according to the type of detective who solves the mystery: the amateur, scientific, medical sleuth; the specialist in chess, cards, or railways; the intuitive detective; and the comic. "The Ebony Box" is classified as a story of sensation; Poe's "The Mystery of Marie Rogêt," as one of analysis; Conan Doyle's "The Adventure of the Prior School," a mixed type. G. K. Chesterton's "The Hammer of God" and H. C. Bailey's "The Long Barrow" serve as examples of mysteries solved by the intuitive detective; E. C. Bentley's "The Clever Cockatoo" features the journalist detective.

The second section has two divisions; the Macrocosmos, tales of mystery and horror, and the Microcosmos, tales of the human and inhuman. In the first division are stories of ghosts and hauntings, such as Dickens's "Story of the Bagman's Uncle" and "The Open Window" by "Saki." Under the heading "Tales of Magic" are stories of witchcraft, vampires, and the Frankenstein theme, as well as tales of possession, doom, and destiny, such as Joseph Conrad's "The Brute" and May Sinclair's "Where Their Fire Is Not Quenched." Tales of nightmares and the borderland of the mind include Le Fanu's "Green Tea" and Quiller-Couch's "The Seventh Man." Eight stories make up the last section, the human and inhuman. Of these, Michael Arlen's "The Gentleman from America" and H. G. Wells's "The Cone," a tale of blood and cruelty, deserve to be better known.

Miss Sayers's next anthology, *The Second Omnibus of Crime*, 1932, published in England as *Great Short Stories of Detection, Mystery, and Horror, II*, has a sixteen page introductory essay covering a variety of topics: explanations for the increasing popularity of the detective story, the distinctive merits of the detective short story and novel, and the role of the fictional detective.[19] Her shrewd, incisive statements reveal her knowledge of the development of the genre and her own experiences as a practitioner. She argues persuasively that the growing tendency to combine the detective story with the novel of psychology and character is a step in the right direction. (Her own commitment to this change is evidenced by *Murder Must Advertise*, *The Nine Tailors*, *Gaudy Night*, and *Busman's Honeymoon*, as has been previously noted.)

Part one, Detective and Mystery, includes nineteen stories by such familiar authors as E. C. Bentley, E. Bramah, A. Christie, W. Collins, and Baroness Orczy. Miss Sayers is represented by "The

Cave of Ali Baba." Part two, Mystery and Horror, has thirty stories by such outstanding authors as S. Crane, A. Bierce, W. W. Jacobs, J. Masefield, Melville, S. Phillpotts, "Saki," and her favorites, W. Collins and Le Fanu. Although the authors are familiar, Miss Sayers in many instances has selected lesser-known works which merit recognition.

The introduction to *The Third Omnibus of Crime* is surprisingly short.[20] The volume contains twenty-one stories of mystery and detection, thirty-one of mystery and horror. About half of these have been reprinted frequently, but of the lesser known works Barzun notes that six are difficult to find and are worth reading. Among these are "The Tea-Leaf," by Edgar Jepson and Robert Eustace; "The Hands of Mr. Ottermole," by Thomas Burke; "Solved by Inspection," by Ronald Knox; "The Elusive Bullet," by John Rhode; and "The Episode of the Nail and the Requiem," by C. Daly King.

Tales of Detection, 1936, includes stories by Poe, Wilkie Collins, Anthony Berkeley, Agatha Christie, and others.[21] Her introduction is significant, for it states her disappointment over the lack of development in the modern detective novel. She had hoped that the elements of mystery and suspense would be combined with some aspects of the novel of manners in the style of the early masters, Dickens, Le Fanu, Collins, and Gaboriau, but few practitioners besides herself were interested or seemed capable of adding psychological insights to the more easily managed structure of plot and suspense. Shortly after writing this introduction, she announced that she did not intend to write any more detective novels.

CHAPTER 5

The Dramas—"Playwrights Are Not Evangelists . . ."

RELIGIOUS drama in England received fresh impetus in 1929 when two new societies were formed. Under the direction of Dr. George Kennedy Bell, later Bishop of Chichester, the Friends of Canterbury Cathedral organized the Canterbury Festival of Music and Drama which, William Spanos noted, "was shortly to culminate in the Church's sponsorship of the Christian poet and the development of a genuine Christian verse drama movement." [1] In the same year another group of clergymen, professional actors, and lay people formed the Religious Drama Society to stimulate interest in the production of plays embodying Christian truths. Most of the work of this group concerned advisory and educational matters. [2]

Tracing the forces that stimulated religious drama in England, Gerald Weales commented that the Canterbury Festival in its first ten years put an official seal on the religious drama festival by utilizing dramatists already well known and commissioning works by new writers, notably T. S. Eliot, Charles Williams, and Dorothy L. Sayers. [3] This practice began in 1935 with the presentation of T. S. Eliot's *Murder in the Cathedral*. For the 1936 Festival, Charles Williams wrote *Thomas Cranmer of Canterbury*; in 1937 *The Zeal of Thy House* by Miss Sayers was given. The next year, with the production of Christopher Hassall's *Christ's Comet*, a drama about the fourth Wise Man, the Canterbury Festival plays ceased to emphasize topics concerning the city or the cathedral. For the 1939 festival, Miss Sayers wrote a version of the Faust legend, *The Devil to Pay*.

Miss Sayers was tremendously interested in the Christian drama movement but was openly scornful of dramas written to edify or to evangelize. In an essay, "Playwrights Are Not Evangelists," she stated that a dramatist must not write with the intention of improving the mind of his audience: "If he writes with his eye on a spiritual box-office, he will at once cease to be a dramatist, and decline into a manufacturer of propagandist tracts. . . . He will lose his professional integrity, and with it all his power—including his power to preach the Gospel." In this essay and in numerous lectures she reiterated her belief that all good writing "springs from the kindled imagination, and after that it is a matter of technical skill, and either one of these is useless without the other. This is always so, and a religious purpose will not make it otherwise." [4] In the introduction to *The Man Born to Be King* she states: "A loose and sentimental theology begets loose and sentimental art-forms; an illogical theology lands one in illogical situations; an ill-balanced theology issues in false emphasis and absurdity." [5]

Although in her lifetime she was better known for her fiction than for her plays, she considered her work in drama as her most significant contribution to Christian thought. Her second book of verse, *Catholic Tales and Christian Songs*, 1918, has her first attempt at drama, a type of miracle play, "The Mocking of Christ," a work obviously not intended for acting. Almost twenty years elapsed before she was financially free to pursue this aspect of creativity. With the exception of the dramatization of a Wimsey novel, *Busman's Honeymoon*, and a light comedy, *Love All*, 1940, she confined her dramatic writing to religious plays.

I   The Zeal of Thy House

The Zeal of Thy House, staged in the Chapter House of Canterbury Cathedral, June 12–18, 1937, concerns the rebuilding of Canterbury Cathedral after its destruction by fire in 1174. [6] The action occurs on two planes: the human and the divine. On the human level, William of Sens, an obscure French architect, chosen to design and to rebuild the edifice, becomes so proud of this honor and so confident of his artistry, that he boasts: "This church is mine / And none but I, not even God, can build it" (68). On the divine level, three archangels, Michael, Raphael, and Gabriel; a recording angel, Cassiel; and a young cherub appear in Canterbury to take an invisible but active part in the Cathedral project. It is through their intervention, for instance, that William is chosen over his competitors, two Englishmen.

After four years, despite the soaring beauty of the almost completed work, both lay workers and monks voice their complaints concerning William's dissolute ways, particularly his dalliance with the wealthy widow Lady Ursula, whose generous benefactions to the church do not prevent tongues from wagging in gossip about her conduct. The Prior refuses to intervene, reminding one informer that it would be wise to allow God to manage His own business, for He was once a carpenter with more centuries of experience than any of them. Perhaps in his own wisdom, the Prior suspects that William's arrogance will lead sooner or later to his downfall.

Explaining to Lady Ursula the intricacies of his craftsmanship, William boasts that he will fly to the top of the scaffold in an ingenious carrier designed by himself, place the keystone of the great arch in its place, and then fly back, "Like St. Paul in a basket." Brazenly flirting while undertaking the hazardous task, William unwittingly distracts the two workers responsible for checking possible flaws in the rope as they wind the windlass. With his eyes on the lovers, Simon sings love songs, too titillated to pay proper attention to the condition of the rope that is to carry William to the heights of the arch. Theodatus, disturbed by the amorous couple, closes his eyes and prays; the flawed rope slips through their heedless fingers. The angels take a more active role. As the onlookers and workers shout joyfully that William is ready to center the keystone, Michael leans forward and cuts the rope. Like Ibsen's Master-Builder, William plummets to the earth.

During months of painful recuperation, William attempts to continue to oversee the building operations, enduring physical discomfort with equanimity but complaining vehemently when his orders are imperfectly executed or changed by insubordinates. Although he contritely confesses his carnal sins, he lacks the wisdom and grace to see that his great fault is one of pride of intellect. The two planes, human and divine, come together in a dream-confrontation when the archangels gather about William's bed. When Michael accuses William of pride, he cries out in protest, insists that God is jealous, and vows that he will never give up his creation for others to finish, but finally he is persuaded by Michael that Christ, too, made the supreme sacrifice, leaving His work to be completed by others. In his final submission, William begs that his work remain unspoiled:

> But let my work, all that was good in me,
> All that was God, stand up and live and grow. (99)

He resolves to return to France, taking Lady Ursula, if she is willing; then he leaves all in the hands of the Divine Architect.

Although as symbolic as Everyman, William of Sens is truly an

historical figure. Miss Sayers followed closely the contemporary
chronicle of Gervase of Canterbury, who recorded in detail the
martydom of Thomas à Becket, the great fire that destroyed the choir,
the rebuilding begun by William, his catastrophic fall, his attempts to
complete the work despite his injuries, and his painful relinquish-
ment of the task to the skill of others.[7] The architect's overwhelming
pride and his liaison with Lady Ursula are the imaginative projections
of Miss Sayers, stimulated, she admits, by the words of Gervase, who
surmised that the fall came from "either the vengeance of God or the
envy of the devil" (10). To create the story element was not the
problem, she comments; the real difficulty was "to supply a supernatural interpretation of a piece of human history" (108).

Because the climactic event, William's fall, is not actually seen but
only described by the excited, dismayed reports of onlookers and
workmen, some critics state that the play lacks dramatic tension, but
Miss Vera Findlay, recounting her experience playing the role of
Ursula in the 1947 production, stressed the theatrical effectiveness of
the scene. "As the masons and carpenters put down their tools, and
the monks and guests crowded around, all watching William's ascent
in his 'cradle-basket,' three angels, eleven feet tall from toe to wing-
tip, majestic in golden robes, stood on the plinth at the back of the
stage, while Michael, high on the scaffold, could be seen to lean
forward, sword poised, ready to sever the rope. The tension was
unbelievably dramatic."[8]

Realistically portrayed relationships also create dramatic interest.
A lesson in compassion and charity is taught by the Prior who,
refusing to listen to a tirade against William, reminds the talebearer
that God founded His church not upon the beloved John, the pure of
heart, but upon Peter: "Peter, the liar, Peter, the coward . . ." (60).
Urged to chastize William, the Prior answers:

> God is a man
> And can defend His Honour, being full-grown
> In wisdom and in stature. We need not
> Play nursemaid to the Babe of Bethlehem
> To shield Him from the harlot and the thief. . . .

As a final injunction, he bids Theodatus:

> Set charity as a bridle on your tongue;
> Talk not of William's nor another's faults,
> Unless to God, Who hears but spreads no scandal. (61)

In the dream-confrontation, visual and aural beauty creates dramatic tension. As the archangels, militantly majestic, gather about William's low pallet, the supernatural and the natural are effectively contrasted. Michael's insistence that man will never be asked to suffer anything which Christ himself did not endure evokes William's contrite submission:

> O, I have sinned. The eldest sin of all,
> Pride, that struck down the morning star from Heaven
> Hath struck down me from where I sat and shone
> Smiling on my new world. (98)

Michael's final speech, addressed to the congregation as he moves down the steps, reiterates Miss Sayers's belief that man's handiwork reflects the heavenly trinity:

> Children of men, lift up your hearts. . . .
> Praise Him that He hath made man in His own image,
> a maker and craftsman like Himself, a little mirror
> of His triune majesty.
> For every work of creation is threefold, an earthly
> trinity to match the heavenly. (103)

(In "Creed or Chaos?" Miss Sayers asserts that this play is a "dramatic presentation of a few fundamental Christian dogmas—in particular, the application to human affairs of the doctrine of the Incarnation. . . . If my play was dramatic it was so, not in spite of the dogma, but because of it. . . . The dogma was the drama.") [9]

One need not, of course, accept the theological concepts presented, in order to enjoy other aspects of the drama, particularly the realistic portrayal of the monks, the grumbling artisans, and the gossiping pilgrims, who tell bawdy jokes, complain about the food at the "Lamb," and pray to St. Thomas almost in the same breath.

The choir not only re-creates the splendor and solemnity of medieval liturgical functions but by hymns, solemn chant, and stylized movements creates moods, hints of coming events, and interprets actions and theme. The archangels are visual reminders of supernatural strength and power as they stand, seemingly invisible to the workers. Miss Sayers's ability to create scenes vibrant with multi-dimensional effects is praised by George Kernodle: "If she lacks Eliot's ear and his marvelous gift of poetic imagery, she has a surer visual sense. In this play her theme is worked out completely in dramatic action, while Eliot depends on the rich fabric of his words." [10]

Most critics agree that it is the prose passages, not the poetic lines, which emphasize the dramatic concepts, but even in these there are some jarring notes. In a matter-of-fact conversation between William and Ursula, when the familiar tone shifts suddenly and heightens, the exchange becomes excessively rhetorical, charged with innuendo:

URSULA: I ought to be offended with you.
WILLIAM: If you are wise, you will be. Let us be plain.
           The first time our eyes met, we knew one another
           As fire knows tinder. You have seen what havoc
           fire works. Let be.
URSULA: I do not fear the fire. (50)

In some passages of angelic dialogue a similar flaw occurs: sublime thoughts are articulated with solemnity, then suddenly change to cloying archness. When a cherub, for instance, asks why God created mankind in two different types if it makes so much trouble, Raphael chides: "Hush! You mustn't ask Why." Gabriel adds: "Only men ask Why" (54). Spanos stated that although the prose is colloquial and modern, it suffers from "a lack of flexibility and sharpness that prose in a verse play must have." [11]

Unlike T. S. Eliot and Williams in their festival plays, Miss Sayers utilized only blank verse, iambic quatrains, and simple folk rhythms. Although the critic in the *Times Literary Supplement* praised the blank verse for being "so flexible and so natural as to show once more that in good hands this ancient form of English dramatic speech can never wither," weaknesses are evident.[12] William's emotional acknowledgment of his sinful pride and his plea for forgiveness are excessively rhetorical, particularly when he begs the Master-Builder and architect, Christ Himself, for forgiveness:

> Let me lie deep in hell,
> Death gnaw upon me, purge my bones with fire,
> But let my work, all that was good in me,
> All that was God, stand up and live and grow.
> The work is sound, Lord God, no rottenness there—
> Only in me. (99)

This excerpt from a speech of twenty-eight lines indicates the intensity of thought and emotion which, although appropriate at the beginning of the passage, becomes dangerously turgid toward the close when William requests that, after suffering in hell, the flames may be blown apart so that he may glimpse "The perfect work, finished, though not by me" (99). Such weaknesses are criticized by Spanos: "The general awkwardness of the blank verse, the archaisms, and the imprecision of the diction, the overformal syntactic constructions and the prosaic imagery: all these not only hark back to older poetic modes but, more important, disperse rather than heighten the emotion of the dramatic situation and thus undermine its intended realism." [13]

This play has enjoyed a modest success through the years. After being well received in London in 1938, it was taken on tour in England by the Religious Dramatic Society the next year, was presented at the Canterbury Festival in 1949, and at various other festivals. A notable production was given at Ely Cathedral in 1960. Undoubtedly the greatest significance of *The Zeal of Thy House* is that it states a theme that runs through the author's writings, particularly in *The Mind of the Maker*: the sacredness of work, when done properly, truly reflects the Trinity of the Godhead.

II   The Devil to Pay

For the 1939 Canterbury Festival, Miss Sayers's version of the Faust legend, *The Devil to Pay*, was given in the Chapter House of the Cathedral, June 10–17. [14] The following month it was produced in London at His Majesty's Theatre.

The legend is given a fresh interpretation, for as the author explains in the Preface, she did not believe that a modern English audience needed a warning against the pursuit of knowledge for its own sake. Instead, she shows Faustus as an impulsive reformer, eager to eradicate physical suffering, poverty, and other social injustices. Discovering that his efforts are in vain, he disassociates himself from the world and its sufferings by signing a pact with the devil. Sayers's version emphasizes the duty of modern man to fight evil and to create a better world, not by means of extraordinary powers but by personal efforts and reliance on God's supportive grace. As the Pope reminds Faustus, in God's plan, mankind and his world are not to be transformed miraculously:

> Hard it is, very hard,
> To travel up the slow and stony road

> To Calvary, to redeem mankind; far better
> To make but one resplendent miracle,
> Lean through the cloud, lift the right hand of power
> And with a sudden lightning smite the world perfect.
> Yet this was not God's way. . . . (156)

The first scene occurs in Faustus's study in Wittenberg where, assisted by his servant Wagner, he conjures up Mephistopheles, who enthralls him with a fleeting vision of Helen of Troy and fills his purse with gold. Flinging the money to the poor and ill, Faustus rages that God must be blind, deaf, and cruel to permit such sufferings. Scene two occurs in Rome. Wagner and Lisa, a serving maid, arrive in the city, where their master has been residing for the past year. Expecting to hear how famous Faustus has become, they are horrified to learn that he is denounced by clergy and laity as an enemy of God and the Church, one whose endeavors bring curses instead of blessings. The crowd tells of its sufferings from Faustus's miracles. A woman to whom he gave gold claims that her husband abandoned her, squandering this wealth on harlots; another wife, barren for years, mourns that she gave birth to a child possessed by seven devils. Wagner and Lisa almost succeed in persuading Faustus to return to Wittenberg, where his ministrations to the sick were truly helpful, but another tempting vision of Helen of Troy prompts him to make a pact with the devil. In exchange for happiness with Helen, or Lilith, as she claims to be, Faustus turns from his commitment to curb the illnesses of the world, accepts the servitude of Mephistopheles for twenty-four years, and promises to forfeit his soul to the devil at the end of that time.

Scene three occurs at the court of the Emperor, Charles V, at Innsbruck twenty-four years later. Faustus entertains the Emperor with magical displays of military power, culminating in a vision of the destruction of Rome by the Emperor's army. After the battle, Faustus fulfills the request of his guest to see famous people of past centuries, but when the Emperor is enamored by the sight of Helen of Troy, Faustus is overcome with jealousy, despite the fact that he discarded her years ago. He assaults the Emperor, and is immediately captured by loyal courtiers and soldiers. On this occasion Mephistopheles does not rescue Faustus: time has run out; Faustus must die. When the devil claims his due, he discovers that the soul of Faustus, deprived of the knowledge of good and evil, has degenerated into the likeness of a small black puppy.

The final scene is in the court of Heaven where before the Judge,

Mephistopheles protests that he has been cheated. Recalled to life, Faustus is given two choices: he may wander for the rest of time, untouched by pain and sorrow except for one deprivation: never to experience the love of God; or, he may again assume the knowledge of good and evil, and accept the full consequences of his past folly. Taking up once again the burden of human responsibility for good and evil, Faustus chooses the punishment of Hell, hoping that in ages to come, his faith and penance will win him forgiveness. The drama ends as Faustus stands at Hell-mouth, listening to the chorus singing, "God will restore unto you the years which the locust hath eaten" (212).

The Devil to Pay is similar to Marlowe's *Doctor Faustus* in many ways: both utilize song, dance, pageantry, comedy, and moral allegory. In both dramas, evil is represented by Mephistopheles, goodness by the angel Azrael, and God the Father by the Judge who conducts the final trial. Miss Sayers does not employ abstract personification as Marlowe does in his allegorical presentation of the seven deadly sins; she utilizes the more modern technique of symbolism. The worthless state of Faustus's soul, for instance, is indicated by its form, that of a worthless black puppy. The teaching authority of the Church is intimated by the magisterial figure of the Pope, who warns Faustus to avoid the greatest error: ". . . that last sin against the Holy Ghost/Which is to call good evil, evil good" (156). Symbolic, too, is the laurel wreath carried by Helen, who says that it is a crown for the victor, one rich in wisdom, honor, and glory. Significantly, she drops it at the feet of Wagner who, clasping it after his master's death, prays: "May God remember all thy willing manhood,/ Not thy refusal" (193).

The conflict between good and evil is dramatically emphasized, visually and verbally, in the scene of the fall of Rome. While Mephistopheles stands majestically triumphant, boasting that Rome's walls are tottering, Wagner sits away from the throng, reading aloud from a medical textbook various cures and remedies for human suffering: "Fumitory. . . to allay fever, herb of grace . . . to combat the plague" (174). His low murmurs are interrupted by the devil's gleeful reports of chaos and carnage in Rome. The juxtaposition of the two figures, one, sadistically triumphant; the other, deeply concerned for man's sufferings; and the counterpoint of their comments effectively dramatize the constant tension in the world between good and evil. In the final scene, the radiant light that illuminates the Gates of Heaven also shines on Hell-mouth, suggesting that the way of purgation can eventually lead to eternal salvation.

The setting of *The Devil to Pay* was modeled on that of the late medieval and early Renaissance stage. To the left of the audience was Hell-mouth, an immense dragon's head, emitting blasts of fire, smoke, thunder, and rumbling noises. On the opposite side of the stage was the area designated as Heaven, an elevated temple of columns reached by eight steps. Between the two structures was a screen with three doors, providing entrances and exits, and a playing area, serving as Faustus's study, the Roman Forum, the court at Innsbruck, and the place of Judgment. On the medieval stage, Hell-mouth was the most spectacular and versatile theatrical device, visually suggesting the presence and power of evil. The earthy buffoonery and preternatural terror so prominent in medieval drama were centered about this aperture. It is effectively utilized in this drama. The jaws of the dragon swing open, and amid thunder and smoke, Mephistopheles emerges in the shape of a lion with the tail of a serpent and the feet of a bull. Devils trip merrily back and forth from Hell-mouth, but Miss Sayers omits Goethe's grotesqueries: Faustus swallowing a span of horses and a wagon of hay, cutting off his leg and then restoring it.

The language is notable for the number of similes and metaphors referring to nature, and aphorisms that pinpoint the folly of vice and the poignancy of lost ideals. Wagner warns Faustus that his soul could slip through the magic circle like a rabbit through a fence; Faustus blames God for allowing the earth to go to ruin "Like an estate farmed by a bankrupt" (136). Asserting that he has wept for men who fight like beasts and are in turn tortured like beasts, Faustus is reminded by his devil-servant that virtue clashes with virtue also: "good savaging good / Like so many lobsters in a basket / Pinching each other's claws off" (137).

The sun, moon, stars, fire, and water are frequent images. After drinking potent wine, Faustus exclaims it gives him life, "As though the vintagers had put in prison / The very sun, and pressed him with the grapes / Till all the vats ran fire." Mephistopheles answers dryly: "And so it should / Seeing what cellars it came from" (135). When Faustus claims that Helen's beauty is beyond the splendor of the stars, he is told that hell-born, hell-named Helen is a mirage, "Thrown on the sky by a hot reality / Far below your horizon" (138). Faustus insists that he will possess her: "Let ruin / Roar like a cataract and drown the world!" (163). When the lovers depart, Wagner and Lisa comment disconsolately on the foreboding darkness: "Like the dusk and silence that creeps before an eclipse." Later, Mephistopheles echoes this:

> The sun is fled, and darkness folds the earth
> Like the chill shade that steals before the eclipse.
> (190)

Animal imagery is frequent: a warrior "strides like a stork"; Helen is a "worm in the brain"; fools, who refuse to face facts, sidle and bridle like a "fretful horse"; the devil jeers at Faustus: "Writhe, my good friend, my toad beneath the harrow" (205), and likens him to a circus horse, dodging the ring master. Mephistopheles voices his contempt for Faustus: "Primitive Brutishness. The fellow's grown mischievous as an ape, lecherous as a goat, giddy as a peacock, cruel as a cat, and currish as a cross-bred tyke" (173). Later he phrases the insult in more temperate language:

> Faustus hath made himself into a beast
> And has no wit to answer more than a beast. (199)

Epigrammatic wit intensifies the theme of man's folly. The devil warns Faustus: "Mark you, mark / How lean men grow who try to save the world" (136); and "Indiscriminate charity is a device of the devil" (143). He confides: "All men are fretful children when they can't get their own way" (159); "Sloth is a sin and serves my purpose; though there are merrier ways to be damned" (160). He denounces man's inconsistency: "When he is innocent, he longs for knowledge; when he is grown wise, he hankers after innocence" (180).

Faustus and Wagner voice significant truths. To Lisa, Faustus comments: "Child, the greater the wisdom, the greater the sorrow" (126). Admitting that self-conceit led him into error, he states: "For all the by-ways run / Down to the circle, the closed circle of self / From which there is no way out" (202). Wagner comments: "To aim at happiness is to miss the mark; for happiness is not an end at all. It is something that comes of itself, when we are busy about other matters" (176). The Judge states succinctly: "There is no waste with God; He cancels nothing / But redeems all" (201).

Throughout the drama, prose is more prevalent than poetry. Realistic dialogue introduces the main characters and establishes mood and theme. The debate between Faustus and Mephistopheles concerning the nature of God and the origin of evil, the Roman street brawl, the sermon on salvation, and Wagner's encounters with Mephistopheles are in prose, ranging in diction and tone from the colloquially familiar to passages of formal eloquence. Blank verse, reserved for scenes of emotional stress and dramatic impact, is particularly effective in the Pope's exhortation to avoid pride, in the Judg-

ment scene in the Court of Heaven, and in the amorous exchanges
between Faustus and Helen. She boasts:

> Thou canst not choose but turn to me again. . . .
> I am the fire in the heart, the plague eternal
> Of vain regret for joys that are no more. (162)

Cadenced lines, embellished with alliteration, onomatopoeia, and
metaphor, appear frequently. The descriptions of the victorious battles waged by the Imperial Armies are vivid:

> A monstrous mine
> Bursts in the breach, and blows them all to pieces!
> Arms, bodies, stones and fragments, nightmare faces
> And shattered engines tumbled together, falling— (187)

Mephistopheles describes how the Romans are beset by the river
Styx, "Bubbling about their feet; bogs of delusion / Snare them about"
(186).

Praising the "ingenious modernisation" so competently worked
into the medieval framework of myth, marvels, and miracles, Ivor
Brown stated: "Miss Sayers is well cut out for her task because she
combines an interest in theological argument with a nice command of
English prose and poetry. The blank verse passages will, of course,
not challenge comparison with Marlowe, but they will stand setting
beside most of English dramatic poetry; they have the right copious-
ness of image and pulse of rhythm and must be agreeable matter for
an actor used to the clipped monosyllabic stuff of ordinary stage
dialogue." [15]

III   The Just Vengeance

Written to commemorate the seven hundred and fiftieth anniver-
sary of Lichfield Cathedral, *The Just Vengeance* was performed at the
festival, June 15–26, 1946. [16] Title and theme derive from the lines in
Canto Seven of the *Paradiso*, interpreting "la giusta vendetta," i.e.,
"the just vengeance." Briefly summarized, the passage suggests that
Adam, by his disobedience, condemned not only himself but all of his
offspring, so that the human race "lay sick for many an age . . . until it
pleased the Word of God to descend to earth," to assume man's
nature and to redeem mankind (279).

In the Introduction, Miss Sayers states that this is a "miracle-play of Man's insufficiency and God's redemptive act, set against the background of contemporary crisis" (280). The action takes place at the moment of the death of an Airman shot down during World War II. His spirit finds itself in his native town of Lichfield, where it meets fellow citizens of the past: from the eighteenth century, Samuel Johnson; from the seventeenth, the Quaker, George Fox; an unnamed sixteenth century Protestant martyr, a band of fourth-century Christians martyred by Roman soldiers, and other citizens from many walks of life. The doubts and questions addressed to this group by the spirit of the Airman have a familiar ring today, for he protests that even when a soldier is trying to do right, unwittingly he harms someone. Ordered to drop bombs, he kills thousands, the guilty as well as the innocent, but what can he do but obey? "I was told to go and I went; I killed; I was killed./ Did any of us deserve it? I don't know" (288).

His query evokes personal responses from the citizens: a martyr tells how he and others were slain outside Lichfield—"and the marketplace appeared like a pool of blood"; a laborer protests, "I never stole the sheep they hanged me for"; a worker tells how he was killed by the poisonous air in the foul potteries. An informer who "ran with the hares and hunted with the hounds" and a judge of dubious merit, admit that they deserved to suffer; but others—hunchback, pauper, sailor, slavey, lunatic—all recount undeserved sufferings, injustices, and ills. Samuel Johnson tells of the scrofulous disease that almost blinded him, then demands to know why the Airman came back to Lichfield.

Asked if he can recite the Creed, the Airman mechanically begins, but when the Chorus picks up the lines, he protests desperately that he does not believe in all this suffering, nor the "sense of a suffering God" (295). Asserting that he believes only in justice, he voices his personal credo:

> I believe in man, and in the hope of the future,
> The steady growth of knowledge and power over things,
> The equality of all labouring for the community,
> And a just world where everyone will be happy. (297)

He insists that the "past has turned the world into a living hell"; only the future holds promise, but the citizens and the Angel of the City,

the Recorder, remind him that he, too, now belongs to the past. They
challenge him: "What did you do with the future we fought and died
for?" His answer is a familiar one:

> But what could I do? I had no time; I was killed;
> It was not my fault, but the fault of the old people. (298)

With tragic intensity, citizens of one generation turn to those of the
past, echoing his censure.

Pleading that he died for the happiness of the future, the Airman
questions why there is no justice, why good turns into horror never
intended. The Angel of Lichfield discloses the past, allowing the
Airman to observe Adam and Eve as they discuss their act of disobedience. Boasting of his new invention, the axe, Adam sees Cain use it as
a murderous weapon, thus beginning the endless chain of good
turned to evil. The theological concepts in this scene are familiar to
Miss Sayers's readers: all men are both Cain and Abel:

> Though you slay innocence and outlaw guilt
> You cannot undo the brotherhood of the blood. (313)

On the upper stage, the *Persona Dei* doffs his royal vesture and
stands in a white alb, while the choir, in song, verse, and chanted
litany, retells the birth of Christ, incidents in His Public life and
details of His trial before Herod, Pilate, and Caiaphas. As in *The
Devil to Pay*, the fluidity of time is significant. Prompted not by
brashness but by twentieth century doubts, the Airman asks the
Persona Dei if it was really worthwhile for God to become Man and to
bid all mankind to be perfect, a seemingly impossible order. The
Persona Dei explains that His law is the law of love; He gave His Body
to be sacrificed for mankind; and man, in turn with Christ, can give
himself, laying down his life for others.

The enactment of the sufferings of Christ is dramatically modern,
for His persecutors are not only historical personages; they also
symbolize the recurring betrayals of common man. Caiaphas sacrifices his honor to expediency, saying piously that the priesthood must
shed no blood, hence he hands Christ over to secular authorities.
Pilate mouths platitudes of situational ethics: "One is always at the
mercy of events and the world-situation; / One takes the thing as one
finds it and makes the best of it; / I do not believe there are any
ultimate standards" (339). In this manner, they assuage their guilt,
and choose the evil that will in time become their hell, not a place but

a condition where, as Cain prophesies, they will all receive what they have chosen, "And can practise on one another to all eternity" (340).

But not all are evil. Asked who will carry the Cross and help bear the pain of the Saviour, Lichfield citizens generously respond. The Harlot says that she will carry the burden of shame; the Lunatic, the fear that shatters the heart and the brain; the mother accepts the sufferings of man's ingratitude; the widow, the grief of loneliness. As they rush forward to help Him, they sing: "Whoso will carry the Cross, the Cross shall carry him" (344). The Airman learns finally that there comes a time when one must not cling to the controls but must let go, receiving from God's hands, not justice but His love and compassion. Asking if it is too late to bring "whatever in me is guilty and ought to be crucified," he is told to bear the pain of bewilderment.

Although Miss Sayers terms *The Just Vengeance* a miracle play, following E. K. Chambers's distinction that medieval dramas based on biblical themes are mystery plays and those that treat the lives of the saints are miracle plays, yet in a sense her audience awaits no miracle, no unfolding of a saint's life, no transformation through grace, no dramatic change except the greatest of all miracles: God's intervention to save man from his just punishment. The pageantry of the processions, the antiphonal responses of the choir, the liturgical music, and the ceremonial dignity of much of the verse suggest both miracle play and masque. Structure and theme combine to develop theological motifs and dramatic movement. The cathedral setting effectively highlighted the central concept: God and man, separated by Adam's sin, are joined together when Christ descends to earth and is acknowledged by men and women willing to help Him bear His sufferings, to accept the new Law of charity, and to follow Him, the Truth and the Light.

The theological ideas are reinforced by striking images. Lichfield, reddened by the blood of martyrs, is every marketplace, at times rife with greed, at times hallowed by suffering, for this town is not only the home of Christian martyrs, of Johnson and George Fox, but it is every town where an individual, for Christ's sake and that of his fellowman, unites with God in acts of atonement. This acceptance of pain and suffering brings an understanding of self, a realization that each man bears within himself the seed of Adam: he is both Cain and Abel. This idea is underlined by the handling of time: past, present, and the future merge as one totality.

The staging of this drama follows closely the manner of presentation of medieval dramas enacted in cathedrals. Acoustical difficulties did not permit the quick flow of dialogue enlivened by the cryptic wit, folk humor, and comic realism notable in *The Devil to Pay*, but the poetry and cadenced prose, the stylized movements of the cast, and the liturgical music gave a sonorous dignity and beauty appropriate for theme, story, and occasion. In the Preface, the author reminds her readers that the play was written for performance in a cathedral, not for reading in a study; the choruses were set to music, and important affirmations were emphasized by dramatic movement. She admits frankly that the play, concerned with doctrines of the Incarnation and Atonement, contains no original thoughts, no new interpretations, but rather echoes the thoughts and words of others, from Dante to Charles Williams to T. S. Eliot.

In this play Miss Sayers employs a greater variety of poetry than in her other works. The opening speech in couplets is spoken by the Angel of the City who welcomes the audience and explains that the chorus represents the citizens of Lichfield who together with him

> . . . at their head
> Wait here to welcome one who is newly dead.
> To him the ageless tale shall all be shown,
> And through his eyes you'll see, as through your own. (281)

Couplets, quatrains, and rhymed lines of five to seven verses occur, but blank verse predominates. Biblical characters, as well as the Lichfield citizens, speak colloquially. The harlot states bluntly:

> They who fouled me
> Scorned me for being foul, and their sleek wives
> Drew back their skirts from me. (291)

The excessive formality of the Persona Dei's rhetorical pronouncement is a startling contrast:

> I the image of the Unimaginable
> In the place where the image and the Unimaged are one,
> The Act of the Will, the Word of the Thought, the Son
> In whom the Father's selfhood is known to Himself,
> I being God and with God from the beginning
> Speak to Man in the place of the Images. (318)

The speech in its entirety is forty-six lines, and as the above excerpt indicates, is heavy with *ploce*, the weaving of several repetitions of one or more words, or close variants, throughout a passage.

"Choose," "chose," "chosen," and "choice" occur fourteen times in quick succession:

> But all this
> Still at your choice, and only as you choose,
> Save as you choose to let Me choose in you.
> Who then will choose to be the chosen of God,
> And will to bear Me that I may bear you? (319)

Alan Fairclough commented that although this may be sound theology, it certainly is not the voice of God.[17]

Present at the first performance at Lichfield Cathedral, Fairclough felt that at the great moments, the language never seemed quite suitable; there was "never for the unique attitudes the unique words." In his review he calls attention, however, to the beauty of Christ's final speech from the Cross:

> Come, receive again
> All your desires, but better than your dreams,
> All your lost loves, but lovelier than you knew . . .
> Instead of your justice, you shall have charity;
> Instead of your happiness you shall have joy;
> Instead of your peace the emulous exchange
> Of love; and I will give you the morning star.
> (350, 351)

Anaphora, the repetition of a word or phrase at the beginning of a series of sentences or clauses, marks the above and occurs frequently in the lines chanted by the choir:

> Speak the coherence, speak the squalors and splendours,
> Speak the skyline and the Cathedral spires,
> Speak order, speak unity, speak the name of the city. (282)

These lines are faintly reminiscent of the plaintive protest voiced by the chorus of women in *Murder in the Cathedral*. This technique of insistent repetition, notable in the plea that the faithful be alert to hear and to help mankind, emphasizes the fluidity of time, and the universality of man's woes. The chorus, for instance, pleads that all listen to

> The feet of the young man, the feet of the fallen,
> The feet of the forgetful running back to remembrance,
> The feet of the future hurrying home to the past
> In the sudden cessation of time, the eternity of the city. (283)

The lack of variety in the placement of caesuras and adjectives, the similarity of end rhymes, and monotonous rhythms mar some passages:

> All that is true in us, all we were meant to be,
> The lost opportunity and the broken unity,
> The dead innocence, the rejected obedience,
> The forfeited chastity and the frozen charity,
> The caged generosity, and the forbidden pity,
> Speak in the mouth of Mary, in the name of the city. (320)

There is, as usual in Miss Sayers's works, the forceful projection of pertinent ideas, expressed with epigrammatic verve. The Airman states calmly that people "have grown used to numbering / Death by the millions" (285). Adam insists that Progress is just the task "of shifting things about from place to place / Quicker and quicker, so as to get more / Of everything at once" (305). Eve admonishes her children: "And do not pray for justice; you might get it" (315).

The Just Vengeance presents theological truths of universal significance: man, whether he likes it or not, is undeniably related to the past and to the future, whereas God sees everything and everyone in the Eternal Now; each person is the brother of both Cain and Abel; man must follow Christ and bear His Cross in order to merit Eternal Life. Dramatized against the contemporary background of wartime suffering, the play had an intense emotional impact upon many in the audience. "I couldn't see the figure of Christ when He took up the Cross," recalled one woman, "but I heard that thumping sound; then He appeared dragging it up the aisle. I just longed to rush out to help lift the cross with the other actors, it all seemed so real." [18] Although a drama for a special occasion, and hence restricted in scope and appeal, *The Just Vengeance* reveals Miss Sayers's talent for projecting theological truths with clarity and vigor.

IV   The Emperor Constantine

Miss Sayers's last drama, *The Emperor Constantine*, was produced during the 1951 Festival of Britain in Colchester, Essex. [19] In the preface of the published text, she poses questions which she attempts to answer in the drama, namely: Who was Constantine? Did he deserve the title "the Great"? Why, since he proclaimed that he was chosen by God to establish Christ's church on earth, did he wait to receive baptism until shortly before his death? He slew his second wife, and his son and heir, Crispus. Were these acts of madness, revenge, or justice? Was Christianity to Constantine "a living faith, a profitable superstition, or a cynical instrument of policy?" (6).

Why did Colchester choose to honor Constantine? Even that question has no simple answer. His mother, Helena, later canonized as Saint Helena, was the wife of Constantius Chlorus, Augustus of the West. Some historians claim that she was a woman of humble birth, perhaps a barmaid, and merely the concubine of Constantius, but tradition records and citizens of Colchester insist that she was a British princess, daughter of the local chieftain, "King Coel" of Colchester, of nursery-song fame. The author attempts to resolve all these ambiguities in a lengthy chronicle, spanning from A.D. 305, when Constantine was twenty-one, to A.D. 326, when he ruled as sole Emperor of the East and West; an Epilogue recounts his baptism and death in 337.

The first two acts trace Constantine's rise to power; the third and final act focuses on two dramatic events: the Council of Nicaea and Constantine's slaying of his son. The first episode, the Council, is streamlined into six impressive scenes, rich in colorful pageantry and personalities, but it is too weighted with abstruse, theological arguments to be dramatically effective. Arius's explanation why Christ should not be considered to be the coequal of the Father is heard and condemned. Then with painstaking circumspection, the Council members formulate phrase by phrase the Nicene Creed. Many of the theological disputations, particularly the fine distinctions inherent in "homousios" and "homoöusios" and other Greek terms, must have been Greek indeed to many in the festival audience. In an attempt to lighten these scenes, Miss Sayers caricatures some of the dominant personalities, shows the clashes between factions, and interjects some bawdy songs defaming Arius:

> Ladies many and various
> Run after Father Arius—
> He knows what's what and he serves it hot—
> How many sons has Arius got? (124)

(This follows a comment that Arius goes about with a following of seven hundred virgins.)

Constantine's personal tragedies reach a climax when he kills his son Crispus, accused of attempting to violate his stepmother. Too late, Constantine discovers that this was Fausta's plot to dethrone him, and he kills her. Contrite over all the blood that he has shed, he

is comforted by Helena's counsel that although evil can not be undone, it may be "purged and redeemed" by the blood of Christ and
true repentance. He promises, as an act of reparation, to provide
money, ships, and men to assist her in an expedition to locate the
True Cross in Jerusalem. The epilogue clarifies one of King Coel's
prophecies that Constantine will become a swimming fish: he is
immersed in the waters of Baptism shortly before his death.

Miss Sayers did not attempt to portray in depth the numerous
political, military, religious, and lay figures who cross Constantine's
path as he ruthlessly achieves his goal of becoming Emperor. She
highlights, instead, Helena's spiritual solicitude for her son, his
devotion to his son Crispus, the festering jealousy of his second wife,
and his anxiety over the theological disputes which threaten the unity
of Christendom. She effectively dramatizes his arrogance and lust for
power. Angrily, he rants: "These theologians are getting swelled
heads. . . . They feel safe, they enjoy the Imperial Favour, they're
exempt from taxation, and instead of looking after the poor and
converting the heathen, they start heresy-hunting. . . . I won't
have it. It's got to stop" (94). His subordinates recognize his pride.
When a Roman soldier comments that the new Greek insignia of the
Emperor's army has a magical look, his comrade answers shrewdly:
"Constantine's magic is to get there first and hit hardest" (61). An old
family servant complains: "He never thinks of the blessed Lord that
died to save us, except as an ally to win his battles for him. My old cat's
as good a Christian as he is—mews when she's hungry and purrs
when she's fed, and knows where her blessings come from" (101).

In an attempt to lighten long passages of detailed historical exposition and to offset the pomp and protocol of court and Council scenes,
Miss Sayers followed her usual technique of utilizing colloquial,
idiomatic speech, but she was not successful. The Cockney exchange
between some soldiers illustrates this. Caught chewing some corn,
one is ordered to "spit it out or swaller it pronto, you disgusting little
slobbering son of a she-camel" (54). At the Council of Nicaea, Arius
answers Athanasius: "Spoken like a giant, little mannikin. You are so
learned in the Scripture you know more about it than Christ Himself
. . ." (146). Such remarks prompted a critic to question: "Did the
soldiers of the imperial legions really speak as only those who have
never seen a barrack-room imagine British conscripts of today to
speak? Was the Council of Nicaea conducted like a branch meeting of
the Transport and Workers' Union? It is only when Dr. Sayers forgets
the imaginary need to flatter her audience and writes simply out of

her own interest that her dramatization of Constantine's life achieves any dramatic distinction." [20]

In the Preface, the author explains that she attempted to remain true to history and tradition: the prayer for the Army is historically accurate although connected with another campaign. Authentic also are Constantine's letter to the Bishops in Act two, his speech at the Council of Nicaea, Arius's letter to Eusebius, and the bawdy songs mocking Arius. Togius and Matibena are imaginative creations; so, too, are the prophecies of King Coel and the idea that Fausta plotted to dethrone her husband. Despite the historical and legendary content, the successful attempt to encompass the complexities of the Council of Nicaea, and the colorful pageantry, *The Emperor Constantine* is a static chronicle on stage, although the theological truths presented are deeply moving. One hundred amateurs and six professional actors were required to enact the twenty-six scenes which lasted four hours. Although cuts and modifications were made after the first performance, the play still taxed the energy of both cast and audience. Reading the play is a more rewarding experience. A shortened version, "Christ's Emperor," was more successful when it was presented under the author's direction the following year at St. Thomas' Church, Regent Street, London.

V   A New Venture: Radio Drama

When the war years almost put an end to the religious festival plays, Miss Sayers became interested in writing for radio, particularly after the success of her one-act play about the Nativity of Christ, *He That Should Come*, broadcast by the BBC on Christmas Day 1938.[21] In the Preface she explains that in order to emphasize the point that Christ's birth took place against a complex social and historical background, she laid the scene, not in the traditional stable, but in a two-storied Oriental inn with a large, bustling courtyard, situated somewhere on the road between Bethlehem and Jerusalem.

Before presenting the hustle and hurry of the inn, she introduces a poetic prologue in which the three Wise Men meet each other and reveal their heartfelt desires. Caspar searches for wisdom; Melchior seeks a religion that works; black Balthazar craves the assurance that he is not alone, bearing the misery of the oppressed. The scene then shifts to the crowded courtyard, where Greek, Hellenized Jew, Centurion, and Pharisee mingle with merchants and their servants. All talk loudly; some demand service, others complain about taxes, the high cost of living, and the prevalence of vice and corruption. The miracle that is to change the values of countless individuals, the Incarnation of the Son of God, is enacted "in a world casual, inattentive, contemptuous, absorbed in its own affairs and completely unaware of what was happening: to illustrate, in fact, the tremendous irony of history" (218).

Joseph's request for a room for his spouse, Mary, is cut short by the Landlady's reply that there is not "an inch of space . . . they're sleeping on the roof, head to tail like herrings in a basket. Indecent, I call it . . ." (237). A place in the stable is finally given to Joseph, but the attention of the crowd is still on its own concerns; conversations reveal social, political, and economic interests. These discussions are cut short by an interlude of songs. The Greek sings of Golden Apollo, who once visited earth and humbly walked with men; the Jew sings a tale of Adam, Eve, and the four rivers in Paradise. Then the landlady bustles in to report that Mary has a Son, and the shepherds return, telling about the angel's message of the birth of the Promised One. The crowd, going off to see the Babe, is warned by the Centurion not to chatter about the event, for fear that the news will come to Herod's attention and arouse his jealousy. As the Nativity tableau ends, the Wise Men, who have followed the star, rejoice that each has found in the Child what he most desired: Caspar discovered the wisdom of the innocent; Melchior, the power of the helpless; Balthazar, God made man.

Miss Sayers made a valiant effort to create a play that would arouse in an audience the realization that Christ, Son of God, actually became Man, not as an exalted, sublime dignitary aloof in a regal court, but as a Child, one of the common people. To achieve a realistic effect, she utilized colloquial expressions and slang. The Merchant, complaining over taxes, answers impatiently, "Vital statistics, my foot!" (232); later, he accuses the manager of "making hay of the accounts." Both Mary and Joseph speak in simple, homey language except when the Child's birth is announced. Joseph's comment, "The dayspring from on high hath visited us" (266) is so stiffly regal that it sounds a bit absurd.

Prophetic statements add an unrealistic note. The Jewish merchant wagers that the new-born Child will probably finish up between two thieves on Crucifixion Hill; later, abashed that he has no gift to bring to the Infant, he promises Mary that if they ever meet again, he will have a present for her Son. He is, of course, Joseph of Arimathea, who gives his tomb for Christ's body. A shepherd offers the Child a twist of flowering thorn for a crown. Gerald Weales commented:

The unfortunate fact is that the inn-yard is full of characters who speak lines full of anachronistic references to the Home Office, colleges, etc., and Jesus manages to be born, not among people, but among stage clichés. The one interesting idea in the play can be found in two songs. . . . The Greek sings of Apollo . . . and Joseph of Arimathea sings of the new tree that grew from the stone of the fruit of the fall of Adam and Eve. The myths apparently become one in Jesus and the idea of Jesus as half-Greek, although familiar to scholars, is unusual to Nativity plays.[22]

Murray Roston in *Biblical Drama in England* praised the work, particularly the realistic language and setting, but disapproved of the verse prologue spoken by the Wise Men and the songs, which, he felt, interrupted the dialogue unnecessarily.[23] The songs, however, serve a useful function, for they accentuate the sublimity of the theme and provide a contrast to the realistic confusion and noise of the inn and courtyard. The prologue, the song to Apollo, and Joseph's one stilted speech are the only elevated passages, and with the exception of Joseph's pronouncement, these are not sentimental or overly rhetorical.

Broadcast year after year during the Christmas season, *He That Should Come* became so popular that Miss Sayers agreed, after many requests, to revise it for stage production. It is broadcast and presented in church and school circles yearly. Its appeal is indicated in a letter written by a cast member: "None of us realized before how much we had just *accepted* the story without properly visualizing it. It . . . brought home to us as never before the real humanity of Jesus" (29).

VI The Man Born to Be King

Impressed by the success of the Nativity play, Dr. J. W. Welch, director of religious broadcasting for the BBC, asked Miss Sayers in February 1940 if she would be interested in writing a series of radio plays on the life of Christ. She welcomed the opportunity but imposed several conditions: she wanted the freedom to treat biblical events realistically, to utilize modern speech, and to introduce the figure of Christ. At that time and up to 1968, the stage representation of any Divine Person was legally forbidden by the Lord Chamberlain's office, except in the case of dramas performed in a church.

Strictly speaking, the prohibition did not apply to radio impersonations but it was characteristic of Miss Sayers to desire that her position
be made clear from the beginning. Her conditions were not only
acceptable to the sponsoring committee but coincided with its plans.

By December 1941 she had completed the first five in the cycle of
twelve plays, *The Man Born to Be King*. It was planned to have the
first play, the Nativity story, broadcast during the Children's Hour
the Sunday before Christmas. At a press conference ten days before
this date, Miss Sayers read excerpts from several of the plays, and
discussed her aims, her reasons for presenting characters and events
in a realistic manner, and some of the difficulties involved in selecting
events and characterization to make each play structurally complete,
and at the same time to fit each into the larger unity of the complete
cycle. Immediately a storm of controversy and censure broke loose.
Vehement protests were directed against the representation of the
voice of Christ and the use of colloquial speech by Him and other
biblical figures. Sensational, inaccurate news reports exaggerated the
aspects of realism. Banner headlines in newspapers protested that
the plays were blasphemous, vulgar, and irreverent. Campaigns
were launched to stop the broadcasts. One paper questioned:
"Should children listen to such unwholesome, American slang as that
spoken to the Apostle Philip: 'The fact is, Philip, you've been had for a
sucker. You ought to keep your eyes skinned. . . . If I was to tell you
the dodges these fellows have up their sleeves, you'd be surprised.' " [24]

Like an avenging angel, Mr. Herbert Martin, secretary of the
Lord's Day Observance Society, began a crusade of protest. To the
BBC he wrote: "My Council desire to inform the B.B.C. that this
proposed theatrical exhibition will cause much pain to devout Christian people, who feel deeply that to impersonate the Divine Son of
God in this way is an act of irreverence bordering on the blasphemous. It is a contemplated violation of the Third Command-
ment which forbids taking the Name of God in vain." In a full-page
advertisement in bold face type, he proclaimed:

This Protest goes deeper than any mere verbal objections to any slang
terms uttered by the Actors. A sinful man presuming to impersonate the
Sinless One! It detracts from the honour due to the Divine Majesty. In the
present instance the man chosen to impersonate the Eternal Son of God—
attributing to Him some words our Divine Saviour never uttered—is a
professional Actor. Could anything be more distressful to reverent-minded
Christians? [25]

Criticism was so widespread and virulent that questions concerning the propriety of continuing the broadcasts were brought before the House of Commons.[26] After serious consideration, the BBC, supported by the approval of leading churchmen of the country, reaffirmed its decision to broadcast the remaining eleven plays in the series. Countless newspapers carried the statement that Miss Sayers had been obliged to eliminate much of the slang, but she stated publicly and reiterates in the published volume of *The Man Born to Be King* that she was never requested to make any such revisions, nor did she do so.[27]

Despite the well-aired opposition by those who considered the words of the Bible so sacrosanct that no expansion, deletion, or imaginative interpretation was permissible, Miss Sayers continued to take the liberties that she deemed necessary to make the plays dramatically effective. To achieve structural unity she distributed Christ's parables and sayings as evenly as possible throughout the plays dealing with the Public Ministry, attempting to provide a suitable context for each, which was not always that of the original. At the wedding feast of Cana, for instance, Christ tells the story of the wise and foolish virgins, and as He finishes, the wine stewards realize that the wine has run out: they, too, were unprepared. Then the miracle of the changing of the water into wine takes place. It is silly, she reasoned, to think that the parables were repeated only on one occasion: "The teacher who thought of such a story as that of the Good Samaritan or the Prodigal Son would be foolish to confine it to a single audience" (32).

To secure unity and to reduce the number of minor characters, she combined two, sometimes three biblical personages. Mary of Cleophas is the sister of Mary, Mother of Christ, and also the "other disciple" on the road to Emmaus; less fortuitously, perhaps, Mary Magdalen is also Mary of Bethany, sister of Martha and Lazarus. Proclus is the Roman centurion whose servant was healed in an early play and the awed spectator who declares after the Crucifixion, "Truly, this Man was the Son of God."

With creative artistry, Miss Sayers harmonized and supplemented the Gospel narrative, giving original explanations and amplifications which aided characterization and unified the plot line that focused on the political and religious tensions between Jew and Gentile. Some cryptic gospel passages were imaginatively clarified. When the crowds, impressed by Christ's power to provide food for the multitudes, desire to make Him their King, they follow all the way to the

Lake of Galilee thinking that He is ahead, only to discover that He is not with the other disciples. The author explains: Jesus was wearing a blue head shawl which clearly distinguished Him; the crowd saw it and followed along; they did not know that James donned it, and that Christ had slipped away.

The portrayal of Judas reveals Miss Sayers's imaginative insight and knowledge of human nature. An intellectual perfectionist, Judas understands better than any of the other disciples the teachings of Christ; he approves and fully supports the Master's Mission until his distrustful nature begins to suspect that Christ plans to betray His Heavenly Mission in order to win political power. In the fifth play, *The Bread of Heaven*, Judas wonders if Jesus is "preaching God's kingdom or merely preaching himself" (145). At Baruch's suggestion that Christ really desires a political, temporal kingdom, Judas mutters: "If I thought you were right, I would kill him with my own hands while He was still uncorrupted" (134). Judas's fundamental lack of trust in humanity and his ungenerous spirit help the plot structure which revolves around Baruch, the only major figure invented by the author. As leader of the Zealots, a political faction gathering strength to overthrow the Roman government, Baruch is convinced that Jesus is destined to be the leader of the national cause, marshaling the Israelites against Rome. Taking John's statement that Judas stole money from the alms-box, Miss Sayers amplifies this, making it a significant element of the plot: Judas steals in order to secure funds to bribe Baruch's men to reveal Christ's plans.

Another dramatic invention, closely related to this, is the explanation of Christ's entry into Jerusalem: Baruch has in readiness both a horse and an ass. If Christ mounts the horse, He signals to Baruch that He is willing to be a political leader of the Jews; if He takes the ass, He proclaims His loyalty to His Heavenly Mission. Aware of Judas's suspicions about Jesus, Baruch deliberately allows the apostle to think that Jesus plans a triumphal military march into the city. It is Judas's misconception and his resentment against this supposed betrayal that motivates him to betray Christ.

The most remarkable characterization in the entire cycle is that of Jesus Christ, a magnetic, virile intellectual, a far cry from the insipid, sentimental, and pietistic idealist envisioned by many. The Great Teacher, Miss Sayers asserts, could never have been static: "He was a lively person. He excited people. Wherever He went He brought not peace but a sword, and fire on the earth; that is why they killed Him . . ." [10]. She gives explicit directives about His changes in mood, voice tones, speech rhythms, and attitudes. In the Samaritan village He is more sad than angry; He is sternly uncompromising when telling the parable of the Unmerciful Servant. As a wise teacher, he argues with the Scribes and Pharisees but when the Heckler starts, "He cracks back at him stroke for stroke, as though to force the issue up to the great challenge."

Such graphic, concrete directives in no way guaranteed that the desired effects would be realized successfully in the broadcasts. Backgrounds, settings, and verbal exchanges were more than adequately rendered; the subtle changes in characterization, the nuances reflecting changing moods and tensions were more difficult to project over the air. The cycle of twelve plays was broadcast at intervals of four weeks; each play lasted forty-five minutes. Budget restrictions and security risks in war-time London severely limited the hours that could be given safely to rehearsals, so Miss Sayers provided copious notes for Val Gielgud, the producer, to peruse. These clarify plot lines, establish links between the individual plays, explain theological issues, historical data, and the psychological reasons for her portrayal of characters. These notes and her suggestions to the production staff reveal her devotion to the project, as well as her training as a novelist. Published in the text, they add to the reader's amusement and knowledge. Note her warning to the Record Librarian:

The "Sea" of Galilee is an inland fresh-water lake, and the boat was a rowing boat. Do not vex the Producer (who has troubles enough already) with the offer of "Schooner in a Storm—Sail-Flap and Shroud-Whistling Effects," or "Atlantic Rollers Breaking on a Cornish Coast.". . . "Squall on Lake Windermere" is nearer the mark; but you may have plenty of wind and waves, because it says so. (125)

Despite the author's determination to avoid sentimentality, some of the dialogue is too emotional, notably in the eleventh play, "King of Sorrows." Recalling Christ's childhood, Mary mourns:

When he was small, I washed and fed him; I dressed him in his little garments and combed the rings of his hair. When he cried, I comforted him; when he was hurt, I kissed away his pain. . . . Now he goes faint and fasting in the dust, and his hair is tangled with thorns. They will strip him naked to the sun and hammer the nails into his living flesh. . . . And there is nothing that I can do. Nothing at all. This is the worst thing; to conceive beauty in your heart and bring it forth into the world, and then to stand by helpless and watch it suffer. (288, 289)

Literary contrivance and sentimentality mark the description of Mary Magdalen's attempt to push through the crowds to secure a place close to the Cross. Pulling off her veil and unpinning her hair, she forces Marcellus to recognize her, pleading: "By the feet that danced for you, by the voice that sang for you, by the beauty that delighted you, Marcellus, let me pass!" Robert Speaight commented forthrightly: "The conception of Judas as a perfectionist undone by pride was especially original. Only in her portraits of our Lady, who was made to talk too much, and of Mary Magdalen, who was made to talk implausibly, was her touch uncertain." [28]

Speaight, as well as many other critics, praised the individual plays in the cycle: "Not only were they brilliant in their characterization, firm in their design and incisive in their dialogue, but they brought home the truths of the Gospel afresh to those who had forgotten them, and they did so at a moment when it was particularly important to recall them." [29] Few critics found fault with the theological content, although in the *Clergy Review* exception was taken to the suggestion that the body of the Risen Christ was not always numerically identical with the body that lay in the tomb, a statement at variance with the teaching of St. Thomas Aquinas in the 54th question in the third part of the *Summa Theologica*. The statement, "There is no need to suppose that Jesus, with his human mind, foresees certainly or in detail what Judas will do to Him" (114), the reviewer points out, is not in accord with the traditional view as expressed in the treatise *De Verbo Incarnato* on the knowledge of the God-Man. [30] It is interesting to note Miss Sayers's statement in the Preface: " . . . There is no more searching test of a theology than to submit it to dramatic handling. . . . Any theology that will stand the rigorous pulling and hauling of the dramatist is pretty tough indeed" (3). The praise of Urban Foster, O.P., in *Blackfriars* must have delighted her, for he commented: "The theologian must testify that Miss Sayers is almost without exception orthodox." [31]

Intimately connected with the play-cycle from its beginning, Dr. J. W. Welch expressed the views of many listeners: "Miss Sayers has put the Christian Church in this country in her debt by making Our Lord—in her fine phrase—'really real' for so many of us. She has made a major contribution to the Church's essential task of revealing Christ. She has also, in my judgment, forced many of us to the grim task of considering afresh the awe-ful implications of the two words: *incarnatus est*." [32]

In lauding Miss Sayers and the directorate of the BBC for having done the English world a great service by presenting the play-cycle with such frank but artistic realism, the *Times Literary Supplement* stated: ". . . the drama of events unfolds in a world of humanity, and the crucifixion . . . takes place not as a part of a religious ritual but as the result of the violent movement of the thoughts of living men. . . . the drama is seen to be one that demands a verdict from the spectator and ceases to be something that can be comfortably ignored. . . . It is not quite easy to place this vivid person in the list of 'The Great Teachers of Mankind' and to have done with Him. To have shown that is considerable achievement." [33]

Frequent transmissions of *The Man Born to Be King* attest to its continued popularity. It was rebroadcast in 1943; in 1944 to 1946 appropriate plays were broadcast during the Christmas and Easter season; in 1947 the entire series was redone with a new cast. This was heard frequently until 1975, when a new production, in stereo with a score for full orchestra, was broadcast as a weekly Sunday feature. Three members of the 1941 cast played their original roles. As a curtain-raiser for this production, an hour-long program featured interviews with Val Gielgud and Robert Speaight, who discussed the sensational outcries which the original production sparked. Audiences accustomed to *Jesus Christ Superstar* and *Godspell* expressed their astonishment that the first plays in the cycle caused such controversy; they could scarcely believe that some outraged listeners blamed the drama for the Fall of Singapore! The 1975 production stimulated queries concerning the possibility of a television production, but this seems unlikely because in 1953 Miss Sayers declared that she never wished "a teleview of *The Man Born to Be King* punctuated by advertisements." She added wryly: "Though, of course, it offers scope; the episode of The Feeding of the Five Thousand, presented by Hovis Bread and Macfisheries, for instance, would be very suitable." [34]

CHAPTER 6

The Essays—"The Mind of a Maker"

I   Begin Here

WHEN Miss Sayers's publisher, Victor Gollancz, suggested in 1939 that her public would welcome advice from her on ways to face the problems of the times, she wrote *Begin Here*. Published in 1940, this book-length essay stresses the need to think about the type of world that men and women wish to build when peace comes to war-torn Europe.[1]

Governments will sit at a table to ratify terms of peace, she states, but it is the ideals of individuals, their ideas of morality, justice, freedom, and charity which will intimately affect the "new new order." She offers no plans for immediate action by individuals or governments, but instead, reviews the main issues and events in European history that created the chaos leading to World War II. Viewing the past, she highlights two basic themes: the changing status of man, which she claims degenerated after the Middle Ages because basic Christian virtues were discarded, and the changes in the concept of authority.

In developing the first theme, she emphasizes that in the Middle Ages, when Christianity was more of a unifying force than it is now, the "Whole Man," as she terms him, was truly Christian in thought, word, and practice. "In this majestic theological structure there was, essentially, nothing that could impair the full development of every side of man's nature" (38). Acknowledging that in practice medieval society never achieved this ideal, she proposes that it is the goal to strive for: "When we press for a United States of Europe, we shall remember that this is no new thing; it existed once, with all the advantages that a common religion, a common culture and a universal authority could give it." Edwyn Bevan in the *Spectator* pointed out that it was inaccurate to claim that the "multitude of kingdoms and principalities perpetually at war with each other," were in any sense, a "United States," for although the spiritual power of the Pope was generally recognized and appeals made to it, such an authority was quite different from the central political authority in the federal system.[2]

Analyzing the changes brought about by new concepts of authority, Miss Sayers traces the loss of its theological character at the time of the Reformation and Renaissance, shows its later identification with the "national" principle, and the subsequent changes brought about by the growth of democracy and by man's demands for greater liberty in every sphere. Europe was dominated in succession by incomplete views of man and society. In the eighteenth century, the rational element in man was overemphasized; the advance of natural science stressed "Biological Man," followed by "Sociological Man," and "Psychological Man" (73). Pleading for a return to the concept of the "Whole" man, not as an ideal but as a reality, she reminds her readers, both English and American, of their shortcomings, too often regarded as twentieth-century virtues, which under no circumstances should be permitted in "the new order." Jacques Barzun summarized these succinctly:

The passion for absolutes, the yearning for an impossible static security, the dread of original thought, the repudiation of Christian morality, the naive faith in machinery—both industrial and administrative—these are so many failures of brain and heart which Miss Sayers berates in words no less justified than eloquent.[3]

The final chapter gives some realistic thoughts on the meaning of peace. There is, she insists, no word, no treaty, no territorial readjustment, nor magic formula that can establish peace and maintain it; peace is achieved by constant effort, for it "is not a static thing: it is the supreme example of balance in movement" (133).

The essay has values that are not limited by its topical matter. Barzun stated: "Two pages on the gaping indifference of the English public to art—the art which that same public fitfully pretends to cherish and defend against totalitarian attack—are worthy of inclusion in the great collection of antiphilistine documents."[4] However, in this essay of 160 pages, there are errors in judgment which cannot be overlooked on the grounds of the essay's brevity. Miss Sayers presents the questionable thesis that the Germans committed the "sin against the Holy Ghost" in so far as they were "in the desperate condition of sin that believes the wrong to be

right" (90); she states that the English may rightly regard the war
against Germany as "just and in a most terrible sense a holy war"
(90). An entire theological treatise might possibly establish some
guidelines concerning the morality and justice of war, but such
simplistic statements only distort the issues. Reginald Rynd, in
pointing out the weakness of this section of the essay, commented:

Apart altogether from the "moral" implications involved in the misery and
mass murder inseparable from war as it is waged today, we must revise not
only our idea of what is "holy" but of the very foundations of "justice"
itself. . . . The fundamental fallacy in all such reasoning lies in the fact that
do what we will it is more often the innocent than the guilty that the bloody
and baneful hand of war reaches, and that to make an equitable distribution
of the burdens it imposes, on victors and vanquished alike, is beyond the
wit of man.[5]

Several other sections, particularly her discussion of the consequences of the Fall and the causes of the Reformation, would have
benefited by a more comprehensive analysis. However, *Begin Here*
is a significant work. Voiced eloquently and persuasively, her ideas
for a peace based on Christian values were read and pondered by
many in England and the United States.

II   The Mind of the Maker

In *The Mind of the Maker*, 1941, Miss Sayers attempts to solve
the greatest of all mysteries, that of the doctrine of the Holy
Trinity.[6] The clues that help to unravel this mystery, she claims, are
found in the nature of man, especially in the creative artist. She
devotes eleven chapters to a detailed analysis of the three-fold
aspect of human creativity, particularly the activity of the imaginative writer, drawing upon her own experience in writing the
Wimsey novels. She then attempts the difficult task of proving that
the three-fold activity of the creative artist corresponds to the
trinitarian nature of the Divine Creator.

Admitting that it may be perilous, and certainly inadequate, to
attempt to explain the mystery of the Godhead by comparing
Divinity with mankind, she reminds her readers that man necessarily measures everything by his own experience, and from ages past
has sought to understand the mystery of God and man's relationship
to Him by falling back on such metaphors as Father, King, and
Ruler. She states that throughout the book, she will be using
metaphorical language, not the familiar analogy of fatherhood or

kingship but one more mysterious, the analogy of God as the Maker of the Universe. Before launching into the three-fold aspect of creativity in God and in man, she reminds her readers of St. Augustine's statement that trinity-in-unity is not an incomprehensible mystery but a familiar truth. The very act of sight involves a trinity: the form seen, the act of vision, the mental attention that correlates the two; every act of thought involves a trinity: memory, understanding, and will (46).

Her thesis is that every work or act of creation is three-fold, an earthly trinity which corresponds to the heavenly trinity. This idea is enunciated in many of her writings, notably in *The Zeal of Thy House* when Michael the Archangel asserts that every creative act involves a Creative Idea, Creative Energy, and Creative Power. It is the first point, she states, that gives the most trouble. When a person says, "I have a wonderful idea for a book," listeners think that the person has sketched out a plot, thought about characters, perhaps even spent some time in research or begun a rough draft. She insists that the planning, the development of characters and plot lines belong to the second step: creative energy. The creative idea, or what might be termed the "writer's realization of his own idea" (48) *precedes* any mental or physical work upon the materials. She emphasizes this point and reiterates that the formulation of the Idea in the writer's mind requires Energy, not the Energy of Composition which will come later, but the Energy of Thought. The creative work, in this case the book, will not take actual form until the creator has utilized his Creative Energy, so it can be truly stated that the idea "cannot be said to precede the Energy in time, because (so far as that act of creation is concerned) it is the Energy that creates the time-process" (48). This is important to her thesis. She hopes that it will clarify phrases in the Creed, making the Trinity more comprehensible: "This is the analogy of the theological expressions that 'the Word was in the beginning with God' and was 'eternally begotten of the Father.' If, that is, the act has a beginning in time at all, it is because of the presence of the Energy or Activity" (48).

From the Idea and Energy together, that is, from a properly conceived and executed work, comes Power which enables the reader to communicate with the thoughts of the writer. She explains that this is a two-fold communication: Creative Power is "the thing which flows back to the writer from his own activity and makes him, as it were, the reader of his own book. It is also, of course, the means by which the activity is communicated to other readers, and which produces a corresponding response in them. In fact, from the reader's point of view, it *is* the book" (50). This Creative Power is the third "Person" of the writer's trinity, proceeding from the Idea and the Energy together. She explains: "In the metaphors used by the Christian creeds about the mind of the maker, the creative artist can recognize a true relation to his own experience . . ." (54).

Some readers may have reservations about Miss Sayers's idea that the three stages of man's artistic creativity are analogous to the creativity of the Holy Trinity, but despite such doubts, many will appreciate in later chapters her illuminating comments on the nature of literary creativity: why it succeeds and why it fails. She asks her readers to accept an essential truth about every honest writer: he transcends his work; hence, he must not be confused with his characters, their ideas, ideals, or actions. "God's in His Heaven/All's right with the world," is often cited as proof of Browning's optimism, she comments, but the song is sung by Pippa in a far from optimistic poem dealing with adultery and murder.

III   *The Writer's Craftsmanship*

How does an author go about creating characters, expressing their intense emotions and complex ideas which may be quite foreign to his own? Miss Sayers analyzes the process:

Actually . . . what happens in the writer's mind is something like this. When making a character he in a manner separates and incarnates a part of his own living mind. He recognizes in himself a powerful emotion—let us say, jealousy. His activity then takes this form: Supposing this emotion were to become so strong as to dominate my whole personality, how should I feel and how should I behave? In imagination he becomes the jealous person and thinks and feels within that frame of experience, so that the jealousy of Othello is the true creative expression of the jealousy of Shakespeare. . . . In this sense, therefore, Shakespeare "is" Othello; but we must allow that he "is" in the same sense, Coriolanus, and Iago, Lear, and Cordelia and every other character is his plays. . . . (59, 60)

A character is not authentic if it is merely the mouthpiece of the author. The writer engaged in composition must allow his Energy to flow with equal fullness into all parts of his creativity, breathing life into all his characters, both major and minor figures, so that they will be incarnated fully; otherwise they will be one-dimensional, devitalized dummies. When writing dialogue, the author must shift constantly from one character to another, considering how John sees Mary, and how she sees and reacts to John—and to others. The audience must be considered: what does it see, hear, and comprehend? The writer must keep before him his original, controlling Idea, and constantly consider: Is it clear to the audience? Will its Power flow out to the viewers, and perhaps from them to others? All these factors, Miss Sayers asserts, are included in that *trinity of awareness* which the competent writer strives to achieve.

The middle chapters develop important ideas concerning the writer's use of his Idea, Energy, and Power. He must not rigidly control the development of his characters nor allow them unrestricted freedom; he must develop them according to their own natures, not the author's whims or the exigencies of plot. Can one really believe, she questions, that shrewish Kate was tamed so quickly? Could inefficient Micawber investigate so competently the knavery of Uriah Heep and bring him to justice? That characters and plots do come together, she shows from her own creative experiences, citing examples from *Gaudy Night* and *Murder Must Advertise.* She warns that the use of a miracle, that is, a sudden change in a character or a situation, is rarely permissible, introduced legitimately only if the transformation is an integral part of the Idea.

Chapter eight, "Pentecost," is an illuminating discussion of the process of literary creativity, showing how the power in a word, a line, or a book, may enkindle in a reader or listener an idea which in turn is manifested to others. It is by this process "that words and phrases become charged with the Power acquired by passing through the minds of successive writers" (116). She gives examples from her experiences. When chided for using the old-fashioned term "dynamite" as a symbol of explosive force instead of the more modern substance, "tri-nitro-toluol," she defended her choice, enumerating some of the literary associations which give the word impact. From the Greek *dynamis* come concepts such as dynamo, dynamic, dynasty, as well as memories of Hardy's retelling of Napoleon's explosion of power in *The Dynasts*, a term recalling also the ancient civilization of Egypt.

She quotes from *The Nine Tailors*: ". . . incredibly aloof, flinging back the light in a dusky shimmer of bright hair and gilded outspread wings, soared the ranked angels, cherubim and seraphim, choir over choir, from corbel and hammer-beam floating, face to face uplifted" (118). She explains that, consciously or unconsciously, a string of passages floated in her memory when she wrote those lines: snatches from Job, "When the morning stars sang together . . ."; from the Prophet Isaiah, "Above it stood the seraphims: each one had six wings . . ."; from David: "He rode upon the cherubims. . . . He came flying upon the wings of the wind"; from Milton, "Where the bright Seraphim in burning row/Their loud up-lifted Angel trumpets blow. . ."; and Keats's lines about the carvèd angels "With hair blown back, and wings put cross-wise on their breasts." Less prominent, but nevertheless in her mind were lines from John Donne, Tennyson, T. S. Eliot, as well as memories of angel-roofs that she had seen in parish churches and in pictures. By quoting at length many passages that inspired her, she adds beauty to this chapter and force to her thesis that creative power transmits creative inspiration to others. She emphasizes: "But what is important and not always understood in these days, is that a reminiscent passage of that type is *intended* to recall to the reader all the associated passages, and so put him in touch with the sources of power behind and beyond the writer. The demand for 'originality'. . . is a recent one" (119). She adds the significant thought that if a reader has the capacity to respond creatively, he will in turn manifest Idea and Energy, and then incarnate a work or an action, which in turn will communicate Power to others, thus continuing the revelations of Pentecost when men were given the gift of understanding each other.

IV   *Weaknesses within an Author's Trinity*

What happens if an author's triadic unity becomes out of balance? The coequality of the Divine Trinity is often symbolized by an equilateral triangle, consequently Miss Sayers chose a scalene triangle, one of unequal angles, to represent the imperfections of the writer's trinity. In the chapter "Scalene Trinities" she discusses the problems that arise when an author's Idea, Energy, and Power are not cosubstantial and coequal, or as she terms these conditions, when the writer is "father-ridden, son-ridden, or ghost-ridden." Those who are "father-ridden" attempt to impose the Idea directly on the mind and senses without the mediation of the son or Energy; these are the dry-as-dust scholars, who deal with lofty but vague thoughts, and those sad figures who have an idea for a book but claim that they have no time to write it. Among the son-ridden are those who, like Swinburne, develop sensuous beauty out of all proportion to the thought, and those who make the simple so complicated that their "manner has degenerated into mannerism" (143). She feels that Joyce's portmanteau words and Cummings's derangement of letters and words place these artists in this category. The ghost-ridden writer thinks that the emotion which he feels is sufficient to call forth a response without requiring him to have a controlling Idea expressed coherently and concretely.

What happens if there is *too little* of the father, or of the son, or of the spirit-or ghost? A serious weakness in the "father" or Idea produces a lack of unity within the work. If it starts with one idea then drifts on to another, or, if the parts, though of interest in themselves, leave no definite impression, there is something lacking in the "paternal Idea." The dramas of Thomas Lovell Beddoes, enchanting fragments but all unfinished, are examples of the unfathered. William Blake represents the opposite extreme, the father-centered artist. Those entirely lacking the sonship are the "mute, inglorious Miltons," who lack the power to express their ideas; the "sonless" are inexpressive and unfulfilled. Not all readers will be totally convinced of the reasonableness of her argument that Energy, when it cannot create, explodes and destroys. She states categorically: "The uncreative artist is the destroyer of all things, the active negation. When the Energy is not Christ, it is Antichrist, assuming leadership of the universe in the mad rush back to Chaos" (153).

Weaknesses, such as bad grammar, banal language, and poorly constructed plots, are failures in the son. To illustrate, she plays a game, labeling such deficiencies artistic heresies. Reminding her readers that Arianism was a fourth-century heresy that denied that Christ was of the same substance as God the Father, she labels artistic Arianism the error of having too much technique and too little vision. French bedroom farces and slick detective stories fall into this category. The Manichees taught the heresy that the body, being material, is evil. Artistic Manichees are those propaganda novelists and dramatists who create characters "that cannot truly live, love, or suffer, but only perform exemplary gestures symbolical of the Idea" (161). Although her examples are witty, instructive, and revealing, nevertheless this section on Christological heresies and their literary counterparts may not be as entertaining to her readers as it was to her. She laments that space and time must limit "this enthralling sport of heresy hunting" (163). Some readers may even suspect that in this section the author herself may be "father-ridden."

Miss Sayers devotes little attention to the complexities involved in a study of the Holy Spirit. She states that a failure in the ghost—or spirit—is a failure in Wisdom, not wisdom of the brain, "but the more intimate and instinctive wisdom of the heart and bowels" (163). Those who lack the spirit are not unintelligent, idle, or unskilled; they lack knowledge and are incapable of ever knowing it. This is the failure of the unliterary writer, the inartistic artist. "A distressing trait of the unghosted is their complacency; they walk, talk, and do not know that they are dead. Neither, of course, are they alive to the deadness of their own creation" (164).

Does this triadic activity have any significance for the individual engaged in work that demands no creativity? Insisting that this trinity is inherent in every one, Miss Sayers suggests that individuals should learn to deal with their lives in a creative manner. The first step is a change in attitude: one cannot look at life as a series of difficult problems to be solved; it must be viewed as the artist sees his work: as a medium for creation. For too long, she states, man has viewed his life as a detective story, replete with problems that can be solved definitively. The final chapter and the Postscript, entitled "The Worth of the Work," make some trenchant observations about world problems: war, peace, unemployment, wasteful productivity, and the failure to believe in the sacramentality of worthwhile work done well.

The Mind of the Maker is a lucid presentation of an artistic and original approach to the doctrine of the Holy Trinity and the tri-unity within the mind and work of the creative artist. Reviewers, however, were quicker to point out their reservations about the theological content than to praise what is, to many readers, a more significant aspect: its illumination of the process of creating a work, particularly Miss Sayers's own experiences in writing specific novels. Thomas Conlan, S.J., commented:

It is truly carping to remark that the revelational nature of the doctrine receives scant attention. Only once . . . does she refer to the basic element of revelation which underpins this Christian mystery. This is the statement that it 'derives from a purely religious experience of God, as revealed in Christ and interpreted by abstract philosophic reasoning. . . .' Knowledge of the dogma of the Trinity is not derived from religious experience; on the contrary, the guarantee of true religious experience is that it should gain its purchase from the twin rocks of doctrine and discipline.[7]

Her statement that there exists "between the mind of the maker and the Mind of his Maker, a difference, not of category, but only of quality and degree" (170), was also refuted:

The Infinite cannot differ in degree from the finite. That is to say, the Infinite would not be infinite. . . . Her study of analogy has, we think, led Miss Sayers to forget that God is, after all, wholly other than the creature, and that whatever likenesses may be pointed out, the unlikeness is always greater. To say that God is a Father means simply that He is infinitely more than the positive value of Fatherhood; to say that He is a Maker, that He is infinitely more than the positive value of human craftsmanship.[8]

In *The Emperor's Clothes*, Kathleen Nott rejects Miss Sayers's idea that before a work is created, the author has some foreknowledge of its impact on himself and others. If this were true, Miss Nott argues, "the world would not be so full of works which have failed to please or have pleased the wrong people for the wrong reasons, wrong at least from the author's point of view. . . . Communication, readers' response, Creative Power, or whatever you like to call it, is something which we discover and judge in experience. It is not something which can be immanent in the Idea of a book, written or unwritten." [9]

Although *The Mind of the Maker* does not explain all the complex issues inherent in the Trinitarian doctrine, it does suggest a novel and instructive approach worthy of consideration. Despite slight theological weaknesses, it is a valuable work: it illustrates how Art in its broadest sense helps to explain some facets of Christian dogma, stimulates thought concerning the nature of the Holy Trinity and its reflection in the creativity of the artist, and reiterates the importance of right attitudes toward work. It not only throws light on the analogy of God as Creator as stated in the Apostles', Nicene, and Athanasian Creeds, but has the additional value of giving revealing glimpses of the personality and mind of Miss Sayers who tells with wry humor some of the problems she encountered while writing *The Nine Tailors*, *Murder Must Advertise*, and *Gaudy Night*.

V Unpopular Opinions

A collection of twenty-one essays, published in 1946, was entitled *Unpopular Opinions*, Miss Sayers explained, because all the ideas gave offense to someone.[10] "Christian Morality," "Forgiveness," and

"Living to Work" were so disliked that they were rejected by those who had commissioned them. With the exception of these three and "Dr. Watson's Third Marriage," the essays in this volume were originally lectures or published articles composed between 1935 and 1945. The author made no attempt to update them or to change those that had a familiar, conversational tone, for she felt that the gain would not offset the loss of spontaneity.

The book is divided into three sections: theological, political, and critical. In a pungent style, the theological essays apply Christian principles to ever-difficult problems: morality, forgiveness, and aesthetics. Political topics range from wartime talks on English life and character to right attitudes toward work and the proper use of the English language. Under the heading "Critical," witty essays parody the style and techniques of Higher Criticism.

The seven theological essays have stood the test of time. In "Christian Morality," Miss Sayers points out that although Christ's contemporaries had a great deal to say against His Messianic claims and His teachings, yet they were able to level only two accusations against His personal life: He broke the Sabbath and consorted with publicans and sinners. With grim humor, she asserts that the Church has tried to obliterate the impression created by Christ's actions by establishing Total Abstinence Societies and insisting that Sunday should be not only a day of prayer but also one without amusement. This has had the very curious result that such words as "purity," "virtue," and "morality" have acquired a very restricted meaning in the English language. Indeed, many Christians believe that true morality consists of three rules: keeping Sunday observance, avoiding intoxication, and not practicing "immorality."

Reminding her readers that Christ gently chided the disreputable, "Go, and sin no more," and reserved His wrath and physical violence for the Pharisees and the money-changers in the Temple, she pleads that the Church and all mankind have the courage to place the emphasis where Christ placed it. Such a revolutionary concept, if truly practiced, would solve economic problems and transform man's attitudes toward work and profits. No longer would it be assumed that the value of work and of people could be assessed in terms of economics: "We might not so readily take for granted that the production of anything (no matter how useless or dangerous) is justified so long as it issues in increased profits and wages; that so long as a man is well paid, it does not matter whether his work is worth-while in itself or good for his soul . . ." (5).

In "Toward a Christian Aesthetic" Miss Sayers states forthrightly that the Church has no Christian philosophy of the Arts, and for almost two thousand years has been trying to reconcile "a pagan, or at any rate a Unitarian, aesthetic with a Christian, that is, a Trinitarian and Incarnational theology" (31). Tracing the origins of European aesthetics back to Plato, she shows that his aesthetic has dominated our critical thinking and influenced the attitude of the Church, perhaps to an unsuspected degree. Acknowledging her indebtedness to R. C. Collingwood's *Principles of Art*, she writes at length on the meaning of art as creation, deplores the popularity of amusement-arts that provide escape and wish-fulfillment, and warns the Church to beware of encouraging artists to create "moral" art, that is, works produced to evoke sentimental piety. She then offers a lucid explanation of a Christian theory of art established on the Trinitarian doctrine of the nature of the Creative Mind, elucidated in *The Mind of the Maker*.

This essay is one of the most provocative in the collection. Many readers will agree with the views of Charles Morgan: "No reader who recognizes that art is a spiritual power and a means of rebirth can fail to value it, however little of a dogmatist he may be." Commenting that the students of Maritain will find the essay of particular interest, he adds that "to one who looks for the Absolute of his Aesthetic to the *Symposium*, it will yield the pleasure of observing once more the parallelism between Platonic and Christian thought." [11]

"Forgiveness" and "What Do We Believe" are directed to war-torn Britain, but the issues raised are worthy of consideration today. The first essay states that forgiveness is not a remission of sin or the obliteration of the consequences of wrong-doing; it is not concerned with reparation due to the aggrieved party; forgiveness is the reestablishment of right relationships. The second essay briefly presents various tenets of the Creed. Doctrinal issues may not be much comfort when one is cowering in a bomb-shelter, Miss Sayers admits, but she suggests that thinking about what one believes concerning life after death should convince one that life must be lived creatively, not free *from* danger and suffering but *in* danger and suffering.

The nine essays under the heading "Political" are varied in tone, topic, and importance. "Plain English" and "The English Language" are trenchant criticisms of the abuse of the language. She cites examples of "telegraphese," that is, sentences laden with confused syntax, wandering clauses, and misplaced modifiers and conjunctions, then contrasts these with quotations from such notable stylists as Donne, Pepys, and Chesterfield. More shrilly denunciatory, the second essay asserts that the English language is in danger of being ruined by the careless speech habits of journalists, politicians, teachers, and radio commentators.

Although delivered in 1938, the address "Are Women Human?" is relevant today. Miss Sayers castigates the practice of imputing certain qualities to men or to women, and deplores the phrase "a woman's point of view." To man's eternal query, "What do women really want?" she answers that *as* women they do not want anything in particular but as *human beings* they want what men want: "an interesting occupation, reasonable freedom for their pleasures, and a sufficient emotional outlet" (138). To support her argument, she cites D. H. Lawrence's admission that most men are willing to accept woman as "an angel, a devil, a baby-face . . . a bosom, a womb . . . an ideal or an obscenity," but will not accept her as "a real human being of the feminine sex" (139). "The Human-Not-Quite-Human" takes its title from the idea that men, including the hierarchy of the Church, refuse to treat women as genuine human beings. Taking the Church to task for failing to follow the example of Christ, she states that He knew how to treat women: He never nagged, flattered, coaxed or patronized them; "never mapped out their sphere for them, never urged them to be feminine or jeered at them for being female . . ." (148).

"Living to Work" points out the folly of regarding one's daily occupation as a means to achieve something else, such as money, leisure, security. Rightly considered, work should be a satisfying, absorbing vocation in itself. Acknowledging that machines cannot, and should not be renounced, she insists that men and women must learn to use technology so that they may work together harmoniously. She makes no attempt to show how this can be accomplished but urges that, in postwar planning, basic questions regarding the nature of work and leisure should be considered. A later essay, "Why Work?", treating facets of the same problems, will be considered in the section on *Creed or Chaos?*.

The third section offers a change of pace; instead of the heading "Criticism," it might well have been entitled "Baker Street," for the essays are witty, pseudoscholarly analyses of aspects of Conan Doyle's writings, a type of "spoof-criticism" begun by Monsignor Ronald Knox to show that by employing the techniques of "Higher Criticism," a modern classic can be disintegrated as speciously as some critics have treated the Bible. With mock solemnity, Miss

Sayers utilizes the methods of Higher Criticism to solve problems about aspects of Holmes's university career, the dates in *The Red-Headed League*, Watson's correct first name, and his life as a widower. Remarkable for its erudition and wit, the final essay deals with facets of Aristotle's Poetics. Employing the same techniques, she quotes passages, infers, twists statements, and in conclusion avows that she has shown that without a doubt what Aristotle really wanted all along was a well-written detective story.

The essays in *Unpopular Opinions* cover a wide variety of topics; each is developed in a style suitable for the audience for which it was originally planned. The tone is often familiar, the manner discursive, indicating that the essays were for "popular" audiences. Understandably, the collection is uneven. Some of the political and social pieces, talks rather than formal lectures or essays, have subjects too large for adequate treatment in the space or time allotted. A few of the wartime essays are somewhat dated, but many, particularly her sound, eloquent defence of a woman's right to be recognized as a human being, are significant today. Despite some shortcomings, many of these essays deal courageously and lucidly with controversial topics, suggesting how social, political, and religious institutions can project in practical ways the Christian values which a mechanized society is always in danger of neglecting.

VI   Creed or Chaos?

The seven essays in *Creed or Chaos?*, 1949, originally lectures, were later published as pamphlets; then when these were out of print, the author gathered them together in this volume to satisfy numerous readers.[12] The collection is named for the fifth essay, "Creed or Chaos?", which stresses the author's conviction that human thought and actions are rooted in dogma, particularly the doctrines of the Incarnation and Redemption.

Insisting that the official Creed of the Church cannot be interpreted with sentimental vagueness in the name of religious toleration, she declares that if England is once again to have a Christian society, it must return to dogma based on Christian theology, stated in language meaningful to the average lay person. Christianity cannot be presented as "something charming and popular with no offence in it. . . . We can not blink the fact that gentle Jesus meek and mild was so stiff in His opinions and so inflammatory in His language that He was thrown out of church, stoned, hunted . . . and finally gibbetted as a firebrand and a public danger" (35). Wisely, she does not confuse the end with the means: she does not make true knowledge, worship, and the daily living of the Christian creed a means to achieve a peaceful society, but argues that where citizens do not know and serve God, social chaos is bound to flourish.

The other essays reaffirm these points. "The Greatest Drama Ever Staged" states that English churches are empty, not because dull dogma is preached, but because it is neglected. Reiterating the truths of the Creed, that Christ was genuine Man and also God, Who experienced poverty, pain, humiliation, defeat, and death, she questions how such a life could possibly be considered dull. In Christ's own day, she asserts, He was considered too dynamic to be safe, but later generations have muffled up that challenging personality: "We have very efficiently pared the claws of the Lion of Judah," and turned Jesus into a "household pet for pale curates and pious old ladies" (5). Language and metaphor reinforce her argument, particularly in her account of Christ's actions which so distressed custom-cranks and Officialdom. In "The Dogma Is the Drama," she pleads forcefully that the drama of Christianity once again be brought into daily life: "It is the dogma that is the drama—not beautiful phrases, nor comforting sentiments . . . nor the promise of something nice after death" (24). Copying the question and answer format of the catechism, she satirically suggests some of the popular misconceptions of Christian orthodoxy; "What does the Church think of Sex?" evokes the response: "God made it necessary to the machinery of the world, and tolerates it, provided the parties (a) are married, and (b) get no pleasure out of it" (22).

"The Other Six Deadly Sins" asserts that although the Church officially recognizes Seven Capital sins, yet, like Caesar, it has shown more concern in the past to condemn Lust than the other capital offenses; quicker to decry sexual immorality than financial chicanery; more vigilant to ban suggestive books or dramas than to censure those who teach that wealth and position are the important goals in life; harsher on excessive drinkers than on those who charge excessive rates of interest. Treating the vice of Gluttony, she returns to a favorite theme: the dangers of gluttonous consumption of manufactured goods. The blame for this "whirligig of industrial finance," based on the wasteful production and consumption of goods, is placed squarely where it belongs: not on producers but on buyers; the whole system would collapse, she insists, if every person limited purchases to the essentials. During the war, necessity forced everyone to conserve and to respect quality, not quantity, but when peacetime returns, she questions whether England will return to "the wasteful consumption of . . . drugs and paper, cheap pottery and cosmetics—all the slop and swill that pour down the sewers over which the palace of Gluttony is built" (71).

Closely related in theme, "Why Work?" denounces the age not only as one of waste and greed but one with wrong attitudes toward work and leisure. To bring about a radical change, she suggests three propositions. The first echoes the ideas of Eric Gill: work must not be considered something one does to earn a living but something that one lives to do. Instead of rushing through one's work, in order to have money and leisure to do the things one longs to do, an individual must find in his work physical, mental, and spiritual satisfaction. To accomplish this transformation of attitude, the work must have quality: whatever is made, whatever service is given, must have beauty, usefulness, and honest workmanship.

The seven essays in *Creed or Chaos?* have unity of tone and content. Riley Hughes praised the author's penetrating analysis of the evils dominant in the twentieth century: "She speaks out against tawdry Church Art, against Christian tolerance of mammon and ungraciousness toward publicans, but most of all against nominal Christians, 'both lay and clerical.' In her view every problem and every struggle is at base a question of theology." [13] The author's knowledge of theology, her ability to express abstruse concepts with clarity and vigor, and her complete dedication to Christian ideals are noteworthy, but as always in essays and lectures designed for popular audiences, there is the danger of treating some aspects of a topic in a simplistic fashion. Mr. Garrison in the *Christian Century* challenged her statements that "heresy is largely the expression of the untutored average man," and that the dogmas of the Church were "hammered out under pressure of urgent practical necessity to provide an answer to heresy." "The creeds," he argued, "were hammered out in the struggle against other opinions but the struggle often had important political considerations." [14]

Whether heard in the lecture hall or read as individual pamphlets, these essays stimulated thought and discussion, particularly during the war years. Edited in a slim volume in 1949, they were again popular; during the fifties both this volume and her earlier collection,

Unpopular Opinions, were out of print but they are available now. Many of the most thought-provoking are reprinted in anthologies or as separate works.

Many of her essays on the art of the detective story, such as "Gaudy Night," "The Sport of Noble Minds," the scholarly introductions to the three volumes comprising *Great Short Stories of Detection, Mystery, and Horror*, and her analysis of the unsolved Liverpool mystery, "The Murder of Julia Wallace," are frequently anthologized in collections dealing with the development and changing status of detective fiction. Her essay on life after death, "Christian Belief about Heaven and Hell," and the provocative "Are Women Human?" and "The Human-Not-Quite-Human," "Towards a Christian Aesthetic," and "The Lost Tools of Learning" are favorites in the United States, appearing in several collections as well as individual pamphlets.

While engaged in translating the *Divine Comedy*, Miss Sayers delighted in lecturing on Dante. She addressed students at Cambridge and Oxford. At the summer schools of Italian at Cambridge University, her lectures were acclaimed "as the best event in the programme and attracted large audiences." [15] Many of these talks were published later in *Introductory Papers on Dante*, 1954, and *Further Papers on Dante*, 1957. These will be considered in the following chapter dealing with her translations of the *Divine Comedy*.

From the early 1930s until her death, Miss Sayers was an indefatigable essayist and lecturer. The bibliography by Harmon and Burger lists some forty public addresses; at the present time there is no complete listing of her book reviews, many of them unsigned, which appeared in the *Sunday Times* and the *Times Literary Supplement*. Letters by C. S. Lewis comment on her active participation in the debates of the Socratic Club while he served as president of this Oxford group of intellectuals which included J. R. R. Tolkien, Charles Williams, and Owen Barfield. G. K. Chesterton and other members of the Detection Club record that, as president, she enjoyed addressing them at dinner meetings; and despite some bitter entanglements with personnel at the BBC, she delighted in giving radio talks and participating in radio serials. Her wry humor and pungent forcefulness were not always appreciated by listeners, just as some readers of *Punch* frowned on the caustic wit permeating *The Pantheon Papers*, her sly mockery of the inanities of society's religious vacuity. Her comments about new saints and holy days provoked smiles from some who understood the serious foolery behind her references to the clergyman, entitled "Perpetual Obscurate of St. Scientia-in-Excelsis," the liturgical calendar with its new holy days, Exhaust Sunday, Trash Wednesday, Cacophany-Tide, and the acclaim given to the paragons of modern virtue, Saints Lukewarm and Supercilia, as well as the observance of the "Gratification of St. Gorge" and the "Beautification of St. Henna"; some readers were not amused.[16]

VII   *Posthumous Publications*

Published in 1963, *The Poetry of Search and the Poetry of Statement* is a collection of twelve papers read by Miss Sayers in academic circles between 1946 and 1957.[17] Six appeared as pamphlets or articles in the publications of the learned societies to which they were addressed; six are printed here for the first time. Five essays, aspects of her study and translations of Dante, will be considered in the next chapter. Two essays are trenchant criticisms of modern education with practical suggestions for remedying the conditions which she deplores. Others range over a number of literary topics: the devil in literature, the merits of writings by her friend Charles Williams, aspects of allegory, and problems in communication.

In the opening essay from which the collection takes its title, Miss Sayers states that there are two kinds of poetry written by two different types of poets. In the Poetry of Search, the poet records his tensions, frustrations, and gropings—a diary of beginnings and mistrials; in the Poetry of Statement, the poet records truths that he has discovered. Keats and Tennyson, she states, are Poets of Search; Dante and Milton, Poets of Statement. Castigating modern education for teaching students subject matter rather than training them to think independently, she pleads in "The Lost Tools of Learning" for educational reforms, outlines a curriculum based on a modern Trivium, and urges that the scholastic tradition, almost lost in England, be revived in order to fulfill the true aim of education: "to teach men how to learn for themselves" (176). In the United States, this essay stimulated such interest after it was reprinted in *Education in a Free Society* that several educational agencies published it in pamphlet form.[18] In "The Teaching of Latin" Miss Sayers pleads that the subject be retained in the curriculum but that emphasis be placed on medieval rather than classical Latin.

These essays have the unique distinction of revealing interesting glimpses of Miss Sayers's life, her methods of work, and the ideals that sustained her. Her amusing account of her father's old-fashioned methods of teaching her Latin, her pride in her ability to chant conjugations and declensions before others in the Rectory, the challenge of learning Greek at Oxford and the dismay over never learning to pronounce Latin fluently, her struggles to create characters who were more than mere puppets, her passion for verse-translation which she called "a congenital disease from which she suffered all her life," and her revealing discussions about translating difficult passages in the *Divine Comedy*—these and many other disclosures reveal aspects of her true self, more trustworthy than any biography. Reading these essays, one becomes conscious of the intellectual integrity that governed not only her search for knowledge but also her own personal development.

Christian Letters to a Post-Christian World, 1969, edited by Roderick Jellema, later published under the title *The Whimsical Christian*, makes available some of Miss Sayers's most representative essays.[19] "What Do We Believe?", "Towards a Christian Aesthetic," "Creative Mind," and "Christian Morality," from the collection *Unpopular Opinions*, express her conviction that Christian truths must be stated dramatically and lived courageously. "The Greatest Drama Ever Staged," "Strong Meat," "The Dogma Is the Drama," "The Other Six Deadly Sins," and "Creed or Chaos?" from the collection of that title, suggest how Christianity has failed to appeal to the postwar generation and some ways to rectify the situation.

Are Women Human?, 1971, includes the essay of that title and also "The Human-Not-Quite-Human." Both essays emphasize the author's views on the subject of women's rights and the role of women in a male-oriented society.[20] Despite the fact she advocated individualism rather than aggressive feminism, the book has been a popular study-club choice of many feminist groups.

A Matter of Eternity, 1973, edited by Rosamond Sprague, has two complete essays, "Christian Morality" and "The Lost Tools of Learning."[21] The remainder of the slim volume is a collection of provocative passages culled from the author's theological, fictional, and dramatic writings. Grouped under such headings as Forgiveness, Evil, Sin, Morality, and Work, these excerpts reveal a remarkable unity of theme notable in early and late writings. Separated from their original context, these affirmations concerning the importance of the Incarnation, the role of Christian dogma in everyday life, integrity in personal relationships, and the evil of sin, gain a new profundity.

CHAPTER 7

Dante for Today

ENCHANTED by the discovery that Dante's *Divine Comedy* was
not a grimly religious poem, intellectual and obscure, but was an
exciting adventure story shot through with satire, romance, spiritual
autobiography, and, most unexpected of all, humor of many types,
Miss Sayers read and reread the poem, then set about the task of
learning the Italian language so that she could enjoy the poem in its
original form. Convinced that Dante wrote his poem for the ordinary
reader and dissatisfied with modern English translations which, she
felt, lacked the joy, verve, and comedy of the original, at the end of
the war she approached Dr. E. V. Rieu, editor of the Penguin
Classics series, about the possibility of making a new translation that
would appeal to students, housewives, office-workers—just ordinary
people—who lacked the background to appreciate the work and, like
herself, avoided it, thinking it too complicated to understand and to
appreciate. This is not to suggest that she intended to write a "popular" translation, for during her first conference with Dr. Rieu she
made it clear that she understood the difficulties inherent in the
poem but was confident that she could clarify abstruse points of
theology, philosophy, history, and other aspects of Dante's thought
so necessary for an intelligent appreciation of the work.

In the essay ". . . And Telling You A Story," Miss Sayers commented diffidently that she came to Dante rather late in life and with
quite an unprepared mind. The truth is quite the opposite. That she
had a genuine talent for languages was apparent from her childhood,
when she began her studies in Latin, French, and German. She
earned First Honours in Modern Languages at Somerville College,
Oxford, where she developed what she termed "her lifelong passion
for verse translation." In 1929, she translated in spirited verse and
prose the twelfth-century poem of Thomas the Anglo-Norman, *Tris-*

tan in Brittany; in 1957, as a relaxing interlude before beginning the task of translating the *Paradiso*, she translated the *Chanson de Roland*; and every reader of the Wimsey novels knows how fluently Lord Peter spoke French. Annoyed by critics who in the past had appreciated her writing talents but now seemed skeptical of her ability to achieve anything of merit in the realm of Dantean studies, she urged her publisher to underplay her reputation as a novelist and to emphasize her background as a scholar. She could have added that her excursions into Christian theology and apologetics in the 1930s had given her insights into Christian teachings inherent in the *Divine Comedy*. Today there is no need to apologize or to defend her contributions to Dante scholarship. Her lively translations of the *Inferno*, *Purgatorio*, and the *Paradiso*, uncompleted at the time of her death, and her scholarly commentaries, *Introductory Papers on Dante* and *Further Papers on Dante*, continue to fulfill her goal: to introduce Dante's masterpiece to the "ordinary reader." Many of the essays in these two volumes shed considerable light on her methods of work. Although she was convinced that no translation could ever reproduce fully the beauty and power of the original, nevertheless she aimed to capture something of Dante's style, tone, and emphasis: ". . . his spare and sinewy strength, his astonishing speed and drive, his salty and astringent humour, his curious mixture of extreme simplicity and intellectual subtlety . . . his lyrical sweetness and his towering ecstasy of song." [1]

To give her readers an appreciation of Dante's poetic power, she utilized his verse form, the ten-eleven-syllable line of the *terza-rima* with its free-flowing, interlocked rhyme scheme that moves from the beginning to the end of each canto, with each terzain or three-line stanza linked by rhyme to the one before and the one following: aba, bcb, cdc . . . xyx, yzy, z. Undaunted by the task of finding several thousand sets of triple rhyme, she insisted that the challenge would force her to probe the meaning of every passage and to select the word that most accurately expressed Dante's thought.

She took the liberty of using every type of rhyme: half-rhyme, eye-rhyme, feminine, unaccented, cockney, and eccentric rhyme, just as Dante did. "I would," she confessed, "rather a thousand times have approximate rhymes than approximate meaning—and in translating Dante into *terza-rima* one must continually choose between the one and the other." [2] She also took considerable license in matters of diction. Although she said that she avoided the use of the obsolete and the archaic, as well as the slangy and ephemeral, these do appear, but for the most part she utilized modern diction for the colloquial passages, the novel and poetic for passages in the grand manner. She reminds her readers that in word choice she simply followed Dante's example, for he used original words, nonsense and "barbarous" words, as well as elaborate Latinisms of vocabulary and syntax.

I   *Some Distinguishing Characteristics*

Many critics agree that Miss Sayers is at her best when translating passages vibrant with swift movement, strident clangor, and emotional tension. Her translation of Canto III of the *Inferno* illustrates how effectively she conveys the misery of the Shades in the Vestibule of Hell. On earth they were so cowardly cautious that they could never decide how to act; here, still indecisive, they rush about aimlessly, blown like weathercocks: [3]

> Tongues mixed and mingled, horrible execration,
>   Shrill shrieks, hoarse groans, fierce yells and hideous blether
>   And clapping of hands thereto, without cessation
>
> Made tumult through the timeless night, that hither
>   And thither drives in dizzying circles sped,
>   As whirlwind whips the spinning sands together.
>
> *Inferno* III. 25–30

When Charon, the Infernal Ferryman, appears, the emotions of the damned are described:

> But those outwearied, naked souls—how gash
>   And pale they grew, chattering their teeth for dread,
>   When first they felt his harsh tongue's cruel lash.
>
> God they blaspheme, blaspheme their parents' bed,
>   The human race, the place, the time, the blood,
>   The seed that got them, and the womb that bred;
>
> Then, huddling hugger-mugger, down they scud,
>   Dismally wailing, to the accursed strand
>   Which waits for every man that fears not God.
>
> *Inferno* III. 100–108

These terzains illustrate several techniques that distinguish Sayers's translations. Most notable is her use of harshly alliterative phrases to convey the stark misery and infernal noise of Hell: "Tongues mixed and mingled," "Shrill shrieks," "whirlwind whips the spinning sands." Unusual words add force: "blether," "gash," "hugger-mugger," and the graphic verb, "scud." She repeats words, especially verbs, to heighten the effect. Dante, for instance, writes: "*Bestem-miavano Dio e lor parenti*" (They blasphemed God and their parents). She emphasizes the virulence of the sinners' despair by repeating the verb: "God they blaspheme, blaspheme their parents' bed." The formal balance of "The seed that got them, and the womb that bred," contrasts sharply with the informality of "Then, huddling hugger-mugger, down they scud." More colloquial than the original, yet Miss Sayers's translation conveys their misery.

Rebuking Dante, his pupil, Virgil begins with strident formality, then ends on a note of familiarity:

> "What error has seduced thy reason, pray?"
> Said he, "thou art not wont to be so dull;
> Or are thy wits woolgathering miles away?"

Inferno XI. 76–78

Here Miss Sayers emphasizes Virgil's irritation in order to accentuate Dante's comic portrayal of himself. Professor Bickersteth's translation lacks this comic touch:

> "Why go thy wits so far astray?" thus came
> his answer: "thou art wont to show more skill;
> or is thy mind pursuing some other aim?"

She effectively approximates Dante's vision of the chaos and cacophony endured by carnal sinners:

> A place made dumb of every glimmer of light,
>   Which bellows like tempestuous ocean birling
>   In the batter of a two-way wind's buffet and fight.
>
> The blast of hell that never rests from whirling
>   Harries the spirits along in the sweep of its swath,
>   And vexes them, for ever beating and hurling.

Inferno V. 28–33

The labials in "bellows," "birling," "batter," "buffet," and "blast,"

and the sibilants in "spirits," "sweep," and "swath" evoke the tumul-
tuous pounding of the winds that make the spirits "cry and wail and
shriek."

Alliteration heightens many passages of violence. The three-
headed Cerberus "Bays in his triple gullet and doglike growls" as he
"rips and rends" the Gluttonous, making the "wretches writhe"
(*Inferno* VI. 14, 18, 21). Attacked by one of the wrathful, Dante
condemns him to remain "Amid the weeping and the woe" and hopes
to see the arrogant brute "soused in the swill" (Inferno VIII. 37, 53).
The Minotaur "reels in the ring," then "falls-afloundering" (*Inferno*
XII. 23, 25). In the Wood of the Suicides, two of the despairing run
with such force that they "snapped to flinders every forest fan"; in fast
pursuit is a throng "Of great black braches, fleet of foot and grim"
(*Inferno*, XIII. 117, 125). Alliteration and meter enliven the description of Geryon's swift departure after depositing his passengers:

> . . . and having shogged our burden off,
> Brisker than bolt from bow away he bounded.
>
> *Inferno* XVII. 135–36

Alliteration also marks the original: ". . . *discarcate le nostre per-
sonne,/si dileguò come da corda cocca.*"

Dante watches a Falsifier who "Puffed his parched lips apart"
(*Inferno* XXX. 55); Hellrakers in the moat, "boil and bubble in the
tarry tide" (*Inferno* XXXIII. 144); when Satan clamps his jaws down
on three sinners, they are "Frayed by the fangs like flax beneath a
brake" (*Inferno* XXXIV. 56). Virgil and Dante trudge with "slow
steps" across a filthy "sludge of souls and snow." Short alliterative
phrases are numerous: "pumpkin-pate," "bloody-minded brute,"
"hideous hole," "slick slither," "wounds and woe," tumble a-tangle,"
and "slubbered smears."

In the passage describing the torrential storm and flood that batters
Buonconte's corpse, Miss Sayers's translation closely approximates
Dante's rhythms that mimetically convey the pounding force of the
waters that tore from the victim's breast the hands that he had piously
crossed in his last moments:

> Then, at its mouth, the Archian's roaring sluice
> Found my stiff frozen body, and it swept me
> Into the Arno, and from my breast shook loose

The cross I made of me when the death-pangs gripped me;
  And rolling me down on its bed, over boulder and brae,
At length with its booty it girded and shrouded and heaped me.
                                    Purgatorio V. 124–129

Miss Sayers's skill in capturing the movement, tone, and feeling of Dante's tempestuous passages is often praised, but her ability to reflect the tranquil beauty and repose of Dante's lines also deserves attention. Particularly effective is her portrayal of the tranquillity of the penitents who joyfully accept their purgative pains:

So, penitent and pardoning and at peace
With God, we passed from that life into this.
                                    Purgatorio V. 55, 56

Her translation echoes the serenity of the original:

  sì che, pentendo e perdonando, fora
  di vita uscimmo a Dio pacificati.

When Lady Pia requests Dante to remember her to her friends when he returns to earth, she adds that he should do this after he is "well rested from the weary way." As softly as a whispered sigh, one of the Envious laments: "I reap the straw whose seed I sowed so rife" (*Purgatorio* XIV. 85). When Beatrice chides Dante for his inconstancy, Sayers's lines, although more alliterative, suggest the gentleness of the original:

And by wild ways he wandered, seeking for
False phantoms of the good. . . .
                                    Purgatorio XXX. 130–31

Determined to write a fast-paced, vigorous translation, Miss Sayers took freedoms with the text, at times shifting the contents of a *terzain*, employing colloquialisms to secure informality, and adding words for emphasis. When Virgil in *Purgatorio* IX tells Dante that he can read his thoughts even if he wore a *hundred* masks, Sayers, to suggest the depths of Virgil's discernment, increases this to a *thousand* masks. In her notes accompanying her translation of *Inferno* XXI and XXII, she admits that here she took many liberties because she wanted to keep the grim satire and comic ferocity of the original. Dante, she states, had good reason to

write such savage descriptions of the barrators suffering in pools of
boiling pitch, their punishment for trafficking in public offices,
because it was an accusation of barratory that served as the pretext
to exile him from Florence. Translating the passage describing the
horrible appearance of the devil who carries a barrator to his fate,
H. F. Cary writes: "Ah, how ferocious was his aspect! And how
bitter he seemed to me in gesture, with his wings outspread, and
light of foot." Miss Sayers's translation has Dante's verve:

> Wow! what a grisly look he had on him!
> How fierce his rush! And, skimming with spread wing,
> How swift of foot he seemed! How light of limb!
> *Inferno* XXI. 31–33

The fiends that torment the barrators are likened by Dante to cats
that torment a mouse: *"Tra mal gatte era venuto il sorco"*—
"Among evil cats the mouse had come." Sayers exaggerates: " 'Twas
cat and mouse—ten cats with cruel claws." When a fiend
commands, "Off with thee, villainous bird," Miss Sayers adds a
slangy note:
"Hop off, thou filthy bird of Hell!"   Never ashamed of what she
termed "honest padding," if it helped her to achieve the desired
effect, she repeats words and phrases more frequently than Dante,
in order to secure emphasis and appropriate rhymes. This is
apparent in the terzain describing the fate of the Suicides:

> We shall take our flight, when all souls take their flight,
> To seek our spoils, but not to be rearrayed,
> For the spoils of the spoiler cannot be his by right.
> *Inferno* XIII.103–105

She gives the literal translation in her notes: "It is not *just* that a
man should have what he takes from himself." (Treating suicide as a
type of self-robbery, Dante states that the robber cannot claim what
he has plundered—in this case, his own body.) Where Dante uses
the word "cerca" - "search" only once in his denunciation of the strife
in Rome, Sayers emphasizes the condition by repeating the word
three times:

> Search, wretched! search thy seas and coasts around;
> Then search thy bosom; see if thou canst hit
> On any nook where pleasant peace is found.
> *Purgatorio* VI. 85–87

In Canto XX of the *Purgatorio*, she very carefully retains Dante's repetition of "I see once more . . . . I see," explaining in her notes that Dante's verse structure here parallels lines written by Boniface VIII, whom the poet despised but nevertheless honored by echoing his prayer to the Blessed Mother. This canto has many examples of her practice of heightening by repetition: "When shall I thrill, my God, when shall I thrill"; "sin-laden, sin crowded"; "now come, now gone." Dante's "*d'antico amor*" becomes "The old, old love."

The necessity of finding rhyming words led Miss Sayers to occasionally use colloquialisms so informal that they detracted from Dante's thought and mood. In Canto XXIV of the *Purgatorio*, Dante's comments on his role in creating the "sweet new style" of Florentine poetry are answered by a contemporary, now a penitent; Dante speaks:

> I said: "I am one who when Love breathes within
>   Give ear, and as he prompts take mode and pitch
>   From him, and go and sing his mind to men."
>
> And he: "O brother, now I see the hitch
>   That kept back me, the Notary, and Guitton',
>   And put this sweet new style beyond our reach;"
>   *Purgatorio* XXIV. 52–57

Although "mode and pitch" are apt terms for lyrical poetry, they only loosely interpret the idea that Dante the poet, inspired by Love, listened, then wrote his song in the fashion and style prompted by this inspiration, but the rhyming word "hitch" in Bongiunta's reply is far too informal to suggest the characteristics that separated his type of Sicilian poetry from that of the Florentine school. In her commentary on this passage, Miss Sayers devotes an entire page to clarify the differences between the two schools, theories far too complex to be dismissed or summarized by the phrase: "I see the hitch. . . ." Dante used the term "*il nodo*," a knot, frequently translated as "hindrance" or "difficulty."

In her attempt to approximate Dante's verve, Miss Sayers expresses at times his idea but not his tone. Would Dante really say that a sinner gave "a walloping blow," and in turn, was "lammed . . . over the face"? When a fiend commands another to stop yelling, Dante's lines, plainly translated, read: "Is it not enough to chatter with thy jaws, but thou must bark too? What Devil is upon thee?" ("*Qual diavol ti tocca*"). Sayers translates:

> Don't thy jaws make enough infernal clatter
> But, what the devil! must thou start barking too?
>
> *Inferno* XXXII. 107–108

Her tendency to intensify Dante's expressions and to slightly change at times his meaning has met criticism. Professor Holmes points out that at the end of the *Purgatorio* Dante is " *'disposto a salire'*—prepared to rise or to climb to the stars, and the whole *Paradiso* is at one in confirming this"; he chides Miss Sayers for saying that Dante is "pure and prepared to leap up to the stars." Holmes notes also that Dante's phrase describing Francesca's grief, "dolci sospiri" —sweet sighs—becomes thick and cloyed by Sayers's translation: "sighing-sweet desires." [4] Professor Singleton sees a distortion in her rendition of Virgil's explanation why he cannot enter Paradise: [5]

> For the Emperor of that High Imperium
> Wills not that I, once rebel to His crown,
> Into that city of His should lead men home.
>
> *Inferno* I. 124–26

Dante's words, Professor Singleton insists, indicate that God wills that *Virgil* should not enter His city, not that he must not lead others there; furthermore, Sayers's translation does not convey the pathos which Dante gives to the poet's exile. He kindly adds that other translators have stumbled here.

In her essay "On Translating the *Divina Commedia*," Miss Sayers tells that she attempted to copy a rhythm used by Dante to achieve some special effect. [6] She used the lilt of "Diddle-diddle-dumpling, my son John," she asserts, to convey the idea of the speed of a lizard:

> And just as a lizard, with a quick, slick slither,
>   Flicks across the highway from hedge to hedge,
>   Fleeter than a flash, in the battering dog-day weather
>
> A fiery little monster, livid, in a rage,
>   Black as any peppercorn, came and made a dart
>   At the guts of the others. . . .
>
> *Inferno* XXV. 79–84

She also used this rhythm to suggest the travelers' laborious efforts to negotiate the steep path from terrace to terrace:

You can mount up to San Leo, or to Noli scramble down,
You can tackle tall Bismantova and clamber to the top
On your two flat feet; but this way has to be flown;
                                        Purgatorio IV. 25–27

Although extremely complimentary about the many fine qualities of
her translation, C. S. Lewis took exception to this experimentation,
terming it a "metrical extravagance" with little resemblance to
Dante's meter.

In *Purgatorio* XXVI, the poet Arnaut Daniel, addressing Dante,
speaks in his native Provençal, a form chosen by Dante to honor
Arnaut's mastery of his mother-tongue, and also to distinguish this,
the last exchange of speech with the souls in Purgatory. To
approximate Dante's lightness and tonal qualities, Miss Sayers
daringly translates Arnaut's speech into Border Scots, a dialect
which she claims bears something of the same relationship to
English as the Provençal does to Italian. Despite her efforts, many
find her translation of the passage jarring and distracting.

A few of her rhymes are unfortunate. She writes:

> Freehold of bliss apparent in his face,
>   The heavenly pilot on the poop stood tiptoe,
>   And with him full an hundred souls had place.
>
> "*In exitu Israel de Aegypto,*"
>   From end to end they sang their holy lay
>   In unison; and so he brought the ship to.
>   *Purgatorio* II. 43–48

Dante's rhyming words, "iscripto," "Aegypto," and "scripto," are in
harmony with the meaning and tone of the passage; Sayers's
translation sounds forced. Her translation of *Purgatorio* XXIV,
37–39, is almost doggerel:

> . . . he muttered and at length he shook a
>   Something from where they feel the fret and fray
>   Of justice most—it sounded like "Gentucca."

Dr. Cunningham cites as examples of bad rhyme:[7]

> Still must sad Cleopatra wail and gasp
>   Because of this that once she fled before
>   To snatch death, swift and fearful, from the asp.
>   *Paradiso* VI.76–78

and also, "Baby Learchus, as he crowed and smiled," obviously designed to rhyme with "wild" and "child." Such lapses are rare.

II   *Dante the Comic Writer*

A storyteller herself, Miss Sayers recognized Dante's superb narrative techniques: structure, pace, details, tone, and style. Her appreciation of his art of characterization is particularly perceptive. Emphasizing that allegory is often boring because it is populated by droves of "frigid abstractions and perambulating labels," she notes that Dante avoided this difficulty by peopling his poem with individuals who do not cease to be themselves because they also typify everybody else's sins and virtues. Dante, for instance, is guided through Hell to Paradise, not by an abstraction named Wisdom, Good-Wit, or Counsel but by Virgil, so human that he shows impatience and a touch of vanity. In telling the story in first person, Dante ran the risk of sounding like a conceited bore, but Miss Sayers notes that he avoided this by a technical device: except where he speaks in a purely prophetic role, he conceives his character in a spirit of comedy.

In the essay "The Comedy of the *Comedy*," she insists that the poem is essentially a humorous one, a theory that has not endeared her to all Dante scholars, particularly Italian critics. However, she did not mean that the entire poem is funny; in fact, she warns readers not to skim, looking for comic bits and pieces, but to look for the spirit of comedy that permeates the entire poem. Laughter, she says, runs like a bright thread from the Dark Wood to Paradise, and is most apparent in the poet's deliberate portrayal of himself as a coward, bungler, nuisance, and inquisitive, brash companion. In the Dark Wood, Dante, distraught with fear, makes himself out to be a ludicrous figure, flattering Virgil, imploring his aid, then cowardly refusing to follow him. Journeying through Hell, he poses questions constantly:

"Sir," said I, "pray tell

Who these are, what their custom, why they seem
So eager to pass over and be gone—
If I may trust my sight in this pale gleam."
Inferno III. 72–75

Dante, to suggest his own ignorance and foolish prattling, allows Virgil to reply impatiently to his many queries:

> "Ah, witless world! Behold the grand
> Folly of ignorance! Make thine ear attendant
> Now on my judgment. . .and understand."
>
> *Inferno* VII. 70–72

When Virgil and Statius are holding a learned discourse, Dante creates this comic portrait of himself trying to break into the conversation:

> And like a baby stork, that longs to fly
> And flaps its wings, and then, afraid to quit
> The nest, flops down again, just so was I—
>
> On fire to ask, but quenched as soon as lit,
> I got as far as making sounds like one
> About to speak, and then thought better of it.
>
> *Purgatorio* XXV. 10–15

Even in Paradise, he makes himself slightly comic by asking questions until Beatrice, "after a pitying sigh," gives him

> A look such as a mother's eyes let fall
> Upon her infant, babbling feverishly.
>
> *Paradiso* I. 101–102

Not all comedy centers on Dante the wayfarer, nor is all the laughter kindly, for, as Miss Sayers points out, there is a type of laughter that shocks and scarifies in the style of Swift. The poet, determined to show evil as it truly is, portrays in the fifth Bolgia grotesque demons: Guttlehog, like a savage boar, plunges his fangs into a victim; Helkin, like a hawk, scratches and chews his catch until they both drop into the boiling pitch; other demons snatch at sinners like rats in a sewer. Can such scenes of degradation, humiliation, and torture evoke laughter? Satiric laughter, yes, she asserts, for when man realizes that mortals, created in God's image and destined by Him for immortality, of their own free will choose to stoop so low, then man's agony of spirit over man's folly can only be expressed by satiric merriment.

Throughout the *Comedy*, Dante evokes contrasting types of humor: the damned shriek with sardonic laughter over the cruelties which they inflict on each other; penitent sinners in Purgatory smile because they have begun their purgation; the redeemed in Paradise sing, dance, and laugh with unrestrained joy as they experience the eternal vision of God. With verve and insight, Miss Sayers explains aspects of the comedy in the *Comedy* and her translations support her view, but some critics censure her for finding humor in passages traditionally considered grim, bitter, and horrific. That humor is present in the *Comedy* few would deny; that her emphasis on the comedy throughout the work has lured readers to tackle the poem with some feeling of security that it is not all grimly gruesome is also true, but perhaps she has erred slightly in seeing humor as an end in itself in some passages. There is, for instance, a touch of the comic in Dante's portrayal of himself as one utterly aghast and speechless when Nicholas III greets him with an abusive tirade, thinking that he is Boniface, but, as Musa points out, the comedy is functional.[8] The tongue-tied, abashed Dante is a foil to the courageous Dante who, once having gained his wits and composure, fearlessly upbraids the Pope for his cupidity; only respect for the office of the Papacy prevents Dante from uttering more grievous accusations.

In Canto VI of *Purgatorio*, Dante seems a comic figure when, in order to escape from a crowd of the Unshriven, he makes promises that he knows that he will not be able to keep, but this episode serves other purposes besides the comic. It effectively modulates the tragic tone of the recital of murder, battle, and misery that ends Canto V, and the garrulous pleas of Dante's petitioners provide a contrast to the affectionate greetings exchanged between Virgil and his fellow poet from Mantua, and to Dante's tirade against conditions in Italy, particularly in Florence.[9]

III *The Image of the City*

In Miss Sayers's commentaries accompanying her translations and in several essays, she reiterates that the subject of the poem is not the story of a journey through Hell and Purgatory to Paradise; the true subject is the relationship between God and man. Dante states, she emphasizes, that the *literal* signification of the poem concerns souls after death, but the *allegorical*, the important signification, concerns man's behavior in this life, for it is by his freely willed actions on earth that he becomes liable to "punishing or rewarding justice." She insists that one must accept Dante's idea that Heaven, Hell, and Purgatory are within the soul, but one may think of the corruption in Hell, she adds, not as the sins of individuals but as the evils which undermine all society, nations, cities, and communities today. This interpretation appeals to many readers who find that Dante's underworld makes more sense to them when viewed as a modern city plagued by every type of moral corruption. Although borrowed from her friend Charles Williams, this interpretation becomes uniquely her own through her succinct comments on the sins of society which are the very same as those trumpeted in the Late News broadcasts and in tomorrow's headlines.

A few examples from the *Inferno* will indicate how she links Dante's portrayal of sin and its consequences with vices rampant in society today.[10] Canto XIX describes the punishment of those guilty of Simony, the buying or selling of holy things. Do not think, she warns, that the vice was confined to medieval folk or to clergymen: "A mercenary marriage, for example, is also the sale of a sacrament" (192). In Circle VII those who corrupted the body suffer for their perverse vices; if Dante were writing today, she asserts, he would place dope addicts, drug pushers, and vicious types of alcoholics there. Charging excessive rates of interest is Usury, greatly frowned upon in the Middle Ages, but today, she claims, society is guilty of other types, such as multiplying material luxuries at the expense of vital necessities (178). In the Eighth Circle, called Malbowges because it is divided into trenches, those who committed Malicious Fraud upon mankind are punished. Malbowges, she states, is an *image* of any corrupted city where relationships, social, economic, personal, and public, have disintegrated. In the Circle of Fraud, Flatterers who on earth abused and corrupted the language wallow in the filth which they once spewed out on the world. "Dante," she says, "did not live to see the full development of political propaganda, commercial advertisement, and sensational journalism, but he has a place prepared for them" (186).

In the *Purgatorio* she continues to show that the vices of the medieval age are those that ravage society today. Gluttony is not always the sin of overeating and drinking; it may be overfastidiousness in matters of food, or too great concern to secure a higher standard of living. Sloth in its modern form is not necessarily idleness of mind and laziness of body; under the guise of Tolerance, it is often passive acquiescence to evil or error; another form is "escapism" or withdrawal from situations which have become difficult. By interpreting the poem on this allegorical level as the "Way of the City," "Miss Sayers indicates how Dante's Hell and Purgatory represent human society characterised by loss of Faith, lack of reverence for life and property, and absence of purpose and direction. Succinctly stated in "The Fourfold Interpretation of the *Comedy*," her summation of the ills of society includes the greedy consumption of goods, exploitation of sex, commercialization of religion, debasement of language, intellectual dishonesty, and other vices that "lead to the cold death of society and the extinguishing of all civilised relations." [11]

These and other shrewd insights into the levels of meaning in the poem, her competent exegesis of abstruse passages, her informative comments on Dante's milieu, and in particular her vigorous, spirited translations make the reading of the *Divine Comedy* a pleasurable, rewarding experience for an audience hitherto unfamiliar with its beauty. Critical evaluations of each *cantica* varied greatly at the time of publication, but there is scant justification for the statement in *Such a Strange Lady* that the first volume met with a storm of disapproval. [12] Her use of *terza rima*, her penchant for highlighting comedy in passages traditionally deemed grim or grave, and her choice of colloquialisms and slang to add vivacity and informality met with some negative reactions, but, as usual, facets viewed with disdain by some critics merited praise from others. Dr. Cunningham's survey *The Divine Comedy in English: A Critical Bibliography, 1901–1966*, indicates that her work compares favorably with the efforts of other recent translators, Binyon, Bickersteth, Ciardi, Hows, and Bergin. [13] Critics and students from the very first have been unanimous in praising the vigor and beauty of her translation and the format of the Penguin edition with its valuable commentaries, notes, glossaries, scholarly introductions, as well as the maps, illustrations, and diagrams by Mr. C. W. Scott-Giles, now Fitzalan Herald Extraordinary. So skillfully did Dr. Barbara Reynolds complete the translation of the *Paradiso*, one scarcely is aware of the break. The informative notes and commentaries by Dr. Reynolds indicate her depth of knowledge as a Dante scholar, as well as her understanding of the mind of her close friend, Miss Sayers.

IV *Essays on Dante*

While working on her translations of the *Divine Comedy*, Miss Sayers frequently lectured on various aspects of Dante's artistry. Published in 1955 as *Introductory Papers on Dante*, these commentaries are valuable studies of Dante's milieu and Catholic doctrines central to the poem.[14] Cautioning that it is not necessary to believe what Dante believed, but that it is absolutely necessary to understand the theological concepts that underlie the poem, she clarifies many abstruse ideas and points out significant aspects of its structure and style. She modestly refers to these informative essays as a "few sign-posts" to guide new readers through the Dark Wood. The titles indicate their wide range: "Dante's Imagery—Symbolic and Pictorial," "The Meaning of Heaven and Hell," "The Meaning of Purgatory," "The Fourfold Interpretation of the *Comedy*," "The City of Dis," "The Comedy of the *Comedy*," and "The Paradoxes of the *Comedy*,"

Aware that many of her readers might not understand the techniques of reading and interpreting allegory, in the first essay she emphasizes that Dante stated that the *Divine Comedy* is an allegory written on four levels: the literal, political, moral, and mystical. She insists that the allegorical subject of the poem is *not* the story of the journey through Hell, Purgatory, and Paradise; rather, it is the *relationship* of man to God. She calls attention to Dante's narrative techniques, such as his method of portraying sin. Sometimes he discusses specific sins; then again he describes not the sin itself but the sufferings of the sinner. In the *Purgatorio*, for instance, he does not dwell on the sin of Wrath but describes the pall of heavy smoke that chokes the breath, hides the light, and blights, blinds, and stings so intensely that the sinner becomes confused, distraught, and unbalanced. By what more effective means, she questions, could Dante have suggested how Wrath clouds the intellect and creates havoc with the emotions?

In "The Meaning of Heaven and Hell" and "The Meaning of Purgatory" she discusses with acumen Catholic doctrines, clarifying many concepts integral to an understanding of Dante's themes. Hell, she insists, is not "medieval"; it is Christ's judgment on sin, but this can only be understood when one has a true understanding of Heaven, which is, as Boethius states, "the perfect and simultaneous possession of everlasting life." In Heaven the Blessed desire only what they possess, never experiencing jealousy or envy toward those who have more. She points out that, for Dante and his contemporaries, this was the ideal pattern of *earthly* order and *should be* the ideal of every individual and nation. "Justice," she states, "is not having as much as the next man but having what one deserves. Felicity likewise is not an abundance of possessions but perfect congruity with one's functions" (59).

In "The Meaning of Purgatory" she traces the historical development of the doctrine of Purgatory, explains the necessity for—and the
nature of punishment for sin, and examines Dante's highly imaginative portrayal of Purgatory. Knowing that some readers would not be
familiar with the doctrine of Purgatory and hence might consider
punishment for sin an act of retribution by an angry God, she emphasizes that these purgative sufferings are gladly accepted by the sinner
who knows that, until properly cleansed, he is not fit to stand before
the Creator. The doctrine of Purgatory, she states, is in accord with
the teaching of Thomas Aquinas in regard to the two elements in all
just punishment: internal amendment and external amends. Both of
these essays are written with insight and verve, unmarred by the
facetiousness that sometimes detracts from her explanations of dogma
and doctrine.

In "The Comedy of the *Comedy*," she states, as has been mentioned earlier, that Dante deliberately portrays himself as a confused
wayfarer on the road to self-knowledge, thereby giving his mentor
Virgil opportunities to offer needed instructions and explanations and
preventing himself from sounding like an egotistical traveler who, on
return, must tell all. "The City of Dis," "The Fourfold Interpretation
of the *Comedy*," and "The Paradoxes of the *Comedy*" explain many of
Dante's concepts. Admitting that Dante is a difficult poet because he
deals with material that cannot be mastered without profound
thought and knowledge, she avers: "When once we have grasped the
assumptions from which he starts and the technical vocabulary which
he uses, he is for the most part lucid as the day. He uses no 'private'
imagery and preaches no esoteric doctrine; his poem is as public and
universal as the Christian Faith itself" (xiv–xv).

As usual, these essays are lively, energetic expressions of her
insights and knowledge. Kenelm Foster, O.P., commented that the
exposition in the essays on Heaven, Hell, and Purgatory is exceeding-
ly well done, "serious and popular, honest and light-hearted." [15]
Some critics deplored her tendency to indulge in sweeping asser-
tions, such as her statement that, with the publication of the *Summa*
of Thomas Aquinas, "peace was established between faith and reason
for several centuries"; or, "Dante's imagery . . . is always functional." Accusing her of a "kind of critical looseness—passionate, knowl-
edgeable, and sometimes brilliant—but generally unrestrained,"
Ciardi nevertheless concedes that "everyone who cares about Dante
will want to read these pages. At her best Miss Sayers sheds light." [16]

Further Papers on Dante, 1957, is a collection of eight essays,
which, with the exception of ". . . And Telling You A Story," were

originally given as lectures.[17] More heterogeneous in subject matter
than those in the earlier volume, these focus primarily on the poetic
and literary aspects of the *Commedia*. Four are comparative studies:
"The Divine Poet and the Angelic Doctor," "Dante's Virgil," "Dante
and Milton," and "The Poetry of the Image in Dante and Charles
Williams." Three pertain directly to the *Inferno* and *Purgatorio*:
"Dante's Cosmos," "The Eighth Bolgia," and "The Cornice of Sloth."
". . . And Telling You A Story" deals with the narrative structure and
artistry of the entire poem.

The essay on Dante's cosmos is an illuminating account of the
physical and mental world of medieval man. An imaginary
conversation between the poet and the late Professor Eddington
leads to a lucid explanation of Dante's metaphysical world, with its
distinguishing marks of hierarchy, order, and purpose. Emphasizing that Man, as the possessor of a rational soul, occupies an
unique position in this system, Miss Sayers considers the problems
of free will and free judgment as seen by medievalists, then adds
some acerbic views of her own on modern man's overweening trust
in science and his ignorance of theological truths.

In "The Eighth Bolgia" and "The Cornice of Sloth," she explains
facets of Dante's structural and poetic techniques. The first essay
shows how his craftsmanship in *Inferno* XXVI relates to the
movement of the entire poem. His sensitivity to tonal qualities and
his knowledge of the psychology of pain prompted him, she
believes, to temper in this canto horrific scenes of suffering, thus
freeing the reader momentarily from visions of misery and despair.
"The Cornice of Sloth" deals with important narrative techniques
and theological concepts of Cantos XVIII and XIX of *Purgatorio*.
The change in the relationship between the two travelers is noted.
No longer brash and egotistical, Dante asks his guide to continue his
discussion of love; Virgil, without a hint of his former impatience,
responds, humbly conscious that he can give only partial answers,
for "the love that reason can analyse is not the love that redeems the
world" (125). Dante must wait for Beatrice to unfold the mystery of
supernatural love. Questioned about the meaning of free will, Virgil
declares that man's free will and judgment allow him to make right
decisions; he may accept, reject, or sublimate desires.

Praising the immediacy, speed, particularity, and coherence of
the poem, she treats in ". . . And Telling You A Story" specific
aspects of Dante's narrative art: his power to create living characters
embodying evils and virtues, his artistry in creating similes that are

earthy, concrete, and functional, his fluid handling of *terza rima*, and his superb narrative structure. The longest in this volume, it touches upon many topics treated at greater depth in other essays, but it serves as an introduction to lure readers to commence—or to enjoy once again—the journey through the Dark Wood.

"Dante's Virgil" offers insights into the personalities of the two poets, their roles and changing relationship as characters in the *Commedia*, and gives Miss Sayers's personal reflections on reasons why Virgil was excluded from Paradise. Claiming that his melancholy kept him from meriting eternal bliss, she asserts that he did not respond fully to the Imagination: "Grace moves, and love responds; Grace, working upon love, opens the eyes of the imagination, and the will responds by faith . . ." (66). "The Divine Poet and the Angelic Doctor" further develops this idea; here she states that Virgil lost Heaven because he had not faith, that is, "imagination actualised by the will" (48). (One might well argue with her that it was not Virgil's melancholy that excluded him from Paradise but that his sadness stems from this deprivation. Did not his imagination prompt him to prophesy the coming of Christ, implicitly, at least, in the Fourth Eclogue?)

"The Poetry of the Image in Dante and Charles Williams" is a study of six of Williams's novels which, Miss Sayers asserts, develop Dante's seminal image of the Beatrician figure who mirrors Eternal Beauty and leads to Beatitude. Criticized for adapting Williams's theories concerning the Way of Affirmation, she insists that his writings illuminate the doctrine of love that permeates the *Commedia*: Love, rightly ordered, makes use of the good things of this world to bring him who loves to the ultimate source of all Love, God Himself; excessive, intemperate love leads away from God to self-idolatry.

Miss Sayers never pretended that these were erudite studies; she frankly admitted that some passages were simply her first excited reactions jotted down for the amusement of Charles Williams, who for years had been urging her to read the *Commedia*. Both the strength and weakness of these volumes lie in this personal approach, but the accusation that the essays indicate that she was either unfamiliar—or ignored—significant Dantean studies is unfounded. While preparing her translations and lecturing on Dante, she read widely, corresponded with scholars, exchanged views with them, questioned various translators, pondered their interpretations, and drew upon her very considerable knowledge of the

Middle Ages. Most important of all, she read and reread the *Commedia* in Italian until she was familiar with its meaning. Since her main purpose in providing these helpful studies, handbooks to read along with the poem itself, was to remove the cairn of scholarship that kept Dante's voice from being heard by so many, she felt no compulsion to encumber these essays with a folly of footnotes so that her erudition could be admired by critics or scholars. (It amused her that some scholars were annoyed by her personal comments that intruded at times, exclamations such as "Dante, dear funny little man," or the note that he was caught "in a preposterous social jam"; she knew that many of her readers enjoyed her familiar asides.) In her Introduction to *The Song of Roland*, she observed pithily: "Simplicity does not mean ignorance."

In the posthumous volume *The Poetry of Search and the Poetry of Statement*, the essay, "Charles Williams: A Poet's Critic" is a spirited defense of Williams's novels which, she affirms, illuminate themes in the *Commedia*.[18] Both poets experienced a romantic, mystical love, she asserts, and because of this mutual sharing, Williams proffers insights hitherto unfathomed by many readers of the *Comedy*. "On Translating the *Divina Commedia*" repeats material in the earlier volumes, but her analysis of passages translated by Bickersteth, Binyon, Longfellow, and others, with her frank evaluations of their work and her own, are instructive. "The Beatrician Vision in Dante and Other Poets" presents parallels in the spiritual experiences of Dante, Blake, Traherne, and Wordsworth. Although not limited to Dante, "The Translation of Verse" restates her aims and methods of translating the *Comedy* and tells how she tried to achieve accuracy and readability, as well as the right tone, style, and emphasis. "For the verse translator with the bug in his veins, prose translation lacks all the fun of the game," she avers; this essay shows she found considerable fun even when choices were difficult. This, like many of the earlier essays, has a casual, humorous air which cloaks her scholarship. The most difficult but rewarding study is "Dante the Maker," which explains how the whole of the *Paradiso* is built like a bridge between the first and last terzain, and how the roads from all the other parts of the poem run together to one point from which to pass over that bridge. The significance of the passage on Atonement Theology in *Paradiso* VII is brilliantly explained.

These illuminating essays, like Miss Sayers's translations of the

Commedia, are a testimony to her scholarship, her original, profound insights, and unremitting zeal to make Dante's thoughts and artistry known to many. It was her hope that having read the *Divine Comedy*, enjoyed its beauties, and found counsel in its Christian themes, readers would be inspired to endeavor to live in such a way that they, too, might experience "The love that moves the sun and the other stars."

CHAPTER 8

"The Worth of the Work"

D URING the lifetime of Dorothy L. Sayers, 1893–1957, her reputation as a writer was quite diverse. To countless readers, she
was the creator of that aristocratic sleuth, Lord Peter Wimsey, who
adroitly solved the perplexing mysteries in her entertaining novels
and short stories. To others, she was the dramatist whose radio serial,
The Man Born to Be King, brought the words of Christ into their
living room and, in many cases, into their lives, as well. To many
students, she was the scholar-translator who not only made *The
Divine Comedy* enjoyable reading but understandable. In the 1940s
and 1950s, many knew her as an essayist and dynamic speaker in the
lecture hall and over BBC radio. But at the time of her death Miss
Sayers's writings, aside from her fiction, were not well known outside
England; yet, in the past ten years, particularly in the United States,
her works are read and admired by many.

Although her reputation is inextricably associated with the inimi-
table Lord Peter Wimsey, it is most certainly not his admirers who
are responsible for this upsurge of interest. Undoubtedly, the BBC
television productions of *Clouds of Witness, Murder Must Advertise,
The Unpleasantness at the Bellona Club, The Five Red Herrings,*
and *The Nine Tailors*, seen over "Masterpiece Theater" in the United
States, introduced Wimsey, Parker, and Bunter to a younger audience that was not reading detective stories when these novels were
first published, but television adaptations alone do not account today
for this widespread interest in Miss Sayers's writings. (It would be
futile to deny that some intimate facts about her private life, disclosed
in Janet Hitchman's *Such a Strange Lady*, piqued a great deal of
curiosity in some—and righteous wrath in others.) However, the
response of genuinely interested readers today centers not on the
trivia of Miss Sayers's dress, deportment, or daring, but on the
sincere desire to learn more about the mind and creativity of a
Christian scholar who in various genres enunciated truths which

were significant for her times but also have an astonishingly pertinent message now.

There are many indications of this enthusiastic interest. In recognition of this growing esteem and desire to know more about Miss Sayers, in 1976 the Dorothy L. Sayers Historical and Literary Society was established in Witham, Essex, where she lived and wrote the last two decades of her life, journeying back and forth to London to keep her commitments there. Acting Secretary, Lieutenant Colonel Ralph Clarke and his assistants have gathered together a noteworthy collection of manuscripts, early editions, memorabilia, and other source materials, now available at the Society's headquarters, Roslyn House, Witham. New material is constantly being added to the archives where visitors and scholars are made welcome. The Society holds an annual seminar on various facets of Miss Sayers's writings, inviting such authorities as Dr. Barbara Reynolds, Mr. James Brabazon, and Dr. Trevor Hall to address the members. The papers are usually made available to members unable to attend the gathering. A bi-monthly, three to four page mimeographed newsletter, sent to members, is a source of information and pleasure for it records vital information and anecdotes, providing glimpses of Miss Sayers's life and insights into her writings. (In England, dues are two pounds yearly, payable to Roslyn House; in the United States, dues are four dollars, payable to Dr. Clyde Kilby at Wheaton College, Wheaton, Illinois, or to Roslyn House.) The aim of the society is well fulfilled: to promote the study of the life of Dorothy L. Sayers, to encourage the publication of her books and the performance of her plays, and to disseminate knowledge about this writer and scholar.

The Marion E. Wade Collection at Wheaton College, with its holdings of the bulk of Miss Sayers's manuscripts with the exception of her Dantean studies, has become the American research center for scholars. Dr. Barbara Reynolds, noted Italian scholar and close friend of Miss Sayers was lecturer-in-residence at Wheaton College in 1977–78. The Dorothy L. Sayers Festival that year featured a production of *The Zeal of Thy House*, lectures by Dr. Reynolds, an address by Mr. Brabazon, and a concert of music in honor of Lord Peter Wimsey. For several years the Writing Conference at Wheaton College, sponsored by the department of English, has highlighted talks on the techniques notable in Miss Sayers's writings, drawing scholars and interested readers, as well as students from the surrounding areas. Tapes of the 1977 Conference are available from the College for a nominal fee.

In 1976, Christie McMenomy launched the *Sayers Review*. Originally a quarterly, it is now published three times yearly; its informative articles, notes, and bibliographies are instructive.[1] R. Harmon
and M. Burger published in 1977 *A Comprehensive Bibliography: An
Annotated Guide to the Works of Dorothy L. Sayers*, the first book-
length bibliography.[2] *Unicorn: A Miscellaneous Journal* published a
partial bibliography in seven sections, 1969–1978, the work of Joe R.
Christopher, Barbara Wood, Karen Rockow, editor, and others.[3] The
issues contain some primary source materials not listed in the study
by Harmon and Burger. Five years of research in British libraries and
bookstores, and intensive study of uncollected letters and notes,
netted Colleen B. Gilbert materials which are published in *A Bibliography of Dorothy L. Sayers*, 1978; Ms. Gilbert is now completing an
edition of Miss Sayers's poetry.[4]

Doctor E. R. Gregory's study and meticulous editing of the
Sayers's manuscripts on Wilkie Collins at the Humanities Research
Center, Austin, Texas, is a model of careful workmanship. His
volume *Wilkie Collins: A Critical and Biographical Study by
Dorothy L. Sayers*, reveals that she had actually written a great deal
about Collins's life and facets of his literary style in his novels;
hitherto it was commonly assumed that although interested in the
undertaking, she had accomplished very little.[5]

Several biographies and critical studies are completed. Alzina
Stone Dale's *Maker and Craftsman: The Story of Dorothy L. Sayers*
is written for young adults.[6] The official biographer, Mr. James
Brabazon, is writing with the approval and cooperation of Miss
Sayers's son, Anthony Fleming; Professor Ralph Hone of Redland
University, California, has published a critical study. Other works in
progress include six bibliographies, two collections of critical essays,
an anthology of her poems, and a definitive study by Dr. Reynolds: an
assessment of Miss Sayers's translations of the *Commedia*, a critique
of her lectures and writings on Dante and the critical reception of
these. (Over a period of eleven years, Dr. Reynolds was in contact
with Miss Sayers's work on Dante; in the *Foreword* to Cantica III,
Paradise, Dr. Reynolds writes: "In conversations and in letters she
discussed in detail her methods of translations, the reasons for her
choice of diction, her preferences as to style and rhythm; sometimes
she sent me as many as ten or twelve trial renderings of a single
passage, and frequently she wrote long letters almost wholly concerned with the technique of verse translation. When I learned, after
her death, that she had expressed the wish that I should continue her

work, I found that I had accumulated a store of information, almost of instruction, as to how to proceed." [7] Undoubtedly, Dr. Reynolds's study will be one of the most rewarding, valuable works to come in the future. New editions of Miss Sayers's works, particularly inexpensive editions of essays pertaining to current interests, such as "Are Women Human?" and "The Lost Tools of Learning," are appearing. Seminars devoted to her creativity have had record attendance at the national and regional conventions of the Modern Language Association of America and those of the Conference on Christianity and Literature.

Although necessarily limited, this enumeration of the varied types of research, writing, studying, and projected works, indicates the widespread interest that is growing steadily in the seventies, some twenty years after her death. What accounts for this genuine interest? Perhaps some reflection on statements made *about her* and *by her* will suggest possible answers.

When she was awarded the Doctorate of Letters, *honoris causa*, by the University of Durham in 1950, the citation specifically lauded her wisdom and artistry in creating stories that were more than mere entertainments because into their plots and themes she subtly wove her own attitudes toward society and its material and moral problems, thereby "making a penetrating criticism of these matters in the guise of an idle tale." One thinks immediately of her castigation of wasteful production and consumption in *Murder Must Advertise*, her unequivocal statements about the need for personal integrity in *Unnatural Death*, intellectual integrity in *Gaudy Night*, where malicious revenge is the result of emotions uncontrolled by the intellect; and *Whose Body?*, in which Sir Julian Freke commits murder without a qualm because he had no regard for moral integrity; relationships were meaningless. Thirty years later, in the introduction to her translation of Dante's *Inferno* Miss Sayers reaffirmed these concepts, denouncing the idea that men and women are slaves of chance, victims of their environment, that conduct and moral views do not matter, that good and evil are relative terms. Individuals, she insists, have free wills and consciously make choices that may be decisive for all Eternity. Acknowledging that the basis of Miss Sayers's moral strength is her lively, uncompromising Christianity, the citation from the university ends with the tribute, "We have in Miss Sayers not only an artist, but a moralist who uses her art to convey a message with a passionate desire to make it tell. This Doctorate of Letters . . . expresses our admiration of her art, gay and grave, and a deep regard

for her sincerity." This accolade expresses succinctly some of the
endearing qualities that readers are discovering today in her fiction
and essays.

On the Sayers Commemorative Tablet at her alma mater, Somerville College, Oxford University, are the words, "Praise Him that
He hath made man in His Own Image, a maker and a craftsman like
Himself." As a maker and craftswoman, Miss Sayers held, and enunciated vigorously, her convictions about the sacramentality of work
and the obligation of every person to utilize his or her talents so that
works and actions reflect the triadic nature of the Divine Trinity. In
Begin Here she states: "Man is never truly himself except when he is
actively creating something. To be merely passive, merely receptive,
is a denial of human nature." Explained at length in *The Mind of the
Maker* and in numerous essays, her views on the creative approach to
life and to work have a persuasive force today when all too frequently,
the pressures of social and economic conditions compel considerations of the financial remunerations of a position or job rather than the
more valid concern: "the worth of the work." It is a measure of her
own creativity and her concern to inculcate right attitudes toward
work that she injected her ideals into so many of her writings: it is the
theme of the short story "Blood Sacrifice," the key concept in many
lectures, the thrust of many notes accompanying her translation of
the *Inferno*. The sins of Dante's age, she insists, are those of today or
of any age when individuals refuse to acknowledge that they are made
in God's Image and hence are duty-bound to be God-bearing images,
witnesses of the truth which they profess to believe. In those powerful essays, "The Dogma Is the Drama," "Strong Meat," "Creed or
Chaos?" and "The Greatest Drama Ever Staged," she expresses her
dynamic faith in Christianity, not as an optional philosophy or way of
life, but as the criterion of all philosophies, the clue to the riddle of
the universe. Her close friend the Reverend McLaughlin, explaining
her conviction that religion was not a mode of feeling but a way of life,
commented: "Her own ambition and desire was always to show the
Faith (to use yet another of her images) not as the *tire* which would
soften one's journey through life on wheels where bare rims might
otherwise jar us, but as the hub or axle upon which the *wheel of life*
turned." [8] The Oxford Commemorative Tablet hints of the richness
of Christian thought that readers are finding now as they contemplate
her most rewarding essays and fiction.

At the Memorial Service held in January 1958 at St. Margaret's,
Westminster, the eulogy, written by C. S. Lewis, praised her as "an

artist and an entertainer who respected her craft." [9] This respect, which she herself might have termed "intellectual integrity," is a hallmark of her thoughts. She had a brilliant mind, a scholar's training and love of learning, an esteem for all that concerned the right use of the intellect. In one of her earliest poems, called simply "Lay," she expresses the idea that because Oxford is an intellectual center, it is therefore "a sanctified city," meriting reverence. This esteem for scholarship and places devoted to its development is notable not only in *Gaudy Night*, but also in numerous lectures and essays where she speaks out against mental slovenliness so blatantly evident in popular illiteracy, the slipshod use of language, religion posing as a consolatory panacea instead of the rigorous, demanding way of life it should be. Clear-minded, forthright, facile, witty, at times truculent in expressing her disgust over intellectual laziness, she used her talents to instruct and to entertain, to encourage and to admonish. She was particularly vocal about the proper use of the gifts of the mind. "I do not know whether we can be saved through the intellect," she told Charles Williams, "but I do know that I can be saved by nothing else. I know that if there is a judgment I shall have to say, 'This alone, O Lord, in Thee and in me I have never betrayed; and may it suffice to know and to love Thee after this manner for I have no other love, knowledge, or choice.' " [10]

In pondering these statements is there perhaps a danger that undue emphasis is given to certain aspects of her life and work, her Christian ideals, for instance, while neglecting other facets? She would be the first to deplore any effort to portray her as one without faults; she was no model of saintly patience, no paragon of virtue—and never pretended to be—but she faced her faults and her trials in life with fortitude and faith, believing firmly in the truth she states in *The Just Vengeance*, "Whoso will carry the Cross, the Cross will carry him." Out of her tribulations, she had the consolation of knowing that she possessed a gift from the Giver of All Gifts; she recognized her talents, stating forthrightly: "I am a writer, and I know my craft." In her lifetime, she had the pleasure of seeing her novels gain recognition: "No single trend in the English detective story of the 1920's," wrote Howard Haycraft, "was more significant than its approach to the literary standard of the legitimate novel, and no author illustrates this trend better than Dorothy Sayers, who has been called by some critics the greatest of living writers of this form." Whether or not everyone agrees with this view, no one can dispute, he claimed, "her preeminence as one of the brilliant and prescient artists the genre has

yet produced." [11] In her efforts to raise the mystery story to the level
of the novel of manners, she weakened the detective element, a step
regretted—and criticized—by some critics and readers, but the significant point is that when she was convinced that this type of fiction
could never be much more than teasing entertainment, she turned
her talents in other directions. Or was there another reason? With
war imminent, did she feel that she could make more vital statements
for readers who might very soon have enough of death, destruction
and the rubble of chaos that no sleuth but only God could solve? What
matters today is that readers are discovering in her later novels in
particular, provocative themes and strong-minded women; Harriet,
Miss Climpson, and the Dowager Duchess are in many ways more
stimulating than Lord Peter who sometimes seems a bit effete in this
workaday world.

"A great work of art," she once commented, "has vitality only when
it speaks to our condition." She would have chortled loudly, no
doubt, at the idea of calling her novels "great" works of art, but
despite her rather scoffing attitude toward these "breadwinners," as
she termed them, her letters to Mr. Gollancz reveal her attitude
toward her fiction, for she stated more than once that she would never
turn out a shoddy piece of work. This is clearly evident, for the same
artistry that marks the translations of which she was so justly proud,
Tristan in Brittany, The Song of Roland, and *The Divine Comedy,* is
notable in the careful construction of *The Man Born to Be King,* in the
dramatic enactment of the Nicene Council in *The Emperor Constantine,* and the weaving together characterization and authentic details
of background essential to the plot in *Gaudy Night, Murder Must
Advertise,* and *The Nine Tailors.* Her best writings in each genre that
she attempted attest to her commitment to utilize her intellect,
imagination, and creativity to glorify the Divine Maker and to atone
for whatever she lacked through human frailty. Her words in *The Zeal
of Thy House* are worthy of consideration:

> Not with the lips alone, but with the hand and cunning brain
> Men worship the Eternal Architect, so when the mouth is dumb
> The *work alone* shall speak and save the workman. . . .

At the present time many efforts are being made to assess the
merits of Miss Sayers's writings and to estimate her significance, but
this can only be arrived at by a very thorough study of her entire
canon. Although gregarious to a limited extent and as a scholar always
eager to share her intellectual pursuits, as a private person she

deplored what she termed "the itch for personally knowing authors." She reminded readers that an author's writings are the truest biography: "When one is dealing with the human maker . . . his chosen way of revelation is through his works." She left very few statements about her personal life, its joys or tribulations. (It seems quite certain she would have been dismayed that a biographer would read into the scenes of tension and friction between the Harrisons in *The Documents in the Case* any intimation that these mirrored marital discord between herself and her husband, Mac; in *Gaudy Night* and *Busman's Honeymoon* she shows only too clearly her dislike of emotions uncontrolled by the intellect.) Whatever aspects of her personal life are revealed in the future, her stature as a writer, as an artist of the spoken and written word, will only be affected if these disclose new aspects of her craftsmanship.

At the present time it is safe to say that Sayers's work as an essayist, and as a scholar and translator of Dante merits the greatest acclaim. When her friend Dr. Barbara Reynolds completed the translation of the *Paradiso*, she wrote in the Foreword: "It was evident from the beginning that she was bringing to Dante studies in this country a new and vitalizing force . . . in her lectures, in her introductions and commentaries on *Hell* and *Purgatory*, and in her translation itself, she brought Dante within the reach of thousands of readers for whom he would otherwise have remained unintelligible." [12] True in 1960, it is even more evident today; thousands of students in the United States on college and university campuses read her translations and commentaries, *Introductory Papers on Dante*, and *Further Papers on Dante*. (When a guest lecturer in a Dante class casually referred to Miss Sayers as a "popularizer" of Dante, a group of students waited after class to insist politely but firmly that she was more than that: she was an interpreter who opened up Dante's milieu: theological, historical, social, economic, and religious views unknown to them. Miss Sayers would have enjoyed that, for her main purpose in translating Dante's poem and providing "handbooks" was to make the work intelligible to the common reader. Like Dante, her all-embracing mind discerned the significance of this world and the irrevocableness of the next; her perceptive interpretation of his ideas about this temporal and the eternal life, particularly her pertinent illustrations of ways that his world mirrors the faults of our contemporary society, is her unique contribution to understanding his universality. In our age, she declared, we do not hear much about alchemists, but Dante did; those alchemists or falsifiers "may be taken to figure every kind of deceiver who tampers with basic commodities by which society lives—the adulterators of food and drugs . . . manufacturers of the shoddy . . . the baseness of the individual self consenting to such dishonesty." [13] Small wonder that students claim that she "interpreted," not "popularized," Dante for them.

In her scholarly introduction to her translation of *The Song of Roland* she states that the voice of Gabriel has "the tart stringency which distinguishes the Divine Word from pious vapourings," and the "authentic toughness which St. Theresa of Avila would have recognised." These qualities aptly characterize her own forceful projection of truths that make her works provocative and appealing today, for whether she was advocating reform of the modern curriculum or a return to preaching—and living—the teachings of the Church, she wrote with clarity, vigor, wit and authority. One of the significant facts that emerges from a close study of Miss Sayer's works is that in her fiction, dramas, essays, and translations there are key concepts which give unity and force to her entire canon. A writer of minor stature, yet she made important contributions to the development of the detective story, to radio drama, and to Dante scholarship. Blessed with a keen intellect, driving energy, a creative imagination, and sincere love for Christian truths, Dorothy L. Sayers was an entertainer, dramatist, scholar, theologian, translator, and above all else, a Christian humanist whose works epitomize her artistic credo: "The only Christian work is good work well done."

Notes and References

Chapter One

1. Stanley Kunitz, ed., *Twentieth Century Authors* (New York, 1942), pp. 1237–38; *First Supplement* (1955), p. 874.
2. "The Teaching of Latin," a lecture presented to the Association for the Reform of Latin Teaching; reprinted in *The Poetry of Search and The Poetry of Statement* (London, 1963), p. 178–80.
3. Letter in the files of Victor Gollancz LTD, London.
4. Vera Brittain, *Testament of Youth: An Autobiographical Study of the Years 1900–1925* (Bath, 1933), pp. 106–107. The sequel, *The Women at Oxford* (New York, 1960), p. 123, gives interesting facts about Miss Sayers's bizarre dress and aspects of her personality.
5. Doreen Wallace, "Miss Dorothy Sayers," *Times*, January 1, 1958, p. 136.
6. Janet Hitchman, *Such a Strange Lady: A Biography of Dorothy L. Sayers* (New York, 1975), p. 46. Writing without the cooperation of the Sayers family, Miss Hitchman pieced together information available from other sources. She is credited with the discovery of the information recorded in Somerset House, which set London talking in 1975.
7. "Gaudy Night," essay, reprinted in *Titles to Fame*, ed. Denys Kilham Roberts (New York, 1937), p. 93.
8. *Gaudy Night*, novel (New York, 1936), p. 306.
9. Maisie Ward, *Gilbert Keith Chesterton* (New York, 1943), pp. 550–51.
10. Mary Ellen Chase, "Five Literary Portraits," *Massachusetts Review*, 3 (Spring 1962), 514.
11. "Thrones, Dominations . . . ," manuscript in the Marion E. Wade Collection, Wheaton, Illinois. In 1975, most of Miss Sayers's non-Dantean manuscripts, letters, and notes were purchased from her son, Anthony Fleming, for this collection.
12. "Church and Morality," a report on a conference at Malvern, *Daily Telegraph*, January 9, 1941.
13. "The Other Six Deadly Sins," an address at Westminster, reprinted in *Creed or Chaos?* (New York, 1949), pp. 73–74.
14. Val Gielgud, "Dorothy L. Sayers," *Sunday Times*, December 22, 1957.

15. "Wimsey Papers; Being the War-time Letters and Documents of the Wimsey Family." *Spectator*, December 1, 1939, pp. 770–71; November 12, p. 673.

16. Excerpt from the citation read at the conferral of an Honorary Doctorate of Letters, University of Durham, 1950.

17. ". . . And Telling You A Story," *Further Papers on Dante* (New York, 1957), p. 1.

18. Ibid., p. 2.

19. Dr. Barbara Reynolds in the Foreword, *The Divine Comedy: Paradise*, partially translated by Miss Sayers, completed by Doctor Reynolds (Baltimore, 1962), pp. 9–10.

20. Val Gielgud, *Sunday Times*.

Chapter Two

1. *Whose Body?* (London, 1933). All subsequent references are to this edition. Page numbers in parentheses follow each quotation.

2. "Gaudy Night," *Titles to Fame*, ed. Denys K. Roberts (London, 1937), pp. 78–80.

3. Howard Haycraft, *Murder for Pleasure* (New York, 1968), p. 136.

4. "Creed or Chaos?" in *Creed or Chaos?* (New York, 1949), pp. 44–45.

5. Michael Underwood, "The Criminal as Seen by the Lawyer," *Crime in Good Company*, ed. Michael Gilbert (London, 1951), p. 34.

6. *Nation*, 117 (Sept. 5, 1923), 247.

7. *Murder for Pleasure*, p. 136.

8. *Clouds of Witness* (London, 1926). All subsequent references are to this edition. Page numbers in parentheses follow each quotation.

9. This custom was abandoned in 1948 when the Lords voluntarily wrote a provision into the Criminal Justice Act abolishing the privilege of trial by their peers which they deemed out of keeping with the egalitarian atmosphere of the times. The last occasion on which this right was exercised was in 1935. "Keen Minds and Coronets," *Daily Telegraph* (December 6, 1974), p. 34.

10. "The Criminal as Seen by the Lawyer," p. 34.

11. James Burleson, *A Study of the Novels of Dorothy L. Sayers*, unpublished dissertation (University of Texas, 1956), p. 40.

12. David Soper, "Dorothy Sayers and the Christian Synthesis," *Religion in Life*, XXI (Winter 1951–52), 128.

13. John Raymond, "White Tile or Red Plush?" *New Statesman and Nation*, 51 (June 30, 1956), 756.

14. Julian Symons, *Mortal Consequences* (New York, 1972), p. 109.

15. *Unnatural Death* (London, 1927). All subsequent references are to this edition. Page numbers in parentheses follow each quotation. Originally published in the United States as *The Dawson Pedigree*, it is now published under the English title.

16. Edmund Pearson, "A Good Thriller," *Saturday Review of Literature*, 4 (April 21, 1928), 790.

17. *Murder for Pleasure*, p. 141.

18. Erik Routley, *The Puritan Pleasures of the Detective Story* (London, 1972), p. 142.

19. R. Philmore (pseudonym), "Inquest on Detective Stories," *The Art of the Mystery Story*, ed. Howard Haycraft (New York, 1947), pp. 423–25.

20. *Mortal Consequences*, p. 108.

21. *The Unpleasantness at the Bellona Club* (London, 1928). All subsequent references are to this edition. Page numbers in parentheses follow each quotation.

22. *Saturday Review of Literature*, 5 (October 27, 1928), 301.

23. *The Documents in the Case*, (London, 1930). All subsequent references are to this edition. Page numbers in parentheses follow each quotation.

24. *Times Literary Supplement* (July 17, 1930), p. 594.

25. D. L. Sayers, Introduction to W. Collins, *The Moonstone* (London, 1944), p. 25.

26. A. E. Murch, *The Development of the Detective Novel* (New York, 1958), pp. 221–22.

Chapter Three

1. *Strong Poison* (London, 1930). All subsequent references are to this edition. Page numbers in parentheses follow each quotation.

2. "Gaudy Night," *Titles to Fame*, ed. Denys K. Roberts (London, 1937), p. 78.

3. Ibid., pp. 79, 87.

4. Sara Lee Soloway, *Dorothy Sayers: Novelist*, unpublished dissertation (University of Kentucky, 1971), p. 190.

5. Letter in the file of Victor Gollancz LTD, London.

6. R. Philmore, "Inquest on Detective Stories," *The Art of the Mystery Story*, ed. Howard Haycraft (New York, 1946), p. 426.

7. *The Five Red Herrings* (London, 1931). All subsequent references are to this edition. Page numbers in parentheses follow each quotation. Originally published in the United States under the title *Suspicious Characters* (New York, 1931).

8. "Gaudy Night," p. 77.

9. Letter in the file of Victor Gollancz LTD, London.

10. In 1975 a great number of Miss Sayers's manuscripts, including short stories, novels, essays, dramas, and unpublished materials, were purchased for the Marion E. Wade Collection at Wheaton College, Wheaton, Illinois. Dr. Clyde Kilby is the curator.

11. William Weber, "Recent Mystery Stories," *Saturday Review of Literature*, 8 (Sept. 26, 1931), 152.

12. Jacques Barzun, Wendell Taylor, *A Catalogue of Crime* (New York, 1971), p. 375.

13. *Have His Carcase* (London, 1932). All subsequent references are to this edition. Page numbers in parentheses follow each quotation.

14. Barzun and Taylor, p. 374.

15. *Times Literary Supplement*, May 5, 1932, p. 333.

16. Letters in the file of Victor Gollancz LTD, London.

17. *Murder Must Advertise* (London, 1933). All subsequent references are to this edition. Page numbers in parentheses follow each quotation.

18. "Gaudy Night," p. 77.

19. *Times Literary Supplement* (March 2, 1933), p. 149.

20. "Gaudy Night," p. 77.

21. Sutherland Scott, *Blood in Their Ink* (London, 1953), p. 56.

22. *The Nine Tailors* (London, 1936). All subsequent references are to this edition. Page numbers in parentheses follow each quotation.

23. John Cawelti, *Adventure, Mystery, and Romance* (Chicago, 1976), pp. 107–25.

24. Edmund Wilson, "Who Cares Who Killed Roger Ackroyd?" *The Art of the Mystery Story*, ed. Howard Haycraft (New York, 1947), pp. 391–92.

25. "The Fen Floods: Fiction and Fact," *Spectator*, 158 (April 2, 1937), 611.

26. *Murder for Pleasure*, p. 221.

27. *Gaudy Night* (London, 1936). All subsequent references are to this edition. Page numbers in parentheses follow each quotation.

28. "Gaudy Night," p. 82.

29. Ibid., p. 86.

30. *Spectator*, 155 (Nov. 15, 1935) 828.

31. "Gaudy Night," p. 87.

32. Edith Hamilton, "Gaudeamus Igitur," *Saturday Review of Literature*, 13 (Feb. 22, 1936), 6.

33. Q. D. Leavis, "The Case of Miss Dorothy Sayers," *Scrutiny*, VI (Dec. 1937), 337.

34. "Gaudy Night," p. 83.

35. *Murder for Pleasure*, p. 138.

36. *Busman's Honeymoon* (London, 1937). All subsequent references are to this edition. Page numbers in parentheses follow each quotation.

37. An introductory letter, a tribute to three friends of Miss Sayers: Muriel St. Clare Byrne, O.B.E., Helen Simpson, and Marjorie Barber, in *Busman's Honeymoon*.

38. *Busman's Honeymoon*, a drama in three acts, produced at the Comedy Theatre, London, December 16, 1936–January, 1937. It played in Westchester, New York, in July 1937 and was published in *Famous Plays of 1937*. Filmed in 1940 with Robert Montgomery and Constance Cummings as Lord Peter and Harriet, and Sir Seymour Hicks as Bunter, the production was disliked by the coauthors.

39. Raymond Chandler, *Crime in Good Company*, M. Gilbert, ed. (London, 1951), p. 94.

40. R. Philmore, p. 433.

41. Q. D. Leavis, p. 336.

42. Introduction, *Tales of Detection* (London, 1936), p. xiii.

Chapter Four

1. *Lord Peter Views the Body* (London, 1928). References are to to this edition. Page numbers in parentheses follow each quotation.

2. Jacques Barzun, W. Taylor, *A Catalogue of Crime* (New York, 1971).

3. Introduction to *Great Short Stories of Detection, Mystery and Horror*, Second Series (London, 1931), p. 27.

4. *Hangman's Holiday* (London, 1933). References are to this edition. Page numbers in parentheses follow each quotation.

5. Letter from Miss Sayers in the file of Gollancz publishers, London.

6. L. A. Strong, *Crime in Good Company*, M. Gilbert, ed. (London, 1951). p. 159.

7. *Times Literary Supplement*, May 11, 1933, p. 328.

8. *In the Teeth of the Evidence* (New York, 1967). References are to this edition. Page numbers in parentheses follow each quotation.

9. *Striding Folly* (London, 1972).

10. *Lord Peter: A Collection of All the Lord Peter Wimsey Stories*, compiled and with an introduction by James Sandoe (New York, 1972).

11. Ibid., Introduction, p. xii.

12. "The Eighth Bolgia," *Further Papers on Dante* (New York, 1957), p. 102.

13. "A Sport of Noble Minds," *Saturday Review of Literature* (August 3, 1929), pp. 22, 23.

14. *The Floating Admiral* (London, 1931).

15. Maisie Ward, *Gilbert Keith Chesterton* (New York, 1943), p. 552.

16. *Ask a Policeman* (London, 1933); *Double Death* (London, 1939).

17. *Great Short Stories of Detection, Mystery and Horror* (London, 1928). American title: *The Omnibus of Crime* (New York, 1929).

18. Howard Haycraft, *Murder for Pleasure* (New York, 1968), p. 273.

19. *Great Short Stories of Detection, Mystery and Horror* (London, 1932). American title: *The Second Omnibus of Crime* (New York, 1932).

20. *Great Short Stories of Detection, Mystery and Horror* (London, 1934). American title: *The Third Omnibus of Crime* (New York, 1935). The number of selections in each of the three American volumes varies slightly from those in the English publications.

21. *Tales of Detection* (London, 1936).

Chapter Five

1. William V. Spanos, *The Christian Tradition in Modern British Verse Drama; The Poetics of Sacramental Time* (New Brunswick, 1967), p. 16.

2. For a more detailed history of the Canterbury Festival and the beginnings of the Religious Drama Society, see Gerald Weales, *Religion in Modern English Drama* (Philadelphia, 1961), pp. 107–21. The final chapter in Robert Speaight's *Christian Theatre* (New York, 1960), pp. 124–33, gives the early history of the Canterbury Festival and other aspects of dramatic vitality in the Anglican church.

3. Weales, pp. 109–10.

4. Sayers, "Playwrights Are Not Evangelists," *World Theatre*, V (1953–1956), 61–62.

5. Sayers, *The Man Born to Be King* (New York, 1943), p. 3.

6. *The Zeal of Thy House* in *Four Sacred Plays* (London, 1948). All subsequent references to this play are to this edition. Page numbers in parentheses follow each citation. (The title comes from Psalm 69, a lament by David: "Zeal for your house devours me," a phrase repeated in the Gospel of St. John when, after Jesus cleansed the temple, the disciples recall this scriptural passage.)

7. Gervase, a Monk of Canterbury (1141–1210), "The Chronicle of the Church of Canterbury," Charles Cotton, ed. (Canterbury, 1930), pp. 7–12.

8. Personal interview with Mrs. Vera Findlay, Canterbury, July 1971.

9. "Creed or Chaos?" in the collection of seven essays, *Creed or Chaos?* (New York, 1949), pp. 20–21.

10. George R. Kernodle, "England's Religious-Drama Movement," *College English*, I (1940), 422.

11. Spanos, p. 132.

12. *Times Literary Supplement* (June 3, 1937), p. 492.

13. Spanos, p. 132.

14. *The Devil to Pay* in *Four Sacred Plays* (London, 1948). All subsequent references to this play are to this edition. Page numbers in parentheses follow each citation.

15. Ivor Brown, *Manchester Guardian* (July 14, 1939), p. 9.

16. *The Just Vengeance* in *Four Sacred Plays* (London, 1948). All subsequent references to this play are to this edition. Page numbers in parentheses follow each citation.

17. Alan Fairclough, "Dorothy Sayers and Religious Drama in England: *The Just Vengeance*," *Christian Drama*, I (Nov. 1946), 6–7. He criticizes the ineffectualness of the Trial scene and castigates the attempt to dramatize the Passion of Christ, stating: "It is doubtful whether any actor can live up to the description of Christ and his effect on men" (p. 8).

18. A Lichfield citizen shares her recollections of the first festival performance. Interview in London, March 7, 1975.

19. *The Emperor Constantine* (London, 1951). All references are to this edition. Page numbers in parentheses follow each citation.

20. *Manchester Guardian* (July 4, 1951).

21. *He That Should Come* in *Four Sacred Plays* (London, 1948). All quotations are from this edition. Page numbers follow in parentheses.

22. Weales, pp. 168–69.

23. Murray Roston, *Biblical Drama in England* (Evanston, Ill., 1968), p. 296.

24. *Daily Mail* (London, December 19, 1941). To the editor of the *Daily Mail*, Miss Sayers wrote: "I shall be obliged if you will correct the ridiculous statement made in your headline of December 11 that my broadcast plays on the life of Christ were 'written in United States slang.' They are written in contemporary English, and any slang expressions which may be called for by the context are such as might be heard in any English town and village at the present day."

25. H. H. Martin, *Life of Faith* (London, December 1941). Similar protests appeared in other English newspapers, notably the *Christian Record*, December 18, 1941, and the *Baptist Times* and the *Star*.

26. In the House of Commons, December 1941, the question was raised whether steps were being taken to stop the broadcasts; the Minister of Information asserted that no measures were being considered.

27. *The Man Born to Be King* (London, 1943), p. 40. This edition has a forward by J. W. Welch and some comments in the Introduction by Miss Sayers which do not appear in the American edition (Harper & Brothers, New York, 1943). Quotations from the radio plays are from the American edition. Page numbers follow in parentheses.

28. Robert Speaight, *Christian Theatre* (New York, 1960), p. 130.

29. Ibid.

30. *Clergy Review* (September 1943), pp. 417–19.

31. *Blackfriars*, 24 (September 1943), 425–28.

32. *The Man Born to Be King*, English edition; Foreword by Dr. J. W. Welch, p. 16.

33. *Times Literary Supplement* (June 19, 1943), p. 289.

34. Janet Hitchman, *Such a Strange Lady* (New York, 1975), p. 138.

Chapter Six

1. *Begin Here*; a war-time essay (London, 1940). All references are to this edition. Page numbers in parentheses follow each quotation. American edition: *Begin Here*, A Statement of Faith (New York, 1941).

2. Edwyn Bevan, "A Book of Good Counsel," *Spectator*, 164 (Feb. 9, 1949), 187.

3. Jacques Barzun, *Nation*, 152 (Jan. 4, 1941), 561–62.

4. Ibid., p. 562.

5. Reginald Rynd, *Hibbert Journal*, XXIX (Oct. 1940), 213–15.

6. *The Mind of the Maker* (New York, 1956). All references are to this edition. Page numbers in parentheses follow each quotation.

7. Thomas Conlan, S.J., *Dublin Review*, 212 (Jan. 1943), 87–90.

8. *Tablet*, 179 (Jan. 10, 1942), 20.

9. Kathleen Nott, *The Emperor's Clothes* (London, 1954), pp. 288–90.

10. *Unpopular Opinions* (New York, 1947). All references are to this edition. Page numbers in parentheses follow each quotation.

11. *Sunday Times*, Oct. 6, 1946.

12. *Creed or Chaos?* (New York, 1949). All references are to this edition. Page numbers in parentheses follow each quotation.

13. Riley Hughes, "A Religion for Adult Minds," *Saturday Review of Literature*, 32 (July 16, 1949), 15.

14. W. E. Garrison, *Christian Century*, 66 (April 13, 1949), 466.

15. Quoted in the Dorothy L. Sayers Bulletin, Biographical summary, 1976.

16. "The Pantheon Papers," *Christian Letters to a Post-Christian World* (Grand Rapids, Michigan, 1969), pp. 3–11. These papers originally appeared in *Punch*, in volumes 225, 226, 227, from November 1953 until January 20, 1954. Excerpts are reprinted in *Christian Letters*.

17. *The Poetry of Search and the Poetry of Statement* (London, 1963). All quotations are from this edition. Page numbers in parentheses follow each quotation.

18. *Education in a Free Society*, ed. A. H. Burleigh (Indianapolis, 1973), pp. 145–67. Reprints of "The Lost Tools of Learning" are available at the Center for Independent Education, P.O. Box 2256, Wichita, Kansas, 67201. This essay also was reprinted in the *National Review*, Jan. 19, 1979, pp. 90–99.

19. *Christian Letters to a Post-Christian World: A Selection of Essays*, edited by Roderick Jellema (Grand Rapids, Michigan, 1969). Later published under the title *The Whimsical Christian: 18 Essays* (New York, 1978).

20. *Are Women Human?* Includes the essay of this title and "The Human-Not–Quite-Human," introduction by Mary McDermott Shideler (Grand Rapids, Michigan, 1971).

21. *A Matter of Eternity*: Selections from the Writings of Dorothy L. Sayers, introduction by Rosamond Kent Sprague, editor, (Grand Rapids, Michigan, 1973).

Chapter Seven

1. "On Translating the *Divina Commedia*," *The Poetry of Search and the Poetry of Statement* (London, 1963), p. 95.

2. Ibid., p. 101.

3. The quotations are from Sayers's translation: *The Divine Comedy* I: *Hell*; II: *Purgatory* in the Penguin Classics edition (Baltimore, 1949; 1955).

4. Theodore Holmes, a review of four translations of the *Divine Comedy*, *Comparative Literature*, 9 (Summer 1957), 275–83.

5. Charles Singleton, a review of Miss Sayers's translation of the *Divine Comedy, Speculuum*, 25 (1950), 395.

6. "On Translating the *Divina Commedia*," p. 105.

7. Gilbert Cunningham, *The Divine Comedy in English: A Critical Bibliography, 1901–1966* (New York, 1966), vol. 2, p. 217.

8. Mark Musa, *Essays on Dante* (Bloomington, 1964), pp. 160–63.

9. Allen Gilbert, *Dante and His Comedy* (New York, 1963). Section three treats of various types of Dantean comedy: the comic hero, comedy in common life, epic figures lowered for comic effects, pp. 61–108.

10. Quotations from the *notes* accompanying Miss Sayers's translation of the *Inferno* are from the Penguin edition. Page numbers in parentheses follow each quotation.

11. "The Fourfold Interpretation of the *Comedy*," *Introductory Papers on Dante* (New York, 1954), p. 114.

12. Janet Hitchman, *Such a Strange Lady* (New York, 1975), p. 57.

13. Gilbert Cunningham, p. 219.

14. *Introductory Papers on Dante* (New York, 1954). Page numbers in parentheses follow each quotation.

15. Dr. Kenelm Foster, O.P., "Review of *Introductory Papers on Dante*," *Blackfriars*, 36 (March 1955), 88–89.

16. John Ciardi, "Dante for the Missionaries," *New Republic* (August 22, 1955), pp. 18–20.

17. *Further Papers on Dante* (New York, 1957). Page numbers in parentheses follow each quotation.

18. *The Poetry of Search and the Poetry of Statement* (London, 1963). Page numbers in parentheses follow each quotation.

Chapter Eight

1. *The Sayers Review*, 3138 Sawtelle Blvd., Los Angeles, California, 90066. Subscriptions: $5.00 per year; published three times a year.

2. R. Harmon, M. Burger, *An Annotated Guide to the Works of Dorothy L. Sayers* (New York, 1977).

3. *Unicorn: A Miscellaneous Journal*; editor, Karen Rockow: 1153 E. 26 Street, Brooklyn, New York, 11210. Subscriptions: $3.50, three issues, published irregularly.

4. Colleen B. Gilbert, *A Bibliography of Dorothy L. Sayers* (Hamden, Connecticut, 1978).

5. E. R. Gregory, *Wilkie Collins: A Critical and Biographical Study by Dorothy L. Sayers* (Toledo, 1978).

6. Alzina Stone Dale, *Maker and Craftsman: The Story of Dorothy L. Sayers* (Grand Rapids, Michigan, 1978).

188

7. Doctor Barbara Reynolds in the Foreword, *The Divine Comedy: Paradise* (Baltimore, 1962), p. 10.

8. The Reverend Patrick McLaughlin, *Christian Drama* (Summer 1958), p. 22.

9. C. S. Lewis, *Daily Telegraph*, January 16, 1958. (The eulogy was read by the Bishop of Chichester.)

10. Quoted by Lord Beaumont of Whitley at the Thanksgiving Service for D. L. Sayers, St. Paul's Church, Covent Garden, June 3, 1978. Reported in Bulletin 17 of the Dorothy L. Sayers Society.

11. Howard Haycraft, *Murder for Pleasure* (New York, 1968), p. 135.

12. Doctor Barbara Reynolds in the Foreword, *The Divine Comedy: Paradise*, p. 10.

13. *The Divine Comedy*: I: *Hell* (Baltimore, 1949), p. 256.

Selected Bibliography

PRIMARY SOURCES

The following list includes only the major publications and pertinent writings referred to in this text. For complete bibliographies, the reader is referred to the book-length study by Robert Harmon and Margaret Burger: *An Annotated Guide to the Works of Dorothy L. Sayers*. Garland Publishing Company, New York, 1977, and to Colleen Gilbert: *A Bibliography of the Works of Dorothy L. Sayers*, Shoe String Press, Hamden, Connecticut, 1978.

1. Poetry Collections

Op. I. Oxford: Blackwell, 1916.
Catholic Tales and Christian Songs. Oxford: Blackwell, 1918.

2. Novels

Whose Body? London: Unwin, 1923; New York: Boni & Liveright, 1923.
Clouds of Witness. London: Unwin, 1926; New York: The Dial Press, 1927.
Unnatural Death. London: E. Benn, 1927; New York: The Dial Press, 1928.
The Unpleasantness at the Bellona Club. London: E. Benn, 1928; New York: Payson & Clarke, 1928.
Strong Poison. London: Gollancz, 1930; New York: Brewer & Warren, 1930.
The Five Red Herrings. London: Gollancz, 1931; American title: *Suspicious Characters*. New York: Warren & Putnam, 1931.
Have His Carcase. London: Gollancz, 1932; New York: Brewer, Warren & Putnam, 1932.
Murder Must Advertise. London: Gollancz, 1933; New York: Harcourt, Brace, 1933.
The Nine Tailors. London: Gollancz, 1934; New York: Harcourt, Brace, 1934.
Gaudy Night. London: Gollancz, 1935; New York: Harcourt, Brace, 1936.
Busman's Honeymoon: A Love Story with Detective Interruptions. London: Gollancz, 1937; New York: Harcourt, Brace, 1937.

3. Novels written in collaboration with others

The Documents in the Case. Written with Dr. Eustace Robert Barton. London: E. Benn, 1930; New York: Brewer & Warren, 1930.

The Floating Admiral. London: Hodder & Stoughton, 1931; New York: Doubleday, Doran, 1932. Written with various members of the Detection Club.

Ask a Policeman. London: A. Barker, 1933; New York: William Morrow, 1933. Written with members of the Detection Club.

Double Death: A Murder Story. London: Gollancz, 1939. Written with members of the Detection Club.

4. Collections of Short Stories

Lord Peter Views the Body. London: Gollancz, 1928; New York: Brewer & Warren, 1928.

Hangman's Holiday. London: Gollancz, 1933; New York: Harcourt, Brace, 1933.

In the Teeth of the Evidence and Other Stories. London: Gollancz, 1939; New York: Harcourt, Brace, 1940.

Striding Folly, Including Three Final Lord Peter Wimsey Stories. London: New English Library, 1972.

Lord Peter: A Collection of All the Lord Peter Wimsey Stories. Introduction and Collection by James Sandoe. New York: Harper & Row, 1972; New York: Avon Books, 1972.

5. Dramas

He That Should Come. London: Gollancz, 1937.

The Zeal of Thy House. London: Gollancz, 1937; New York: Harcourt, Brace, 1937.

The Devil to Pay. London: Gollancz, 1939; New York: Harcourt, Brace, 1939.

Busman's Honeymoon. New York: The Dramatists Play Service, 1939. Produced in London, 1936.

The Man Born to Be King: A Play-Cycle on the Life of Our Lord and Saviour Jesus Christ. London: Gollancz, 1943; New York: Harper, 1943.

The Just Vengeance. London: Gollancz, 1946.

Four Sacred Plays. London: Gollancz, 1948. Includes *The Zeal of Thy House, The Devil to Pay, He That Should Come, The Just Vengeance.* London: Gollancz; New York: Harper Brothers, 1951.

Love-All, a light farce. Produced in London, April 1940. Publication doubtful.

The Emperor Constantine: A Chronicle. London: Gollancz, 1951; New York: Harper Brothers, 1951.

Christ's Emperor, shortened version of *The Emperor Constantine.* Performed at St. Thomas Church, London, 1952. Unpublished.

6. Book-Length Essays

Begin Here: A War-Time Essay. London: Gollancz, 1940; New York: Harcourt, Brace. 1941.

Even the Parrot: Exemplary Conversations for Enlightened Children. London: Methuen. 1944.

The Mind of the Maker. London: Methuen, 1941; New York: Harcourt, Brace, 1941.

7. Collections of Essays

Unpopular Opinions. London: Gollancz, 1946; New York: Harcourt, Brace, 1947.

Creed or Chaos? And Other Essays in Popular Theology. London: Methuen, 1947; New York: Harcourt, Brace, 1949.

Introductory Papers on Dante. London: Methuen, 1954; New York: Harper, 1954.

Further Papers on Dante. London: Methuen, 1957; New York: Harper, 1957.

The Poetry of Search and the Poetry of Statement; and Other Posthumous Essays on Literature, Religion and Language. London: Gollancz, 1963.

Christian Letters to a Post-Christian World; A Selection of Essays. Grand Rapids, Michigan: Eerdmans, 1969. Collected and Introduction by Roderick Jellema. Re-issued: *The Whimsical Christian: 18 Essays.* New York: Macmillan, 1978.

Are Women Human? Grand Rapids, Michigan: Eerdmans, 1971. Introduction by Mary McDermott Shideler. Includes the title essay and "The Human-not-Quite-Human."

A Matter of Eternity. Selections from the Writings of Dorothy L. Sayers. Oxford: A. R. Mowbray, 1973; Grand Rapids, Michigan: Eerdmans, 1973. Selected and introduced by Rosamond Kent Sprague.

8. Selected Essays

"Gaudy Night," in *Titles to Fame*, Denys Kilham Roberts, editor. New York: T. Nelson, 1937, pp. 75–95.

"Fen Floods: Fiction and Fact," *Spectator*, 158 (April 2, 1937), 611–12.

"The Psychology of Advertising," *Spectator*, 159 (November 19, 1937), 896–98.

"The Wimsey Papers," *Spectator*, Vol. 163, 672–74; 736–37; 770–71; 809–10; 859–60; 894–95; 925–26; and Vol. 164, 8–9; 38–39; 70–71; 104–105 (November 17, 1939–January 26, 1940).

"The Pantheon Papers," *Punch*, 225 (November 2, 1953), 16–19; 226 (January 6, 13, 1954), 60, 84; and 226 (January 20, 1954), 124.

"Playwrights Are Not Evangelists," *World Theatre*, 5 (1955–56), 61–66.

"Christian Belief about Heaven and Hell," *Sunday Times* (January 6, 1957). Reprinted in *The Great Mystery of Life Hereafter*. London: Hodder & Stoughton, 1957.

"Trent's Last Case," essay in the Marion E. Wade Collection manuscript collection; recently published as an introductory essay: *Trent's Last Case*, E. C. Bentley (New York, 1978).

9. Introductory Essays

Introductions to *Great Short Stories of Detection, Mystery and Horror*, first, second, and third series. London: Gollancz, 1928, 1931, 1934. Published in America as *The Omnibus of Crime*, first, second, and third. New York: Harcourt, Brace; Payson & Clarke, 1929; New York: Coward-McCann, 1932; 1935.

Introduction to *Tales of Detection*. London: J. M. Dent & Sons, 1936.

Introduction to *The Moonstone* by Wilkie Collins. London: J. M. Dent & Sons, 1936.

Introduction to *The Surprise*, by G. K. Chesterton. London, New York: Sheed and Ward, 1952.

Introductions to Miss Sayers's translations of the *Divina Commedia*, Cantica I, *Hell*; Cantica II,*Purgatory*. Harmondsworth, Middlesex: Penguin Books, 1949, 1955; Baltimore, Maryland: Penguin Books, 1950, 1955.

Introduction to *The Song of Roland*. Harmondsworth, Middlesex: Penguin Books, 1957; Baltimore, Maryland: Penguin Books, 1957.

10. Translations

Tristan in Brittany, Being the Fragments of the Romance of Tristan, by Thomas the Anglo-Norman. London: Ernest Benn, 1929; New York: Payson & Clarke, 1929.

The *Divina Commedia*, by Dante Alighieri: Cantica I: *Hell*, 1949, 1950; Cantica II: *Purgatory*, 1955; Cantica III: *Paradise*, 1962; completed by Doctor Barbara Reynolds.

Chanson de Roland, The Song of Roland. Harmondsworth, Middlesex: Penguin Books, 1957; Baltimore, Maryland: Penguin Books, 1957.

11. An Unfinished Study

Wilkie Collins: A Critical and Biographical Study, edited from the manuscripts at the Humanities Research Center, Austin, Texas, by Doctor E. R. Gregory. Published by The Friends of the University of Toledo Libraries, 1977.

SECONDARY SOURCES

BASNEY, LIONEL. "God and Peter Wimsey," *Christianity Today*, 17 (September 14, 1973), 27–28. Emphasizing the ethical overtones in the novels, this suggests a parallel: like Dante, Lord Peter undergoes a conversion when he recognizes his inadequacies and accepts Harriet's love, which transforms him.

BERGIN, THOMAS G. *Dante*. New York: Orion Press, 1965, pp. 251–52. Utilizes Miss Sayers's definition of allegory, quoting directly from *Introductory Papers*.

————. *Dante's Divine Comedy*. New Jersey: Prentice Hall, 1971, p. 40. Commends Miss Sayers for her percipience in judging Francesca an

articulate and persuasive egoist who speaks so movingly that many are
deceived by her version of things.

BRITTAIN, VERA. *Testament of Youth; An Autobiographical Study of the Years
1900–1925.* New York: Macmillan, 1933. Gives an amusing, affectionate
picture of Miss Sayers at Oxford University.

_____. *The Women at Oxford: A Fragment of History.* New York: Mac-
millan, 1960, pp. 122–24. Adds further information about the university
years. Traces the beginnings of *Whose Body?* to a parlor game in which
each player adds an incident. Miss Sayers added the corpse in the
bathtub.

BURLESON, JAMES B. *A Study of the Novels of Dorothy L. Sayers.* Ann Arbor:
University Microfilms, A Xerox Company, 1969. Unpublished doctoral
dissertation. A study of the detective novels leads Burleson to conclude
that Miss Sayers was a skilled craftsman, but not a novelist of great
significance.

CAREY, GRAHAM. "The Unity of Artistic Experience," *Catholic Art Quarterly,*
XXI (Christmas 1957), 28–31. A comparative study of the ideas in
Etienne Gilson's *Painting and Reality* and *The Mind of the Maker*; states
that Sayers's book succeeds where Gilson's fails because, concerned
with artifice, she bases her commentaries on her own creative experiences.

CAWELTI, JOHN G. *Adventure, Mystery, and Romance: Formula Stories as Art
and Popular Culture.* Chicago: University of Chicago Press, 1976, pp.
106–38. A comprehensive study of *The Nine Tailors* as a classical detective story in which character, social setting, and thematic significance
are interwoven into the structure of the mystery.

CHRISTOPHER, JOE R.; ROCKOW, KAREN; DUNLAP, BARBARA; and others. "A Sayers
Bibliography," *Unicorn: A Miscellaneous Journal,* I–III (1969–1977).
Has significant material not contained in Harmon and Burger's book-
length study; the annotations are very helpful.

CIARDI, JOHN. "Dante for the Missionaries," *New Republic* (August 22, 1955),
pp. 18–20. In a review of *Introductory Papers on Dante,* Ciardi takes
Miss Sayers to task for overstating and overarguing her points with
"missionary" zeal. He finds much that is illuminating, particularly her
technique of pointing out parallel passages, such as the speeches of
Francesca and Ugolino, both drawn from the same passage in the
Aeneid.

CONLAN, THOMAS, S.J. "Review of *The Mind of the Maker,*" *Dublin Review,*
212 (January 1943), 87–90. Praising Miss Sayers's artistic approach to the
doctrine of the Trinity and the triune elements in human creation set
forth in this work, he expresses dissatisfaction that scant attention is paid
to the revelational nature of the doctrine and that she attributes the
"Idea" to the Father rather than to the Son.

CUNNINGHAM, GILBERT. *The Divine Comedy in English. A Critical Bibliography, 1900–1966.* Two volumes. New York: Barnes & Noble, 1965–1966;

Vol. 2, pp. 211–20. This thorough assessment of Miss Sayers's translation of the *Divine Comedy* praises her versatility and industry, cites
passages of effective translation and others with specific weaknesses:
overinventiveness, exaggeration, uncertainity of tone stemming from
the mingling or archaic and modern diction, and weak rhymes. Summa-
rizing the critical comments from seven periodicals, Cunningham concludes that the shortcomings and the merits of her translation have
contributed to its popularity.

CURRAN, TERRIE. "The World Made Flesh: The Christian Aesthetic in
Dorothy L. Sayers' *The Man Born to Be King*." *Sayers Review*, I
(September 1976), 14–25. Sees Proclus as Sayers's employment of Idea,
Energy, Power, but believes that the portrayal of Judas is more suc-
cessful.

CURTAYNE, ALICE. "Dorothy Sayers on Dante," *Studies*, 54 (Summer-Autumn
1965), 222–26. States that Miss Sayers's critical acumen and accurate
scholarship are apparent in the two volumes of critical essays on Dante.
The translations have the merit of fast pace and vividness but the *feeling*
of the poem is largely lost because of the difficulties inherent in the form,
the *terza rima*.

DALE, ALZINA STONE. "*The Man Born to Be King*, Dorothy Sayers' Best
Plot," *Sayers Review*, I: no. 2 (January 1977), 1–16. Examines Sayers's
craftsmanship notable in Judas and Jesus.

————. *Maker and Craftsman: The Story of Dorothy L. Sayers*. Grand
Rapids: Eerdmans, 1978. Highlights Sayers's Christian ideals and
indefatigable zest for creative scholarship.

DUPREY, RICHARD. *Just Off the Aisle*. Westminster: Newman Press, 1962, p.
191. This study of the dramas of Henri Gheon points out that the
medieval heritage prominent in his works is evident in *The Zeal of Thy
House*; the major difference is Sayers's formality and Gheon's
simplicity.

FAIRCLOUGH, ALAN. "Dorothy Sayers and Religious Drama in England: *The
Just Vengeance*," *Christian Drama*, I (November, 1946), 3–9. Contains
negative criticisms of this drama; castigates the attempt to dramatize
the Passion of Christ.

FAIRMAN, MARION E. *The Neo-Medieval Plays of Dorothy L. Sayers*.
(Unpublished dissertation) University of Pittsburgh, 1961. This study
of *The Man Born to Be King*, *The Zeal of Thy House*, *The Devil to Pay*,
and *The Just Vengeance* states that although the theological ideas are
vividly dramatized, they lack an imaginative beauty; as an effective but
minor dramatist, Sayers deserves esteem for breaking away from
naturalism and for making religious thought an important element in
the English theatre of the 1930's.

F[OLIGNO], C[ESARE]. *Studi Danteschi*, 30 (1951), 226–32. C. F., undoubtedly Cesare Foligno, praises Miss Sayers's translation of the *Inferno* and
her background in medieval studies, but suggests that she neglected

the works of Italian scholars. The quality of *zeppe*, frowned upon by many critics, meets with his approval, but he questions her emphasis on humor in specific passages.

FOSTER, KENELM, O.P. "Dorothy Sayers on Dante," *Blackfriars*, 38 (October 1957), 426–30. Disagrees with Miss Sayers's reasons for Virgil's exclusion from Paradise, and her analysis of voluntary human action in *Purgatorio* xviii, 19–75.

FULTON, ROBIN. "Two Versions of Ulysses' Last Voyage," *Studies in Scottish Literature*, II: 4 (April 1965), 251–57. A comparative study of Miss Sayers's translation of the Ulysses voyage in the last half of Canto XXVI of the *Inferno* and one by Tom Scott written in unrhymed iambic pentameter in tercet form utilizing Lowland Scots (in *The Ship and ither poems*, 1963), cites passages where Sayers's translation sacrifices meaning or emphasis in order to keep the rhyme of the *terza rima*, hints that Lowland Scots is particularly effective in securing primitive, forceful effects; "gurled" and "gart her birl" can suggest the rugged force not found in English equivalents.

GILBERT, ALLAN H. *Dante and His Comedy*. New York: New York University Press, 1963. Contains only a brief, negative criticism of one passage of Miss Sayers's translation of the *Inferno*; sections on "The Comic Hero," "Generally Recognized Comedy," and "Epic Figures Lowered" add new dimensions to Sayers's theories concerning the comedy in the *Comedy*.

GILBERT, COLLEEN B. *A Bibliography of the Works of Dorothy L. Sayers*. Hamden, Connecticut, Shoe String Press, 1978. Arranged chronologically in seven sections, this is a storehouse of information; much of the material has not been collected hitherto.

GILBERT, MICHAEL, ed. *Crime in Good Company*. London: Constable, 1951. Essays by Raymond Chandler, Cyril Hare, Jacques Barzun, and others estimate the weaknesses and strengths of the modern detective novel with critical comments on Sayers's work. Chandler states that she gave up writing the detective story because she realized it was an arid formula, a second-grade literature.

_____. *The Mystery Writer's Handbook*, ed. Herbert Brean. New York: Harper, 1956. In a chapter, "Technicalese," excerpts from a letter by Miss Sayers shed light on the construction of *The Nine Tailors* and Gilbert's criticism.

GREEN, MARTIN. "The Detection of a Snob," *Listener*, 49 (March 14, 1963), 461–64. Praising Sayers's inventiveness of detail, particularly in her portrayal of Lord Peter, Green accuses her of exploiting interest in snobbery: the "Fanny Hill of *class* distinction."

GREGORY, E. R. "From Detective Stories to Dante: The Transitional Phase of Dorothy L. Sayers," *Christianity & Literature*, XXVI: (Winter 1977), 9–17. Rightfully sees Sayers's abandonment of detective fiction and her turning to drama, aesthetics, and then to her study of Dante, her translations of the *Divina Commedia* and her perceptive essays on this masterpiece, as a natural progression in keeping with her intellectual training and interests. Dr. Gregory is the editor of *Wilkie Collins: A Critical and Biographical Study* from the Sayers' manuscripts in the Humanities Research Center, Austin, Texas. See entry under Primary Sources: An unfinished study.

GRELLA, GEORGE. "Dorothy Sayers and Peter Wimsey," *University of Rochester Library Bulletin*, 28, (Summer 1974), 33–42. Gives a negative view of the value of Lord Peter and the writing talent of his creator.

HANNAY, MARGARET. *As Her Whimsey Took Her: Critical Essays on the Work of Dorothy L. Sayers*, edited by M. Hannay. Kent, Ohio: Kent State University Press, 1979. An authority on the writings of Sayers, Doctor Hannay has brought together in this collection significant studies which illuminate the mind and artistry of the author. Without a doubt, it is the best introduction available at the present time to her complete canon.

—————. "Harriet's Influence on the Characterization of Lord Peter Wimsey," *Sayers Review*, II: 2 (June 1978), 1–16. Traces Peter's development from the silly-ass-about town to maturity. Also published in the collection named above.

HARMON, ROBERT, and BURGER, MARGARET. *An Annotated Guide to the Works of Dorothy L. Sayers*. New York: Garland Publishing Company, 1977. This first book-length bibliography is comprehensive, well annotated, and expertly indexed.

HARRISON, BARBARA GRIZUTTI. "Dorothy L. Sayers and the Tidy Art of Detective Fiction," *Ms*, 3 (November 1974), 66–69, 85–89. Says that Sayers's radical views on work, love, and the role of women make her an early feminist whose ideals are portrayed by Harriet Vane and the Oxford dons. Omits *Have His Carcase* in the discussion of the Wimsey-Vane relationship.

HAYCRAFT, HOWARD, ed. *The Art of the Mystery Story*. New York: Simon and Schuster, 1946. A collection of critical essays, edited and with a commentary by Howard Haycraft, provides informative material on Sayers's techniques. Includes "Gaudy Night," and her introduction to *The Omnibus of Crime*.

—————. *Murder for Pleasure; The Life and Times of the Detective Story*. New York: D. Appleton-Century, 1941. Haycraft discusses Miss Sayers's contribution to the development of detective fiction and her scholarly introductions to her three notable anthologies of detective stories.

HEILBRUN, CAROLYN. "Sayers, Lord Peter and God," *American Scholar*, 37 (Spring 1968), 324–30. An informed treatment of Sayers's life and writing with special praise for the combination of murder, manners, and wit in the novels.

HITCHMAN, JANET. *Such a Strange Lady: An Introduction to Dorothy L. Sayers (1893–1957).* New York: Harper & Row, 1975. The first biography of Miss Sayers reveals aspects of her personal life hitherto unknown, except to a small circle. Receiving no cooperation from the Sayers family, Hitchman had to rely on varied sources for information.

———. "On Writing *Such a Strange Story,*" *Sayers Review,* I:4 (July 1977), 16–21. Version of the report given at the Sayers Seminar, November 1976, Witham, England.

HOLMES, THEODORE. "Book Review," *Comparative Literature,* 9 (Summer 1957), 275–83. Assessing the merits of translations of the *Divine Comedy* by Professors Bergin, Bickersteth, Ciardi, and Miss Sayers, Holmes states that Miss Sayers is at her best in passages where she heightens the cruel, the frightening, or lurid, but archaic diction clogs some lines; her exaggerations change Dante's meanings.

HONE, RALPH E. *Dorothy L. Sayers: A Literary Biography.* Kent, Ohio: Kent State University Press, 1979. A perceptive account of Sayers's life, the milieu which influenced her development and an appreciative evaluation of her importance in various genres, Doctor Hone's study, the work of years of research and careful reading of available material, will appeal to the general reader and to scholars as well.

KERNODLE, GEORGE. "England's Religious-Drama Movement," *College English,* I(February 1940), 414–26. Brief but excellent survey, complimentary to Miss Sayers's early dramas.

LASSANCE, R. A. "Review of *Creed or Chaos?*" *Thought,* 26 (December 1951), 621–22. Praises the penetrating analysis in "Creed or Chaos?" and "The Other Deadly Sins," but raises questions concerning her meaning of "official creeds."

LEAVIS, Q. D. "The Case of Miss Dorothy Sayers," *Scrutiny,* 6 (December 1937), 334–40. Criticizes *Gaudy Night* as an unfair, romanticized, misleading "Peepshow" of university life; expresses scorn and pity for readers so ignorant as to see literary qualities in Miss Sayers's novels which, Leavis asserts, sink to the meretriciousness of Marie Corelli and Ouida.

MARTIN, HERBERT H. "Radio Impersonation of Christ: Appeal to Christian Men and Women," *Life of Faith,* January 1942. As a protest against the radio cycle, *The Man Born to Be King,* H. Martin, secretary for the Lord's Day Observance Society, in a full page advertisement, asks prayers that "these God-Dishonouring Impersonations—at this critical hour in our Nation's History—may be made to cease." (Similar blasts appeared in other newspapers; see the *Christian Record,* London, December 18, 1941.)

McLAUGHLIN, REV. PATRICK. *Christian Drama* (Spring 1958), pp. 11–13. In a moving tribute, mention is made of the disillusionments and sufferings that marked Miss Sayers's life. That statement and a quotation from Professor C. S. Lewis's panegyric, written for the Memorial Service—

"she never sank the artist and entertainer in the evangelist"—elicited questions, answered vaguely in the summer issue, pp. 22–23.

McMenomy, Christie. "A Glossary of Foreign Terms and Quotations in the Wimsey Novels," *Sayers Review*, I:3 (April 1977), 8–20. French, Latin, Greek, and German phrases culled from the novels and short stories; origins and sources of many are given.

Morral, John B. "Review of *Further Papers on Dante.*" *Studies*, 46 (Winter 1957), 493. Sees unbalanced partisanship in "Dante's Cosmos" and "Dante and Milton"; accuses Miss Sayers of ignoring previous scholarly studies on Dante, and basing conclusions on speculation rather than facts.

Murch, A. E. *The Development of the Detective Novel.* New York: Philosophical Library, 1958, pp. 221–23. Discusses the importance of Miss Sayers in the development of the detective story in the Golden Age, the late twenties and early thirties; in various chapters comments on the role of Lord Peter Wimsey.

Nott, Kathleen. *The Emperor's Clothes.* London: Heinemann, 1954, pp. 253–98. Negative reactions to many of the ideas in *The Mind of the Maker*; less caustic observations of Miss Sayers's fictional work make the chapter "Lord Peter Views the Soul" provocative reading.

Patterson, Nancy-Lou. "Images of Judaism and Anti-Semitism in the Novels of Dorothy L. Sayers," *Sayers Review*, II: 2 (June 1978), 17–24. Citing numerous examples of bias in nine works, concludes that Sayers was guilty of prejudice, although no Jew is a villain or rogue in her novels.

Reynolds, Dr. Barbara. "The Origin of Lord Peter Wimsey," *Times Literary Supplement*, April 22, 1977, p. 492. Expanded version in *Sayers Review*, II: (May 8, 1978), 1–21. Includes a transcript of the discussion following the reading of this paper by Dr. Reynolds at the D. L. Sayers Conference, Witham, November 1976. Dr. Reynolds's "Foreword" to *The Divine Comedy*, III: *Paradise*, is a revealing tribute to Miss Sayers. A series of Dr. Reynolds's informative lectures on Sayers's short stories, novels, and literary techniques are available on tapes from Wheaton College, Wheaton, Illinois, for a small sum. A close friend and collaborator, Dr. Reynolds reveals, as no one else has done, the full stature and artistry of Miss Sayers.

Rickman, H. P. "From Detection to Theology: The Work of Dorothy Sayers," *Hibbert Journal*, 60 (July 1962), 290–96. Traces Miss Sayers's development as a writer of detection fiction to that of a Christian apologist.

Roston, Murray. *Biblical Drama in England.* Evanston, Ill: Northwestern University Press, 1968, pp. 294–298. Discusses *The Man Born to Be King* as a work that revitalized the message of the Gospels and by its realistic treatment succeeded in reaffirming faith in the mystery of Christ.

Routley, Erik. *The Puritan Pleasures of the Detective Story.* London: Victor Gollancz LTD, 1972. Discusses Sayers's contribution to the evolution of the detective story.

SANDOE, JAMES. "Contributions toward a Bibliography of Dorothy L. Sayers," *Bulletin of Bibliography*, 18 (May-August 1944), 76–88. The first extensive bibliography, now superceded by the work of Harmon and Burger, and that of Colleen B. Gilbert.

SCOTT, SUTHERLAND. *Blood in Their Ink: The March of the Modern Mystery Novel*. Foreword by A. Beverly Baxter. London: Stanley Paul and Co., LTD, 1953. Classes *Murder Must Advertise* as Miss Sayers's best, because of its authentic background.

SCOTT-GILES, C. W. *The Wimsey Family*. London: Victor Gollancz, 1977. Designer of the Wimsey crest, maps and diagrams in the Dante translations, Mr. Scott-Giles traces the Wimsey family history in an amusing style.

SINGLETON, CHARLES. *Speculuum*, 25 (1950), 394–95. States bluntly that Miss Sayers's translation is a failure, for it is impossible to translate the poem in its original *terza rima* without "padding at every turn." Criticizes her for utilizing Williams's "jargon" which, he says, obscures rather than illuminates Dante's meaning; commends her for her cogent pages on Dante's allegory and symbolism.

SOLOWAY, SARA LEE. *Dorothy Sayers: Novelist* (unpublished dissertation), University of Kentucky, 1971. Gives a sophisticated explanation of theories and techniques that supposedly influenced Miss Sayers's novels.

SOPER, DAVID WESLEY. "Dorothy Sayers and the Christian Synthesis," *Religion in Life*, 21 (1951), 117–28. Soper's insights prove that Sayers was a Christian humanist or integralist, deeply conscious of man's need to achieve a balanced relationship in three areas of knowledge: theology, philosophy, and natural science.

SPANOS, WILLIAM V. *Christian Tradition in Modern British Verse Drama: The Poetics of Sacramental Time*. New Brunswick, New Jersey: Rutgers University Press, 1967, pp. 81–134. A balanced critique of Miss Sayers's religious plays, particularly *The Zeal of Thy House*.

SPEAIGHT, ROBERT. *Christian Theatre*. New York: Hawthorn Books, 1960, pp. 130–31. Praises the characterization, dialogue, and structure of *The Man Born to Be King*.

SPRAGUE, ROSAMOND KENT. "Introduction," in *A Matter of Eternity: Selections from the Writings of Dorothy L. Sayers*. Grand Rapids, Michigan, William B. Eerdmans Publishing Company, 1973, pp. 11–14. States that Miss Sayers's Christian thought and her ideas regarding women and humanism are factors which make her works relevant today.

SYMONS, JULIAN. *The Detective Story in Britain*. London: Longmans, 1962, pp. 26–28. Tracing the development of the detective story in Britain, Symons recognizes the importance of Sayers's fiction but states that her rebellion against restrictive rules, prohibitions against introducing love interests or utilizing special backgrounds, was noteworthy but not very successful.

_____. *Mortal Consequences: A History—From the Detective Story to the*

Crime Novel. New York: Harper & Row, 1972. (English title: *Bloody Murder*. London: Faber, 1972.) Convinced that Wimsey does not change essentially, Symons sees a "breath-taking gap" between Miss Sayers's intention to write novels of literary distinction and her actual achievement. He rates her short stories higher than the novels.

THURMER, JOHN. "The Theology of Dorothy L. Sayers," *Church Quarterly Review*, 168 (October-December 1967), 452–62. Outdated in the statement that Miss Sayers's theological works are not known, the essay presents a lucid explanation of key ideas in *The Mind of the Maker* but terms these concepts "*secularized* Christian theology."

WARD, MAISIE. *Gilbert Keith Chesterton*. New York: Sheed & Ward, 1943. Provides glimpses of Sayers's activities in the Detection Club.

WATSON, COLIN. *Snobbery with Violence: Crime Stories and Their Audience*. London: Eyre & Spottiswoode, 1971. Refers frequently to Miss Sayers's work, defending her against charges of anti-Semitism and social snobbery, praising her adroit characterization and satiric thrusts at fads and fashions. Chapter twelve is excellent on Harriet Vane.

WEALES, GERALD C. "Charles Williams and Dorothy Sayers," in *Religion in Modern English Drama*. Philadelphia: University of Pennsylvania Press, 1961, pp. 164–77. Severely critical of Miss Sayers's deficiencies as a poet, Weales states that her achievements never match her aims. A detailed study of *The Man Born to Be King* gives no hint of its revolutionary uniqueness nor of its continued popularity today. Chapter VI, on the development of religious drama in England during the 1920s and 1930s, and Chapter XIII, on various religious plays, mention aspects of her aesthetic creed, notably that religious drama must be judged by the same standards as those applied to secular drama.

WEBSTER, DEBORAH. "Reinterpreter: Dorothy L. Sayers," *Catholic World*, 169 (August 1949), 330–35. This survey of Miss Sayers's writings up to the publication of *Creed or Chaos?* indicates that at the foundation of all her works is dogma: the nature of God and His relationship to men and the universe.

WINN, DILYS. *Murder Ink*. New York: Workman Publishing Company, 1977. A far from laudatory view of Miss Sayers's fiction; mention of the new Dorothy L. Sayers Society, Witham, England, has created a flurry of interest.

Index